CHARLIE

RED STAR

GRANT CAMERON

CHARLIE
RED STAR

True Reports of One

of North America's

Biggest UFO Sightings

DUNDURN
TORONTO

Cover image: istock.com/standret
Printer: Webcom
Unless specified otherwise, all images are the property of the author.

Library and Archives Canada Cataloguing in Publication

Cameron, Grant, 1954-, author
    Charlie Red Star : true reports of one of North America's biggest UFO sightings / Grant Cameron.

Includes bibliographical references.
Issued in print and electronic formats.
ISBN 978-1-4597-3780-8 (softcover).--ISBN 978-1-4597-3781-5 (PDF).--
ISBN 978-1-4597-3782-2 (EPUB)

    1. Unidentified flying objects--Sightings and encounters--Manitoba.
2. Unidentified flying objects. 3. Ufologists--Canada. 4. Cameron, Grant,
1954-. I. Title.

TL789.6.C3C34 2017   001.942097124   C2017-901623-7
                                                    C2017-901624-5

1 2 3 4 5   21 20 19 18 17

We acknowledge the support of the **Canada Council for the Arts**, which last year invested $153 million to bring the arts to Canadians throughout the country, and the **Ontario Arts Council** for our publishing program. We also acknowledge the financial support of the **Government of Ontario**, through the **Ontario Book Publishing Tax Credit** and the **Ontario Media Development Corporation**, and the **Government of Canada**.

Nous remercions **le Conseil des arts du Canada** de son soutien. L'an dernier, le Conseil a investi 153 millions de dollars pour mettre de l'art dans la vie des Canadiennes et des Canadiens de tout le pays.

Printed and bound in Canada

VISIT US AT

 dundurn.com | @dundurnpress | dundurnpress | dundurnpress

Dundurn
3 Church Street, Suite 500
Toronto, Ontario, Canada
M5E 1M2

To Bob, Elaine, Freddie, Mark, Rolande, Eleanor,
Peter, Jean in Sperling, the Dufferin Leader staff,
and the adventurous film crew from CKY-TV in Winnipeg.
By looking up in the sky, you provided a wonderful story
for the world to read.

Contents

Acknowledgements

I would like to thank all who have helped on this project over the past several decades. Their input and suggestions helped a reluctant author make sure this book finally got published.

My very special thanks to Rob Diemert and his wife, Elaine, who helped me for the two years I was in and out of Carman investigating and talking to witnesses. Rob set up interviews for me, and because he was at the centre of the entire rash of sightings, there was almost nothing he didn't know.

Elaine helped me edit and typed up the very first manuscript that was done shortly after all the sightings stopped. If it hadn't been for her, there would have been no manuscript.

Thanks to all the people in southwestern Manitoba who talked to me knowing they would get ridiculed if their stories ever got out. Thanks also to others who were ridiculed after they talked but continued to talk. Many of the witnesses in this book are now dead, and because the names have been changed, their children and grandchildren will never know the historic role their parents and grandparents played. I, sadly, am one of the few people who got to hear their experiences. I am eternally grateful; their stories changed my life greatly.

The biggest thank-you probably goes to my oldest sister, Pat. She is the historian of the family. Long ago, when the manuscript didn't get published, I gave it to her, and she kept it for a quarter century, years after I'd forgotten I'd ever written it. When she gave it back, I realized she had saved the story, since I had long since discarded most of the notes used to write it.

Finally, a big thank-you to those who pushed to have the manuscript published. It was my younger sister, Sandra, who encouraged me to publish it when I had no interest in doing so. Then it was Teza Lawrence, a TV producer in Toronto, who really pushed for *Charlie Red Star* to be published. She actually took her valuable time to find Dundurn and negotiate with them when I still didn't believe.

Thanks, too, to Brian Westbrook and Laurie Rosenfield for early editing, and for their enthusiasm, which prevented me from scrapping the project. If not for this chain of people pushing the book to the finish line, it wouldn't have happened, since I fought against publishing it the whole time. In many ways, I consider myself the person who worked the least to get *Charlie Red Star* published.

Introduction

> Americans assume that facts are solid, concrete, and discrete objects like marbles, but they are very much not. Rather they are subtle essences, full of meaning and metaphysics that change their color and shape, their meaning, according to the context in which they are presented.
> — Dwight Macdonald, *Esquire*, March 1965

This book is the recounting of my work investigating the numerous unidentified flying object (UFO) sightings that occurred in the Canadian province of Manitoba in 1975–76. The investigation initiated a long trip into the mystery of UFOs that has never ended.

I have held this manuscript for thirty-six years. The reason it is being published now is to put the events on the record. It is not to prove anything, but to detail a series of incredible events that occurred in a small Prairie town.

When the flap[1] of sightings broke out in 1975 around Carman, Manitoba, I was a political studies student at the University of Manitoba. Prior to my first sighting, I can't recall ever having thought about UFOs.

I certainly don't remember reading anything on the subject. The only reason I can recall venturing out on the first night to Carman was to observe what everyone else was reportedly seeing.

Once I was involved in the Charlie Red Star story, an evolution began in my thoughts on the subject of UFOs. When I first glimpsed the object, I went from ignorance to absolute amazement. My increased awareness and belief crystallized after speaking with many of the major witnesses in the flap area. It became apparent to me that something very extraordinary was going on.

The Charlie Red Star story is a unique tale. In terms of time and the number of sightings involved, it was one of the biggest UFO flaps ever to have occurred. It is perhaps for this reason that the *National Enquirer*, an American tabloid newspaper based in Lantana, Florida, considered calling Manitoba the UFO capital of the world after its initial investigation in the spring of 1975, followed by a two-week study of the sightings in 1976.

Despite the number of sightings that occurred, not many people have ever heard of the flap, since almost none of the sightings were publicized beyond local TV, radio, or newspaper reports. Even the largest local book publisher failed to help spread the word. When approached with a manuscript that would tell the rest of the world the story, the publisher wrote: "Mr. Cameron. You may believe in this sort of thing. Consider me among the unbelievers."

The stories that follow will hopefully replace those constantly repeated in ufology, which have become thin through their constant retelling. It is hoped these stories will provide some researcher somewhere new information that might help solve the UFO mystery.

The majority of this book is simply a retelling of the many tales told to me by citizens involved in the sightings. Together, the witnesses and I agreed that the only proof existed in what we had seen.

Therefore, instead of this book being a vain appeal for others to believe what we saw, it looks at how others treated the witnesses, their personal opinions, and above all, their emotional reaction to a story that is personally theirs. The two-year flap is unique and worthy of being documented in book form.

In many circles the prevailing attitude is that sightings occur through-out a scattering of civilization when the witnesses are "in the wrong place at the wrong time." In other words the general position is that "you don't find UFOs — they find you."

In Manitoba there was sufficient evidence to say that this model didn't apply. On at least five occasions, mobile TV crews from Winnipeg "went out to find UFOs" and did indeed do so. That was how CKY-TV in Winnipeg captured what came to be considered one of the most famous UFO nocturnal light movies in the world at that time. Nine different photographers made it a point to regularly seek out UFOs and photo-graph them. Hundreds of other people did likewise.

The story of Charlie Red Star is also a look at what has been learned with the perspective of more than 40 years after the sightings happened. It appears that the Manitoba experience didn't follow the general rules in a number of categories. Most UFO studies have shown that sightings are random, and yet for some reason the Manitoba ones weren't.

The Manitoba UFO flap was also different from other historic ones in that the UFO became personified. The object that appeared almost nightly became known as Charlie Red Star. People and newspapers alike called it Charlie rather than a UFO. Charlie became a legend and was even part of advertisements placed in a local Carman newspaper by companies selling their goods.

As to what Charlie was, no one really pushed a pet theory. Many thought it was extraterrestrial, some believed it was an angelic phenom-enon, and a few were convinced it was demonic. Usually, the object was simply Charlie, who meant no harm to anyone and whose course for the night just happened to bring him into the Pembina Valley, around Carman where the vast majority of the sightings took place.

THE ARRIVAL OF
CHARLIE RED STAR

Once you see the thing, you know it. When you see this thing
once, you never forget it. Just the way — the heartbeat of
the thing. It's a luminous light. You'd like to see through it, but
you can't.

— Art Stagg, Resident of Carman, Manitoba

Except for some of the world's best wheat, the Winnipeg Jets hockey team,
and being among the coldest regions in the world, the city of Winnipeg,
and the town of Carman 35 miles southwest have been famous for
very little. It was therefore unusual when, in February 1975, Manitoba
suddenly become the focus of a series of almost nightly UFO sightings
that lasted nearly two years. During that time, the province was on the
map as the place where aliens came to visit.

Manitoba, however, wasn't totally unfamiliar to UFO phenomena.
There had been a flap of sightings in 1967 that included one of the most
famous UFO cases ever — that of Stefan Michalak, the Polish-born
prospector who came in contact with a UFO that had landed outside
Falcon Lake.

The Michalak case occurred on May 20, 1967, about 40 miles north of the U.S. border on the edge of Whiteshell Provincial Park. The area where the event took place is desolate, hilly, rocky, and treed.

Michalak was prospecting for quartz veins associated with silver deposits when the incident happened. Just after noon he heard the cackling of geese, sounding as if they had been disturbed. Looking up, he spotted "two cigar-shaped objects with 'bumps' on them."[1] They were descending from high above him.

One of the two objects landed on a large, flat rock about 160 feet away. The other object "hovered for a short while, then departed as well, flying into the west, where it disappeared behind the clouds."[2]

Shortly after the approximately 40-by-10-foot craft landed, Michalak noticed that a two-by-three-foot door had opened on the side of the craft. He could see light inside the door "and heard two humanlike voices, one with a higher pitch than the other."[3]

Believing the object to be an experimental American aircraft, Michalak walked up to the vessel and called out, offering help. When he didn't get a reply, he tried other languages he knew but got no answer in Russian, German, Italian, French, Ukrainian, and then once again in English.

Still not receiving a response, Michalak walked up to the craft and stuck his head inside where he saw "a maze of lights on what appeared to be a panel, and beams of light in horizontal and diagonal patterns. There was also a cluster of lights flashing in a random sequence 'like on a computer.'" Then, as he moved back, "three panels slid over the opening, sealing it 'like a camera shutter.'"[4]

At that point Michalak touched the side of the craft and noticed no joints or welds. It took only seconds to realize that his rubber glove had melted.

Next, the vessel began to lift off. As it rose, it started to spin, and as it did, a six-by-nine-inch grid like a vent shot out a blast of hot air against his chest as it rotated by him. The hot air ignited his clothes, prompting Michalak to tear them off as the craft flew away.

Once he had removed his burning clothes, he had a new problem. He had become very sick and was vomiting, and struggled to get back through the rugged terrain to the Trans-Canada Highway.

THE ARRIVAL OF CHARLIE RED STAR 19

After returning to his home in Winnipeg, he made many hospital visits for his burns and other physiological effects. The case was investigated by several government and UFO organizations, became one of the most investigated UFO cases ever, and has been the subject of numerous articles and documentaries.

The 1975 Manitoba UFO flap was the second big UFO event in the province. When the sightings first began, the phenomena went unstudied for quite a while before people started to visit Carman and record the events. Most media and UFO investigators didn't really get involved until May 1975 after the nightly flybys had been occurring for a couple of months.

My personal involvement in the flap was similar to that of the media. I had heard reports of sightings in the Carman area, but like most people, I watched with curiosity from afar.

At that time in my life I was a member of a group of young men in their early twenties who spent most of their free-time hours driving around Winnipeg doing not much of anything. None of us had an interest in UFOs. No one was a science fiction buff, and none of us had any scientific leanings. Our interests were focused on football, baseball, and playing cards. My only related activity was the field of parapsychology,

Map of southern Manitoba.

particularly the stories surrounding the psychic Edgar Cayce, and in research related to the study of death and dying.

The only UFO story I knew that was connected to my interest in parapsychology came from research I had done into the life and "readings" of the "sleeping prophet" Edgar Cayce. It was an account that still pops into my mind when people talk about the possible date for UFO disclosure. In a book about Cayce, author Jess Stearn describes a strange dream Cayce had about what appeared to be a UFO:

> As happened so often in his life, a significant dream came during a great emotional crisis. Cayce had been arrested in Detroit for "practicing medicine without a license," and had been subjected to the ignominy of public trial as a charlatan.
>
> On the train back to Virginia Beach, he had one of his most singular dreams. He had been born again in 2100 A.D. in Nebraska.
>
> "The sea," he recalled, "apparently covered all the western parts of the country, as the city where I lived was on the coast. The family name was a strange one. At an early age, as a child, I declared myself to be Edgar Cayce who had lived two hundred years before. Scientists, men with long beards, little hair and thick glasses, were called in to observe me.
>
> "They decided to visit places where I said that I had been born, lived and worked in Kentucky, Alabama, New York, Michigan and Virginia. Taking me with them the group of scientists visited these places in a long, cigar-shaped metal flying ship which moved at high speed."[5]

It was partly these words spoken years before the initial Kenneth Arnold UFO sighting in June 1947 that convinced me UFO phenomena were real, and that by the year 2100 humans would possess its technology. I was now poised to become involved.

In May 1975, the media had been reporting since March that sightings were being made in Carman almost every night. I realized there was a chance I might see the UFO making such a stir as reported in local newspapers. It was a rare opportunity comparable to being given the opportunity to see Elvis Presley perform live, or to attend a royal wedding.

I suggested to my friends that instead of driving around the streets of Winnipeg aimlessly, we should head for Carman to see what everyone was reporting. The decision was made to go, but nothing happened until more than two weeks after CKY-TV in Winnipeg filmed the object. Three of us left late one evening to join hundreds of people crowding the roads around Carman, waiting for a flyby of the UFO residents were calling Charlie Red Star.

Like the general population, I had the impression UFO sightings were a random event that occurred to people who weren't usually planning to see anything. Prominent researchers in the UFO community had clearly stated that one couldn't isolate the UFO phenomena. UFOs, it was concluded, couldn't be studied in a laboratory. They were random events among a scattering of civilization in the wrong (right) place at the wrong (right) time.

Because I also believed UFOs found you and not the reverse, I had grave doubts we would actually spot anything when we arrived in Carman. However, there was nothing better to do that night, so at 10:30 p.m. on May 29, 1975, we headed off to see a flying saucer or whatever the hell everyone was making so much noise about.

In Carman during April, May, and June 1975, it seemed that many people had abandoned their television sets to catch a glimpse of Charlie Red Star. Numerous cars were parked on the roads outside town.

Upon arriving in Carman, we drove around looking for the UFO. My friends and I had no idea what to search for. We knew many people had seen the object at the local airport known as Friendship Field, but we couldn't find it because it was dark and the runway lights were off. Like typical men, we didn't bother to stop anyone in town to get directions.

Then we saw what turned out to be Venus setting in the west. It appeared brighter and brighter as it neared the horizon. At the time we didn't know exactly what it was but realized it had to be a planet or star because it wasn't moving except in relation to the other planetary objects. We thought that maybe this was what everyone was talking about. If it was the reported object, though, it wasn't very impressive.

Anthony and Rachael Britain's Friendship Field airstrip in Carman, Manitoba.

Doug Wheeler, my long-time friend and the driver that night, finally put an end to the hunt. "We'll drive back into town one more time," he said. "If we don't see anything, we'll go home." The rest of us quickly agreed. The whole episode seemed a total waste of time.

We were about two miles east of Carman when Doug made the final turn back into town. Then it happened. About a mile from Carman everyone saw it. "There it is!" one of my friends yelled. It was moving from left to right, coming from the south and crossing the road in front of the car.

As I have explained literally hundreds of times since in lectures and seminars, there was no question that what we were now gazing at was indeed Charlie Red Star as described in media reports. The red pulsing and bouncing object was quite low. It flew in front of us about a half mile down the road and was unlike anything we had seen before.

The mood in the car turned from silent pessimism to one in which the home team had just scored the winning touchdown.

What is important to remember is that there was no belief involved. There was no analysis of what we were seeing. No one asked, "Is that what everyone's reporting?" We all *knew* UFOs were real and we were looking at one. Instantly, we left behind the percentage of people who had never seen a UFO and therefore could only choose to believe or disbelieve the existence of unexplainable UFOs through the accounts of others.

The object was so low that as it moved to the north side of the road it seemed about to disappear behind a set of school buses parked beside the road in a lot. I clearly recall that I was so excited by what was happening that I tried to get out of the car before it fully stopped. All three of us raced to the buses and watched as Charlie darted away from us, bobbing up and down into the northeast away from Carman.

It was at this point that my friends stored what they had seen in the backs of their minds and went on with their lives. I, on the other hand, fell off the planet and became infected with the obsessive feeling of mission that has affected many in the UFO community.

I was completely transported by the experience and could think about little else except going back and getting a better look. Two nights later Doug and I returned to Carman, hoping to see Charlie again.

As on the first night, we tried to find Friendship Field, which was owned by Anthony Britain, the aviation legend. But we still couldn't locate it even though we now knew it was in the southwest part of town. Later we discovered we had parked just down the road from the airport without being aware of it.

I had alerted all my friends from the city to show up for the spectacle of their lives. I was very evangelistic about it and convinced a number of people to drive out. They did make the trip, but after an hour of waiting they had had enough and retreated to Winnipeg at 12:30 a.m., saying, "We're hungry and we're going back to the city for pizza." I pleaded for them to stay, but no one would listen.

Hundreds of people were driving around the area. Many were looking for Charlie and some were merely teenagers cruising or searching for a quiet place to drink beer.

When we first arrived on the road west of the airport, there were 25 people gathered on the dark gravel road. By the time the object arrived just before 1:00 a.m., only eight people were left.

Our car had four people, and there was another vehicle with four others in their early twenties. On the side of their vehicle was a large decal for a Winnipeg courier company. All the people who remained were about to experience something extraordinary.

In our car we had brought Doug's younger brother, Rob, and Danny, one of Rob's friends from down the street. Rob and Danny were sitting in the field scanning west toward the hills. Suddenly, one of them called out that he had spotted something. I looked and thought I also saw a flash. It seemed as if a flash on a camera had gone off about a mile away.

Moments later there was a second flash, which both Rob and Danny saw. They started to yell, and I confirmed to them that I could see it. The problem was that the second flash was nowhere near the first one. Perhaps there were two objects. A third and fourth flash followed, each in a different part of the western sky. The flash moved around like a bouncing ball. The young children of the McCann family eight miles north of Carman later described this as the "bouncing Ping-Pong ball."

By now seven of the eight witnesses could see the object. There was lots of excitement and shouting. As had happened with my first sighting, everyone immediately knew this was a UFO and became instant believers.

One young girl in the other car couldn't see the object. After all, it was jumping all over the sky. She began to cry and said, "I can't see it. Someone show me where it is." Everyone, however, ignored her. They were too busy watching the incredible show.

One of the men in the second car had a camera with a motor drive. He used the top of the car to brace the camera and took pictures as fast as he could.

As on the first night, no one asked, "Is that it?" We all knew this was the object everyone was talking about.

While the seconds ticked by, the flashes became brighter and closer together. The girl could now see it and stopped crying. It appeared to be right before us.

I don't recall how it happened, but the object changed from the white strobe flash to a blood-red pulsing ball of light exactly like the object we had seen two nights before. It was very low to the ground and still coming at us. The yelling and the sound of the clicking camera continued.

When the object was about half a mile away, it turned left toward the north side of town. It was only a couple of hundred feet off the ground. As it turned, a green glow could be seen on the back bottom side. The object shape couldn't be determined because of the intense red glow surrounding it. All that could be established was that it was longer than it was high. It looked like a glowing heart with a slow-pulse heartbeat.

Once the object made the turn north, it moved away from us. The people in the other car jumped into their vehicle, declaring they were going to chase the object. With gravel shooting out from behind spinning tires, they sped away.

I had now had my second dramatic sighting in two days. Other people who had seen Charlie Red Star were as impressed as I was. Although the sighting had been an ongoing event for two months, there had only been a few newspaper articles describing what was happening. I wondered why no one else was investigating and talking to all the witnesses, so I decided I would take on the task.

More Media Attention

Media outlets in Winnipeg were beginning to acknowledge the existence of UFOs, and because of the regularity of Charlie's appearances, movie crews started to visit the area, hoping to capture him on film.

The *National Enquirer* also became involved. It had heard from J. Allen Hynek, a prominent ufologist and director of the Center for UFO Studies in Chicago, that something unusual was occurring in Manitoba. The *Enquirer* decided to assign a reporter to do a story and gave the job to Daniel Coleman, its leading UFO reporter.

In his assessment of the Manitoba flap, Dr. Hynek had distinguished in a statement made in early June that the situation was unique:

> We have had for the past six weeks a fair amount of activity in southern Manitoba [in] an area about 55 miles south of Winnipeg. We've had some very interesting sightings from there. The pattern has been in the past that an area can remain "UFO hot" for several weeks and then things just die down. This thing

is unusual in that it has lasted so long. It's beginning to look as if northern Wisconsin, northern Minnesota, and southern Manitoba form one large area.[6]

The sightings continued day after day throughout the summer and in all types of weather. Definite patterns of time and place could be established from the numerous reports that came in.

Media coverage didn't seem to have an effect on sighting reports as one would expect. For example, some towns in Manitoba reported no sightings at all, even though they were reading the same newspapers as everyone else. One town, Steinbach, had a large UFO convention while the flap was going on, but investigators didn't uncover a single UFO sighting in that town.

The idea that UFO sightings were a random event was now a long-dead idea. In the first eight nights I was in Carman, I had had six sightings. The evidence seemed to indicate that at least in this situation the phenomena could be isolated.

Sightings were so commonplace, in fact, that Anthony Britain took Winnipeg crews out on Carman's back roads, trying to film Charlie Red Star. In four trips they had four sightings but were only able to document one. That footage, shot by Martin Rugne (then a film editor with CKY-TV), became one of the most important UFO movies of the day.

There were nine photographers I knew of who attempted to get pictures. It was in the days before digital cameras and videotape recorders. A lot of work and expense went into getting shots. Yet they persisted because they saw something that was unique and unidentified — something worth photographing.

Anthony Britain

Anthony Britain and his wife, Rachael, were at the centre of the UFO flap. Their airport, Friendship Field, was on the southwest side of town and had a clear view of everything. Anthony was a local hero known to everyone and a person with whom people shared their UFO experiences.

Anthony Britain working in an airplane hangar at Friendship Field in Carman.

Anthony had made his reputation as a restorer of Second World War planes. He was the first to restore a "war bird," as they are now called, in what is now a multi-billion-dollar business. In 1962 he reconditioned a Hawker Hurricane, a fighter aircraft that was a significant factor in the Allied victory in the Battle of Britain. In fact, Anthony flew his, one of only three at the time, in the 1969 movie *Battle of Britain*.

The Carman native had also restored other very rare planes such as the Japanese Zero. At the time he rebuilt a Zero he had the only flyable one in the world. He had also done the same for a Japanese Val dive bomber, which he hauled out of a jungle and restored.

Already famous for rebuilding vintage aircraft, now Anthony became celebrated as the Carman expert on UFOs and acted as the tourism office for anyone who had questions or wanted to see Charlie Red Star.

The *Apollo* Story

Years after the Carman UFO flap Anthony Britain had a chance meeting with one of the men who had walked on the moon. The *Apollo 15* astronaut was in Carman lecturing at a local high school. In talking with the people hosting the lecture, Irwin mentioned he would like to meet Anthony while in town. Like Anthony, the moon walker had an interest in restoring Second World War aircraft and wished to speak with Anthony, who had pioneered the business.

Anthony didn't attend the lecture but did meet with the astronaut at Friendship Field after it. He recounts what occurred:

> He told me the story here in the hangar … as soon as we were by ourselves [Rachael, Anthony's, wife, had just left the hangar]. He turned to me and he looked at me and said, "I'm going to say something that is top secret. If you repeat it I will deny ever having said it." He said they weren't there [on the moon surface] an hour and a saucer landed a mile away from them and we asked Houston if we could motor over and say howdy. They said "no ignore them and pretend they're not there, and carry on about your business." He said that all the time we were there they saw no sign of movement, and they were still there when we left.

As dramatic as this story is, there are other accounts that back up the idea that a UFO incident was witnessed by the *Apollo 15* crew while on the moon.

A few years after Anthony had told the story to me a couple of times I learned that Dr. Frank Stranges, a minister and UFO researcher, had experienced a similar encounter with James Irwin. I contacted Stranges by phone, and he confirmed the report I had heard.

In 1976, Stranges was hosting a UFO convention at the Anaheim Convention Center. The keynote speaker was this *Apollo* astronaut who was, according to Stranges, going to "inform us of the strange things that he saw on the surface of the moon."

The fact that Irwin was scheduled to speak clearly demonstrated that he had an interest in UFOs, something had occurred, and he was prepared to reveal what had happened. Stranges recalls his encounter:

> You want to hear something interesting about our astronauts? We put on a space convention some years ago at the Anaheim Convention Center and one of our top speakers for the convention was [James Irwin] — United States astronaut. He was all set to come to inform us of the strange things that he saw on the surface of the moon.
>
> The day before the convention started I got a telegram from him saying "I'm sorry. I'm not able to come. I am returning the check that you sent — the honorarium." Plus we had to cancel his hotel reservation. When I questioned him after the convention in Colorado Springs he said, "Look I have a pension to worry about. I have a family to take care of, and they told me to just back away from this entirely — or else." That was a cold slap in the face to say the least.

The final piece of evidence supporting the fact that James Irwin had UFO experiences on the *Apollo 15* moon mission came in an interview he gave to a Japanese film crew doing a UFO documentary. The interview was public, and therefore the astronaut was much more conservative in what he revealed. His story was akin to the National Aeronautics and Space Administration (NASA) version of events. Here is what he said:

> We travelled back and saw strange things around us. We could call them UFOs — they're Unidentified Flying Objects. What they were I do not know. They could have been other spacecraft, perhaps satellites, perhaps part of the spacecraft that came floating with us, part of the fuel that we dumped or ice crystals. We were surrounded by a beautiful cloud of ice crystals as we travelled … it was hard to discern. Very few would say that they are spacecraft from another world.

The Personification of Charlie Red Star

During 1975, people living in the Pembina Valley told many stories about the UFO sightings being made. Yet in all the stories rarely was the term *UFO* used. Instead, the glowing, pulsating disk became known as Charlie Red Star, the toast and talk of every town in southern Manitoba. Conversations in cafés and pubs were abuzz with Charlie's name, and no one thought for a moment that it was a child's game to personify the thing.

Even local newspapers and television and radio stations played along. At first they — the media — called it a UFO, but after countless interviews with those involved, they, too, named the object Charlie Red Star. The Carman press even used *him* as a way to entice customers for businesses advertising with them. Ads were headlined: SHOP WHERE CHARLIE RED STAR SHOPS.

What was Charlie? Most people thought he was extraterrestrial, but no one really cared, not even those who saw him. As Frances Stagg of Carman put it, the whole affair was fast becoming the legend of Charlie Red Star.

Charlie was seen as a friendly guy, evidenced by the fact that he never hurt anyone. Those who caught a glimpse of Charlie as he dropped into the valley wondered why he came to Carman of all places. No one really wanted to expound on a theory and then be forced to defend it. It was decided that Charlie lived in the west near Roseisle. He remained in the hills during the day and flew into the valley at night, perhaps to pick up a case of beer and then return to the hills for the night. This jokingly became known as "the beer run."

To most residents, Charlie was a lazy sort, evidenced by the fact that he flew very slowly. The nightly flight into the valley was, therefore, not so much a mission of a businessman driving down the freeway to work but of a man picking up his beer for a night of television watching.

Yet, when the people of Miami and Carman attempted to chase Charlie with cars, they learned first and foremost that he was far superior to everyone in knowledge and technology. They discovered that Charlie was able to dodge and tease them, or was capable of disappearing at the first sign of a chase.

Ultimately, Charlie was considered the property of southwestern Manitoba. He was a one-time occurrence in history. Few of those I talked to bothered to reflect on whether Charlie was the same craft that nabbed Travis Walton, or the vessel that blasted Thomas Mantell's airplane out of the air in 1948.[7] He certainly wasn't one of those ships with the ugly little greys that flew around abducting people.

It seemed that southern Manitobans subconsciously behaved as if Charlie had been created solely for their entertainment. He was born, visited the province for 18 months, and now resided in a paradise for flying saucers in the sky. He was the one and only Charlie Red Star.

"Words, Words, Words"

The chapters that follow are intended for the entire spectrum of society. Skeptical scientists struggling to maintain their research budgets and stagnant ideas might be the exception. Hopefully, then, I have prepared a complete banquet for readers.

Most of the ensuing chapters simply tell people's encounters with UFOs. They are stories that readers may regard or disregard as they see fit.

The reports of UFOs in Manitoba are, I believe, valuable additions to the overall history of UFOs, and I hope the small piece presented here will greatly enrich the picture as a whole. In 1977 there were, according to the computer files at the Center for UFO Studies, 5,000 UFO reports from Manitoba over the previous 10 years.[8] My estimate is that there were probably 4,000 reported and unreported cases from 1975 to 1977 in Manitoba alone. Consequently, due to the heavy numbers of sightings, I gave up two years of university studies to collect and file the many UFO stories. I spent an estimated $7,000 to keep up with a flap that at times appeared to have no end.

To me the whole series of events was never anything to take too seriously. I had lived in a world where the paranormal wasn't supernatural but merely things that lay undiscovered by humans. I had heard the stories people were telling and I had seen Charlie Red Star myself. But to me these things were just symptoms, and it didn't appear as if anyone was looking for the cause.

As with cancer research, it seemed as if everyone was merely collecting case studies in the same way a hobbyist amassed stamps, coins, or matchbook covers. When I found that I, too, was compelled to do little else, I began to gather the stories for what they were — stories that should be told to all who wished to hear them.

There was, hidden somewhere in the maze of sightings, a cause. At the end of my two-plus-year search I made my guess. My hypothesis was that the sightings in Manitoba represented an extraterrestrial visitation.

Most ufologists, however, didn't hypothesize, because it meant too much to them to be called scientific. Ufologists are scientists, and scientists must be objective. They mustn't speak until they know they are right. To do so and be wrong would mean the end of their attempts to be accepted by scientists in other disciplines.

On this and many other points, I disagreed with scientific ufology, and I did all in my power not to become part of it. Scientific ufologists have stifled research by believing that UFOs had to be understood to exist. Science knows less about the mind than it does about UFOs, but then who would dare stand up to deny the mind's existence?

Scientific ufology has as much as any field built its ivory towers. It is safe to say that the majority of ufologists are uncooperative and evasive in their dealings with one another. In ufology the bosses greatly outnumber the workers.

UFO groups are like countries of the world. Each is out to protect its information and interests. Like the world around us, there is always a war going on, and each group sticks a knife in the back of another, given the opportunity.

From all of this, I have tried to protect myself. I call myself a storyteller first and a ufologist second. I have made a point to tell as much of the story as I can, and it appears that most people want it this way. To them it has become more important to hear all the stories than to know what the stories mean. Mystery, after all, is still the storyteller's prime weapon.

So sit back as I relate stories of Manitoba UFOs that are, as far as I know, truthful and complete. But don't take them for anything more than they were intended. For in the end, perhaps Hamlet was right: "There are more things in heaven and earth, Horatio, than are dreamt of in your philosophy."

WITNESSES AND TESTIMONIES TO CHARLIE RED STAR

It's funny, but I was downtown telling a friend about the first sighting on March 27. This was just after it happened. He said, "You know that could be the start of a rash of sightings." You talk about a prophetic statement.

— Anthony Britain, Owner of Friendship Field in Carman

I received five reports out of seven nights last week, and a lot casually mention it to you without filing a report. There are a considerable number of reports, and people who are seeing them are pretty reliable people.

— Corporal Glen Toews, RCMP Officer in Carman

It is a constant complaint that no two descriptions of UFOs are ever the same. A similar grievance is made about photographs. But for every rule there is an exception. When it comes to the Manitoba flap, most people around Carman, where most of the sightings took place, described a "red, glowing, pulsating, bobbing disk that flew ever so slowly and quite close to the ground."

There were, of course, other types of UFOs spotted in the area, but they were few and far between. The descriptions were so similar in the early 1975 depiction that the object was given the name Charlie Red Star.

At times there were variations in the exact portrayal of Charlie, but these can be accounted for by the angle at which the object was seen, or by human nature. The story changed in its telling as any account that is passed around does. The person might not have been paying attention to the detail, or forgot to tell part of what was seen, or added something to make the story sound a bit more impressive.

UFO researcher Coral Lorenzen, who acted as co-director of the Aerial Phenomena Research Organization, explained this reporting problem as follows:

> I've discussed this problem with psychiatrists and psychologists. They say that no two people seeing the same thing, no matter what it is, are going to describe it the same way exactly. All people perceive things differently.
>
> When people are observing UFO phenomena, they're seeing things they've never seen before. They're completely bewildered.[1]

Good evidence to support this drawback to the reporting of sightings can be seen in a quick survey of statements made by 190 of the approximately 400 witnesses to the John F. Kennedy assassination in Dallas, Texas. Estimates of the time from the first shot to the last ranged from a few seconds to five minutes; 52 percent believed the shots were fired from the grassy knoll, compared to 39 percent who thought the shots had come from the Texas Book Depository. The number of shots mentioned by witnesses ranged from two to more than four.[2]

Hence, in something as critical as the assassination of President Kennedy, the testimonies of witnesses must be questioned. That is, until the testimonies are viewed as a whole. Then, using the majority positions, we find that were three shots, two directions, and a time period of four to six seconds.

In Manitoba an overall profile reveals that the majority of people described a "red, pulsing disk, flying low, bobbing, and flying at a low speed." Like the Kennedy assassination evidence, an overall profile is not totally conclusive but is sufficient for intelligent speculation, and pretty hard to dispute.

Sightings of Charlie were restricted to the southern part of Manitoba near Carman, Sperling, and the Miami-Roseisle area. His first documented appearance was on March 27, 1975, and the last for that year was November 17.

The number of sightings wasn't known for sure, but polls taken in the area indicate it was consistently high. In a poll conducted on November 30, 1976, at Carman Collegiate, I asked: "How many of you believe that you have seen something in the past two years that could be considered a UFO?" In response, 52.9 percent indicated they had. August 1974 polls, on the other hand, reported that just 11 percent of Americans "report having seen something they thought was a UFO."

The figures in Carman, therefore, are almost five times the national average. In Roland, a small town of 400 southwest of Carman, a poll taken at a local school indicated that 80 percent of the students claimed to have seen something — seven times the national average.

According to those polled at Carman Collegiate, more students and teachers claimed to have witnessed UFOs in their life (62.5 percent) than those who had seen a Boeing 747 jumbo jet (54.8 percent). This turned out to be rather astonishing. It demonstrated that in Carman the phrase "seeing is believing" wasn't necessarily true. If that were the case, then UFOs would be more real than jumbo jets.

The qualities of the sightings reported at Carman Collegiate were much better than would be expected. Of those who had seen a UFO, more than 50 percent claimed to have been close enough "to see an actual object, as opposed to a light in the sky."

As with any poll, it was conducted to confirm already-existing suspicions. The factors that led to believing the results would indicate a high number of sightings are as follows:

- Charlie Red Star flew right by the town on many nights between April and July.
- This odd pattern attracted a great deal of attention. Local citizens went out of their way to go out and look, hoping to get a glimpse of Charlie.

- The length of the rash of UFO flybys took place over many months, as compared to the usual two weeks that was the pattern of other flaps around the world.
- Charlie moved very slowly (10 to 60 miles per hour). Carman residents weren't the only ones who saw the object, but they were able to witness it up close.
- Charlie was always reported below 1,000 feet, which made him easier to see well.

Since many citizens made it a habit to stay outside and watch for Charlie, it wasn't unusual to talk to people around town who had over 80 sightings of the object in one year. Of those involved during the two years of activity, I was aware of 25 people who claimed they had at least a dozen sightings of Charlie.

It was because people knew they could go out and see it that made the results in the poll in Carman so high. UFO watching had become a pastime. Everyone got involved.

There were even stories about how the name Charlie Red Star evolved. Charlie personified was brilliant red and came from the stars. The object was so familiar and so unique it became like a person's face.

"It was just a big red ball," Frances Stagg told me from her house on the northwest side of town. "It was just like a heartbeat. It was pulsating. It didn't make any sound at all and it was very low. It was silent and floating. The timing of the pulsation wasn't too regular or anything. It was like a heartbeat. That's the only way that I can describe it, and it was so red."

"It was off to the northwest," reported Constable Ian Nickolson, a Royal Canadian Mounted Police (RCMP) officer in Carman. "I'd say it was three to four miles away and 1,000 feet up. There was an oval-shaped light. There was a white X-shaped halo around but not connected to it. The red was the colour of a traffic safety light, a stop light."

"It was a big red ball coming right at us," reported Anthony Britain and his wife. "It was like a big landing light, and it was loafing along. It was close enough that you could actually see the dome on top, but it was all pulsing red."

"It was hovering not far from the horses," Anna McCann told the *National Enquirer*. "They stampeded at first, but later calmed down some. That light from the object was shining down on one of our brown horses and he looked bronze because the light from the object was pink. The object itself was a very bright, bright red colour. It was revolving slowly."

"We were driving west," stated a reporter for the *Dufferin Leader*, "and we saw to the northwest a relatively large bright red light that seemed to be hovering about 50 to 100 feet off the ground. It was very, very bright red."

"It was lower than the [grain] elevator," said Jennette Frost of Sperling, describing one of her many sightings of Charlie. [Jennette had so many sightings that she kept a journal recording everything she saw.] "It was as red as could be. It was just going up and down as these things go [bobbing motion]. It was going up and down and then it rose up at [a grain] elevator and down on the other side."

"It was so stupid," Jennette added. "It seemed that it would even wobble from side to side. It was really an odd-looking thing, but it was as red as could be. This was definitely a disk-shaped sort of thing."

"I was about a mile west of Roland when I saw that red thing glowing over Roland," Travis Taylor told me. "It was quite low to the ground ... and it was a huge saucer-shaped sort of thing. It was glowing red, like I suppose metal would when it's hot. The lights were out in Roland because of the storm and the sky was black, so it really showed up well, really well."

"We were looking west down Klondike," Lacy Christian told me, "and we saw Mrs. McCallum's place, and it looked like it was on fire. Travis hurried out. He started walking and by the time he got to Main Street, the big red thing was below the level of the buildings. Yes, we've seen it [Charlie Red Star] many times. You know what fire looks like through a window. That's it."

These are some of the many descriptions people in and around Carman gave me of their sightings of Charlie Red Star. The accounts seem to parallel one another, which makes it hard to believe all the witnesses made them up. Having seen Charlie myself more than a dozen times, I knew how important their reports were. Their common descriptions built a strong case for the repeatable phenomenon that was Charlie Red Star.

Charlie's First Visit

It was 2:00 a.m. on March 27, 1975. Most Manitoba residents had long since gone to bed. One man from Graysville, however, was still up watching television.

Suddenly, he noticed a huge red ball pass by the kitchen window. He jumped up and caught a glimpse of the object moving slowly over his house. When it was out of sight through the window, he raced outside and watched the object slow down and fly south.

The man didn't tell his wife about this or any of his friends. The only person he told was Lloyd Hebert because he saw the object travel toward the house Lloyd was living in. It had been reported that Lloyd and his wife had seen and heard the object already. Therefore, he figured he and Lloyd could safely talk together about it.

It was Lloyd's daughter, Darlene, who saw the object at the Bourgeois household where the Heberts were staying. She was awakened and immediately noticed that the house was shaking. She also thought the house was on fire. Darlene had been sleeping in the living room on the main floor of the two-storey house, and her bed was in front of the window and the drapes were open.

When she opened her eyes, she caught a glimpse of the red ball as it moved south past the window. She described it as a "loud and fast noise." It was a "steady" noise. It was like "a real shrill, pulsating siren."

"Then again maybe it wasn't like that," Darlene's mother stated, "because I have never heard anything like it before. But it was loud because it woke up the whole family, even grandmother who isn't hearing so good these days."

The front living room was red, and Darlene figured that whatever it was it had set fire to the house. She called to her mother upstairs to come quickly. While she waited, she glanced out the window and saw the huge red object sit itself down in the pasture.

"She was so sure," Mrs. Bourgeois said. "She was positive it was right out there in the pasture. She went out the next day and looked. That's how positive she was. She said it was right beside the trees, sitting right there in the pasture."

Like children racing downstairs to open their Christmas presents, the Bourgeois family came down to the living room one after another. Mrs. Bourgeois was the first to arrive and the only other person to see the object. "I thought it was something tangled up in the evergreen trees," she said. "I didn't know what it was. The noise woke me up. I didn't know if I was dreaming or not, so I got up and looked out the window to the south where the noise had gone. It seemed to come over the house from the north. By the time I got there, the object was way in the south on the horizon. It looked like the sun coming up. It was orange and it looked like it was just over the bush, about three miles away."

And so that was how Charlie Red Star arrived in the Pembina Valley — with a bang, scaring two families half to death. So scared was Darlene Hebert that for three weeks she slept on an air mattress in the hall outside her parents' room upstairs.

The Blast-Off — The First Night

It was the last few days of June 1975. The weather was hot and extremely dry. The Pembina Valley was experiencing its fourth flap of UFO sightings in two months. The people in Carman were again taking up their nightly watches for Charlie Red Star.

Anthony and Rachael Britain had posted themselves at the top of a steep hill in the Pembina Hills just southwest of Miami, Manitoba. This location provided a beautiful view for 70 miles into the Pembina Valley, and it also offered a hideout to avoid the huge crowds gathering at the Britains' airstrip in Carman.

In the early months of the 1975 Carman flap, Charlie was seen at the U.S. border about halfway between the former KCND-TV tower on the border and the town of Walhalla, North Dakota. After crossing the border, Charlie started to drop altitude until at Roland, Manitoba, he wasn't more than 1,000 feet off the ground.

The plan of those who watched from this loft in the hills was to spot Charlie early and then attempt to drive into the valley toward Roland to cut him off. The Britains had seen this flight path numerous times — over the border, up to Carman, back south along Highway 3, past Jordan, and then back into the United States. Most of the time the object pulsated red and resembled a beating heart with a bluish-green field on the forward side.

That night, however, a new lighting formation appeared. "When we first saw that thing from the hill at Miami, it had a blue light and a white light," Anthony said. "As a matter of fact, this night we thought it was an airplane. Paul Sanders was with us, and so was Ian Harris. Rachael said, 'That's a UFO.' And we said, 'It's a plane.'"

Continuing his story, Anthony said, "I don't know why we said that. Because of the lighting, it was all wrong. We were convinced it was an airplane even though it made no sound. We chased it across country and we chased it quite a ways and got fairly close to it because it made its usual swing up to Carman. We caught it cross-country and waited for it. As it came up, we got fairly close to it.

"We hit a dead-end road and watched it with binoculars, and we figured, hell, that's got to be an airplane because it's not going fast enough. The next day, about 2:00 p.m., I got a phone call from a woman who lives south of Roland." She said, 'You know, I don't like to bother you, but last night a UFO scared me and my two kids.' So I said, 'Okay, where were you?' And she told me, 'Well, we were driving home to the farm. We were about two miles south of Roland. This thing came over us and lit up the whole road. It made no noise, and it was about 1,000 feet up. It had a white light and a blue light on it.'"

Anthony asked her what time this had happened. She answered, "About 10 minutes to 11:00."

"Lady," Anthony said, "at about 10 minutes to 11:00 we were watching the same object just four miles west of you. We came to the conclusion that it was a plane."

"That was no plane!" she exclaimed.

"The time and position are identical," Anthony told her.

"I shut off the engine," she continued. "It didn't stall. Then I rolled down the window."

"Did you get out?"

"No way. I looked up at it. There was just no sound."

I asked Anthony what the woman's name was. He said she had given it but that he hadn't written it down. Therefore, I had a good double-witness sighting but had nothing to back it up. A year after the sighting, however, I was in Roland Elementary School, spilling forth my tales to the grade fours, fives, and sixes. Even before I began, a small girl in the first row put up her hand. "I've seen a UFO."

"Where was this?" I asked.

"Just south of town."

"Where was the UFO?"

"Right over the truck."

"Who was with you?" I probed.

"My mommy and sister."

Bingo, I thought to myself. *I haven't even begun to talk and I have what I came to Roland for.* The trip to the elementary school had been a long shot in finding the family, but it had paid off.

The woman turned out to be Jean McMahon. She confirmed the story to me. She also confirmed phoning Anthony Britain with regard to what she had seen near the end of June.

A Saucer Visits Aspen Air Base

"You see something like what I saw," said Peter Chociemski, "and there's no doubt in your mind. Two hours ... you couldn't follow an aircraft that long."

"We're the ones that saw it," added Linda, his 23-year-old wife. "It was a red light. Every time I think about it I get scared."

Peter, his wife, and four-year-old daughter were driving north to their home in Gimli, Manitoba, after a night of shopping in Winnipeg. It was around 10:00 p.m. and they had driven 20 miles when Peter spotted the object near a microwave tower northeast of Clandeboye.

"When I first spotted it, it was just a blinking red light," Peter told the *National Enquirer*'s Daniel Coleman. "It looked like an airplane, but after a couple of miles I noticed that I was passing the light. I was going approximately 60 miles per hour and started passing it. It didn't really seem to have a speed to it. Most of the time it was just standing still."

"Peter never showed it to me for a long time," Linda stated. "Then he said, 'Look at that light in the sky — it's going the same speed we are and it seems that we're keeping up with it.' So we followed it up to Gimli and got about a mile from town or so when it crossed the road and was going into town. Then it went into the Aspen Air Base [west of town] and crossed over the road [east] and continued on. We followed it north of Gimli to Walter Zdanowicz's place."

The object was going so slow that Peter decided to pass it. Pulling into Walter's yard, Peter summoned him to come and see the object.

In conversation with Daniel Coleman and me, Walter confirmed the whole incident and described how the object made two passes over his house from the highway into the west. He made it in time to see the triangle of lights fly over his house the first time and agreed with Walter's interpretation of what the object was.

"Peter said that he was going after it again, so he went back to his car and I went back to my shed," Walter told us. "A couple of minutes later I noticed that Peter was still in the driveway. The thing had made a big circle and was coming back. It flew over the house a second time, and that's when Peter started chasing it again."

Meanwhile, in the car, Peter and his family watched the erratic movements of the craft. "We were watching it and it seemed that every time lights would come down the highway, the object would back up," Linda Chociemski said. "When there were no lights, it would come closer to us. We didn't have any lights on in the car and were just watching it. We couldn't hear a sound. Peter was watching with binoculars and then it started going back [south], so we followed it without lights for a while."

The object headed south down Highway 8, turned west, and continued on Highway 231. When it arrived in Gimli, Peter and his family were hot on its tail.

"The object was within one-tenth or one-eighth of a mile from the highway," Peter said. "It went over to David Roman's place. That's when I really saw it close. I pulled into David's yard, and it was close … maybe 50 yards. It was just on the south side of his house, and it was so low you could have hit it with a rock if you threw hard enough. It was about the height of the TV antenna."

Peter jumped out of the car, ran to David's house, and pounded on the back door. David was alone inside, watching television when he heard the noise. Thinking it was his son, he made no move to answer the door. As the banging continued, however, he got up to see who it was. Finding Peter standing there urging him to come outside, he figured the visitor had had an accident or was drunk. But at Peter's insistence he decided to see what the emergency was. In a later conversation with Coleman and myself, David admitted, "I'm sure sorry that I didn't hurry."

While Peter got David out of the house, his wife and daughter waited in the car 50 yards from the hovering object. For them the night's fun was over.

"When Peter went to the house," Linda told Coleman, "it started coming lower and lower, and that's when I saw it. It was the shape of a saucer and had these little windows. It came down and landed, and when it landed, the lights went out and we couldn't find it. Sherri was so scared. She was saying, 'Let's go home.' When Peter got back into the car, I told him that I wanted to go home. I was pretty scared. I wanted to leave it, but Peter didn't want to. He wanted to follow it, but I was too scared to look at it."

Returning to the car a few minutes later, Peter shone the car lights on the field south of the farm to see the landed saucer. They couldn't find it, so they switched off the lights and waited for David Roman.

"About two seconds after we shut the lights off the craft lit up and it took off again and landed on the runway. [Aspen Air Base was a half mile east of David's farm.] It went east and landed like a helicopter."

Finally, David appeared, and Peter tried to point the object out to him. "But I couldn't distinguish it from all the hangar lights at the air base," David recalled. "He knew which one it was, but I couldn't see it."

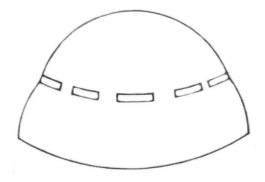

Peter Chociemski's drawing of a UFO with windows.

David got into his truck, Peter returned to his car, and they started after it, heading east toward the base.

"We went driving around," Peter said, "with no lights or anything, and we came back to the yard and talked for a while. Roman still didn't believe me. All of a sudden the lights came back on, blinking. It went along the ground maybe a hundred yards and lifted off and went south. The funny thing about it was that Roman said, 'It's an airplane,' but it gave a roar when it took off and then went silent."

"Now that I saw," David said, "it was a light rising into the south of the base. It made a low, rumbling noise, but this only lasted for a few seconds. I worked at the base for 21 years [clearing snow from the runways], and it didn't sound like a plane to me. Which runway it came off, I don't know. I couldn't tell because of the distance. It was moving too slowly to be a plane, and it was moving off into the south."

Upon seeing the light take off, Peter hopped into his car and sped off after it again. David, still uncertain what was happening, declined to go.

"I followed it for miles," Peter said. "It was going back to Winnipeg Beach, four, five miles from here. It was after midnight when we left it. My car was running low on gas, and my wife was after me to leave, so we just left it, hovering over the treetops."

The *National Enquirer* was extremely interested in this case and in a landing that occurred south of Doris People's farm four miles east of David Roman's place. When Coleman and I talked to Doris, we found that she, too, had been involved in the Chociemski sighting.

Doris and her 13-year-old daughter had been driving home, west on Highway 231 one night, which she was sure was the same evening as the Chociemski encounter.

"Whatever it was, it was sitting in Roman's yard," she told us. "From the road it was about a block. Not even a block, because I said to the girl, 'It's funny that they're having a wiener roast at this time of the night.'"

Doris estimated the object to be about half the size of the barn. Peter and his wife had described the object as taller.

"It was about 30 feet in diameter," Peter told us, "roughly … I don't know … 15 feet … 12 feet high. You could see the outline when it was lit up. It had rectangular windows [wider than tall] around it, four or five on the side that I could see. They were about two-thirds the way up the craft. The lights coming out of the windows were different colours. They would get brighter and duller."

Doris, however, only got a brief glimpse of the object. "I drove right on by," she said. "I didn't take notice of it until after I saw this thing [referring to the object that landed down the road from her farm] and I heard that Peter had seen it."

Asked whether she had discussed the event with Roman, she answered, "No, because no one would believe me. I thought, *No, I'm not going to say anything*."

There were strong indications from my sources at Gimli Collegiate that a number of students had been involved in the Chociemski affair, but those people didn't wish to get involved. Still, with the number of witnesses, the similar times, and the closeness of the sighting, the Chociemski case must be considered a classic.

Four days after Peter Chociemski sighted the first object, he and five others made a spectacular sighting at the plant they were employed at north of town and east of Highway 8 where Peter had chased the first object. This was a fairly lengthy sighting, and the RCMP was involved.

Peter told the story to me but then stated a couple of months later to the *National Enquirer* that he couldn't talk about it. I recognize Peter's desire not to do so and include reference to the incident only to show there were quite a few sightings in the Gimli-Fraserwood area during that week in April 1976.

The Second Night — Charlie Takes Off

On the second night a car salesman named Sam Brazil, one of the few night pilots in southern Manitoba, joined the Britains at their private sighting spot high in the Pembina Hills.

"After that night," Anthony Britain told me, "Brazil's life would never be the same."

It was the usual routine. Charlie appeared at the border and started his descent toward Carman. Tannis Major, the photographer, and the Britains were off to the car in a shot. They moved quickly to cut Charlie off.

Brazil, the rookie, wasn't so sure. "He felt sorry for us because he was sure that we were chasing an airplane," Anthony told me with a chuckle in his voice.

They headed into the valley after Charlie, but as if Charlie had seen the posse coming, he cut short the loop and continued back long before he got to Carman. "Consequently," Anthony and Rachael Britain told me, "we were behind him by the time we got to the highway in the valley."

Nevertheless, they sped south down Highway 3 after him. As with the sighting the night before, the lighting formation had begun as a blue-and-white light. "As we chased it," Anthony said, "the light changed to a pulsating red light, and from then on we never lost sight of it. Then it went from a pulsing red to a steady red, so it changed configurations three times while we watched it."

Brazil, however, was still convinced it was a plane. He told the Britains that it would go back to the west and land at Jordan. Instead, Charlie headed south into North Dakota. "It disappeared over the horizon into the U.S.," Anthony said, "and the four of us decided that the night's fun was over, so we turned around and started back for Carman. Suddenly we noticed that it was coming back at us, and as it was coming back, it wasn't pulsing. It was solid red."

Everyone got out of the car and watched as the object moved north, closer and closer to their position. As Anthony watched it with his 7x50 binoculars, Tannis set up her camera for a picture she would never get.

"It almost got close enough for Tannis to get a picture, but not quite," Anthony said. "She got the camera set up, trained on it, tele-photo lens and all, but what are you going to take a picture of? One little light? She waited too long. She was waiting for it to get a little closer, and all of a sudden one, two lights went off, the other dimmed, and she was beat."

The whole episode about the lights dimming down and then shutting off was a complex affair, and the inquisitive mind of Anthony Britain had a lot to say about it. As the object approached, Anthony handed his binoculars to Brazil, whose plane theory was now shot down in flames. He watched it for a while and then cried out, "It's changing its altitude!"

When Anthony got his binoculars back, he confirmed Brazil's observations. "It had shifted itself on its edge. Just as it flipped on the angle, many other things happened. It got close enough so that I could actually see it against the starlight — the shape of the thing. You know. The disk shape of the thing ... you put together two plates and you get sort of a cigar shape. It had two lights on the edge of the disk."

Anthony continued. "It had two running lights from each side. When it went on an angle, the bottom light went out and the top light sucked down. The top light was the only one that remained. Everyone thought it had disappeared. I could see with the binoculars that it was still there. It had just sucked down its light the same way as when you short out a welder." He referred to a drawing he had just made. "There was a haze here. Like St. Elmo's fire. Some type of field, but it was actually like little fingers of flame, just the same as the one that we saw at the tower."

To prove his point, he got a colour drawing that had been done by Brian James of Winnipeg. Just as Anthony was now telling me, there was a field protruding out the side of a cigar-shaped object.

"It disappeared from us as it moved in a long arc upward," he said. "The lights started to come on as if it no longer needed the power. As the power came back on, it got brighter and brighter. Brazil told me that without the binoculars he could see it getting brighter as it moved off into space. It picked up speed. Soon it was going so fast that I said, 'See, it's going from that star to that star to that star. It achieved orbit in 35 seconds from the time it flipped on its side, which is faster than any man-made machine.'"

From this observation, which was one of the best Anthony Britain made from his numerous sightings of Charlie Red Star, he drew up a list that outlined the things he believed were going on.

1. It was manned because it went out in a long, large arc.
2. I believe the drive is electronic because of the sucked-down light and the fact they shut the other one off to conserve power.
3. They weren't using anti-gravity because they wouldn't have put on the

angle and the long bank. They were setting up the best G angle.

4. They conserve energy because they didn't go into orbit to the south, the direction it was travelling, but arced to the east so they could use the spinoff off the ground.

5. Their most economical cruising speed is between 60 and 80 miles per hour.

6. They like to fly not more than 1,000 feet or usually less. When they set up for blast-off, they were below 1,000 feet.

7. It had a halo under it after an angle. It looked like St. Elmo's fire, or blue mist, some type of magnetic field.

8. Power came back on [light got brighter] as it achieved orbit. This would mean less power drain.

9. Orbit in 35 seconds, counted from suck-down until it was gone. No noise. We were within five miles, maybe as little as three miles. It was hard to tell at night.

The Third Night

According to Anthony Britain, Sam Brazil saw the same thing again six months later in December 1975. Brazil and his wife were driving east to Winnipeg on Highway 2 and had just passed through Starbuck, Manitoba. Near the Starbuck tower, his wife saw an object on the ground and pointed it out to Sam, asking him whether it was a yard light.

They slowed the car and watched it. It didn't look right. It was little and red and didn't have the same halo found around a yard light.

"All of a sudden it took off," Anthony said. "Same circumstances. It went into orbit, but this time he was on the other side of it. It went into orbit over them." It made a bank and headed up and into the east just as the one at Morden had done. "This time, Anthony added, "it left a definite trail."

And Now Others See

It was April 10, partway through Darlene Hebert's recuperation period, when Charlie appeared again, this time swooping east into the Pembina Valley toward Carman.

There were many witnesses this time, including the Britains. This was the first time they saw Charlie Red Star, but it wouldn't be their last. They probably had more sightings than anyone else who came forward as witnesses in the Carman area.

Looking back at the April 10 sighting, Anthony Britain commented, "That is probably the closest we've ever been to the thing. It was close enough so that you could see the dome on the top, but it was all red — pulsing red. It was a big red light coming at us, like a big landing light. You couldn't miss it. It was right at eye level, and it was just loafing along. I looked at it, and even after it was by us, I still didn't want to believe it. No way had I wanted to believe it."

The object headed along the river and then north of town. Rachael Britain urged Anthony to chase it, but as he said, "It was at a low level, and when you are low like that, it is soon over the horizon. You don't have much time."

At the same time the Britains were watching the object head north out of town, Maria Rhodes was sitting in her living room crocheting and gazing out the window toward the airport where the Britains were standing.

"I saw this red ball go by the trees," Maria stated. "It was low down by the trees. I just happened to look out, and I just saw that big thing. It was low and it was a great big thing. You know — like fire. It looked like a red ball. It was very red — that's one thing that I noticed."

As Anthony described it, Charlie followed the Boyne River through Carman on the way out of the north side of town. It was at this point that Freda Waterman spotted the object as it flew over her house along the river.

"It was exactly as Anthony Britain described it," she told me. "That was the first time that I saw it, and it disturbed me. I didn't know what to do, so I didn't report it. It was a couple of days later that Anthony told his story. That's when I realized it was the same time as mine."

That ended Charlie Red Star's April 10 flight, but it wouldn't be his last. Charlie was seen many times and often by Anthony Britain around his small airstrip. Once, as Anthony explained, Charlie flew low along the runway, just feet off the ground. There were also many more witnesses, some who made it a hobby to hunt UFOs every night.

The reported sightings over the next couple of weeks were scattered. May brought with it sightings all over the province. A particular one occurred south of Morden near the U.S. border.

It was 4:15 a.m. on May 4 near the farm of James and Tina Stevens. The couple had just returned from closing down and cleaning the drive-in movie theatre they ran in Morden. Shortly after going to bed, Tina was awakened by a bright light passing north into the valley over the house.

"It was suddenly like a bright sunny day," she told me. "I was really scared by what was happening and I tried to wake up James to see the light, but he didn't get up in time."

The object moved low over the Stevens's house heading toward Howard Rempel's farm a mile down the road. "The dogs woke us up with their barking," Mrs. Rempel told the *National Enquirer*. "We looked out the upstairs window and immediately noticed there was a bright light in the corner of the driveway out there about 50 yards from the house."

"It wasn't a bright light," Mrs. Rempel added. "It was more like a fluorescent glow with no focus to it or anything. It was twice the size of a car, maybe 15 to 20 feet long and 10 to 12 feet high. I didn't notice any edges to it, so it's hard to say exactly what."

The Rempels watched the object for 45 minutes until shortly before the sun began to rise. "In a very short time," Mrs. Rempel said, "the glow just faded away and was gone. There was no movement that we could see. It didn't take off or anything. It just faded and was gone."

Two days later in another part of the province there were other sightings. In a major one, Roger Pitts and two other pilots spotted three disks in daylight flying right at their plane one after another.

"There were two pilot sightings reported the day before," Pitts stated. "We were southbound from Churchill, Manitoba, with a DC-3 at 6,000 feet and we were coming up on Berens River. There were three of us on board. All of us were pilots, and we spotted an aircraft coming at us at quite a distance. It drew closer and closer. We were both watching it [pilot and co-pilot], trying to determine what it was. We noticed that it wasn't flying straight and level. It was flying on a 45-degree angle, but it was still flying straight at us. As we watched, it didn't turn around. It just went directly the other way straight away from us. It just went off into the distance away from us, and a puff of smoke appeared — an odd shape, like a small cloud, and it disappeared in that."

Then a second object appeared, flew at the plane, reversed its direction, and disappeared in a puff of smoke. A third one appeared with the three pilots watching. It did the same thing.

The evening after the pilots were being challenged by the UFOs, the Britains, along with Wayne Teal, Bob Skelton, and David Rosenfield, were repairing the landing lights on the runway at Friendship Field when they noticed Charlie coming toward Carman from the west again. As quickly as they could, they scrambled into a car and chased Charlie out to the north end of town where he sped up and continued northeast toward Winnipeg. The time was 11:15 p.m.

The next night the Britains, Teal, Rosenfield, and a member of the Royal Canadian Air Force were again at Friendship Field when they spotted Charlie approaching the airport. Wayne and Anthony climbed onto the roof of one of the hangars to watch the object fly. "This night the object was lower than the previous night and proceeding at 60 to 80 miles per hour," Anthony told the local newspaper.

This made three sightings for the Britains in only a couple of days, all of the same red bobbing and pulsating ball.

"The first time we saw it," Anthony recalled, "it was 10 minutes before we phoned the RCMP. We were sort of debating whether we should report the thing. We didn't get much reaction the first time. It wasn't until I phoned on the eighth that there was a reaction. I was sort of kicking my tail for phoning because it kicked up such a hornets' nest."

RCMP Constable Ian Nickolson drove out to Friendship Field to see what was going on. As he arrived, he spotted the object in the west, three to four miles away, about 1,000 feet high.

"I drove a mile north to Highway 245, which goes west out of town," he told the *National Enquirer*. "Then I went another mile west where I stopped the car. Off to the northwest, there was an oval-shaped red light. There was a white halo around it, not connected to it. The light was somewhat like the colour of a traffic safety light — a stop light.

"I sat there for two to three minutes just looking at the object, which appeared stationary at the time. Then I decided to get a closer look at it. I drove west on Route 245 in my police car — and I can say it was moving pretty fast. As I was going west, the object seemed to be flying in a northeasterly direction. I continued for approximately 12 miles, keeping the object in sight, trying to get somewhat abreast of it so that if the opportunity arose, I could have driven north toward it. About 16 miles west of Carman I stopped the car. I'd seen that there was no way that I was going to catch up to it, so I stopped the car and watched the object go out of sight over the treeline on the horizon."

The next day, May 9, the Canadian Broadcasting Corporation (CBC) phoned Rachael Britain and the story was out of the bag. "Of course," Rachael said, "half the town of Carman was at the airfield when dusk fell."

The runway lights were on, and one of Anthony's planes stood ready should Charlie appear. The large group of onlookers waited, and soon it was near midnight with no sign of Charlie.

"Everyone had gone," Anthony recalled, "when suddenly Paul Sanders came driving up. He was just shaking."

Sanders was sitting a half mile southwest of the Britains' house near the garbage dump. As a reporter from the *Dufferin Leader* recounted in a story about Sanders's sighting, Sanders had seen the object flying from east to west. He also had his field glasses with him, and as it turned to veer north, he observed potholes on the underside. In Sanders's estimation it was as big as a DC-3. Then it disappeared from his sight below the trees at the cemetery.

Charlie seemed to take May 10 off, but on May 11 he made a major sweep through the valley. The first people to spot him were the Britains, Wayne Teal, and Barry Johnson. They chased the saucer-shaped object as it flew north on a 20-degree angle. In a line between Haywood and Carman, the object hovered for a few minutes. It then flew toward the Southport Air Base at Portage la Prairie. It was 12:20 a.m. as the group drove to Carman.

Those who had chased him in Carman had now gone to bed, but it appeared that Charlie hadn't quite finished his work for the night. At 1:30 a.m. Jennette Frost spotted him from her kitchen window 12 miles east of Carman, flying over Sperling.

The brilliant red object was reported just above the horizon and spent 20 minutes dropping four small blue saucer-shaped craft to the ground. (See Chapter 4, "It's Funny They Should Be the Same.")

On the night of May 12, a large group gathered at the CBC tower on the northeast corner of Carman. They included pilots, professional photographers, and a crew from CKY-TV in Winnipeg. Although Charlie did show up and was seen by the group, he never got close enough for CKY to get good nighttime film.

That same night Carl Major was travelling south out of Carman toward Roland when his wife said, "See, what's that?" Later that evening he joined the large gathering at the tower and reported he "was pretty darn sure he had seen the darn thing because it was the shape of a Ferris wheel with lights all around."

The next night 10 people, including the television crew, showed up north of town. They spotted an object that appeared to sit northwest of town and wondered if they would be able to film it.

At 11:00 p.m. they were certain the object was on the ground. While the television crew stayed at the tower, two groups left to surround the object. By the end of that night, the group had obtained one of the most important nocturnal light films in history. It became known as the CKY-TV movie.[3]

Once the footage was played on TV, many of the staff at the station wanted to come out and get more. On May 14, the now-larger CKY crew arrived to obtain further film of Charlie but came up empty-handed. If they had stayed a few more nights, they would have had greater luck. At 2:00 a.m., on May 16, Charlie visited the same area one more time.

This dramatic sighting took place at Stephenfield Dam, only three miles west from where the object filmed by the CKY crew had jumped off the ground. It was early Sunday morning, and the Saturday night beach party was dragging on. Twenty-five people from the Carman area were gathered on the north shore of the Stephenfield Dam Reservoir.

At 2:00 a.m. five men left the party and walked over the dam to the south side of the reservoir. They stood on the dock, overlooking the water. Suddenly, a huge, glowing red object the size of a full moon appeared over the dam a couple hundred feet away from the dock. The object remained there motionless for a few seconds and then shot a white beam into the reservoir between two buoys.

The beam remained at that point in the water for a few seconds before the five men noticed that a smaller white object, six to 10 feet across, had formed below the spot where the beam had touched the water, about 100 feet from shore.

Next, the glowing white object beneath the surface of the water started to move slowly toward the dock on which the men were standing. It was extremely luminous, lighting up the water in the reservoir to such an extent that the bottom of the lake could be seen. The lake at that location was 15 feet deep.

Ripples formed on the water as the object moved closer to the dock directly at the stunned five witnesses. When the object came within 15 feet of the dock, Wiebe, one of the five, picked up a rock, and in desperation, threw it at the approaching object.

The rock hit the object, and in an unbelievable fashion, split it into four pieces. These broken four pieces then slowly assembled in a straight line. The row of pieces subsequently moved back, as if on a conveyor belt, to a place halfway between the two buoys where they had first appeared.

The beam was still pointed into the water, and moments after the four objects arrived back at the point between the buoys, the beam and objects disappeared. The five men then turned their attention to the red object perched on the dam and witnessed a second incredible occurrence.

The huge red disk abruptly broke into two pieces. These two pieces then flew east toward Carman. Each piece exhibited flight characteristics that would become commonly tied to descriptions of Charlie. They zigzagged back and forth, up and down, and appeared to play a game of tag with each other as they flew away.

The five stunned young people raced back to Carman and reported their encounter to the RCMP.

"Things were just starting to heat up in the two weeks previous to May 24," Anthony Britain told me. "We were spending most of our time out at the CBC tower north of Carman."

Each night different people met to wait patiently for Charlie to appear. Some brought along sandwiches and coffee. Anthony was armed with a movie camera, the Majors with a still camera.

Many good sightings were made in mid-May near the tower. In one case, five people watched as a huge 200-foot object resembling a Ferris wheel raced toward the tower, then reversed direction 180 degrees without anyone seeing it stop or turn around. In a second case, two people witnessed Charlie suddenly materializing out of dense fog to fly east close to the tower. It occurred only moments after the majority of the group returned home. In the most spectacular sighting reported during the middle weeks of May, Charlie was reported sitting at the top of the 570-foot tower, jumping back and forth from one side to the other.

Tannis Major, the photographer, spent 26 nights in May and the first couple of nights in June trying to obtain a photo of Charlie. In those 26 nights, she witnessed 19 sightings and took close to 60 pictures. "A lot of them are too far away," she told me. "All you get is a dot on the film."

The week following May 24 marked the heaviest part of the flap in the valley, and Tannis was finally able to get photographs of Charlie that were good enough to place in her slide collection.

The sightings made from May 24 to June 1 numbered close to 100. It was an extremely hot week with temperatures in the high eighties. The media was on the Charlie Red Star story enthusiastically, and as a result, hundreds of people from Winnipeg drove around Carman every night attempting to see the object.

Some people knew exactly where to be to get a good sighting. In the northwest corner of town, numerous people watched nightly as Charlie flew low past their neighbourhood.

"The first time we saw Charlie," Frances Stagg told me, "was when it flew low over our house. That was late May. I forgot the exact dates. Mrs. Major photographed that one. She was at the CBC tower, and it was one of the good pictures that she got. I phoned her afterward and she said that it was 11:06 or 11:07.

"We were just having coffee, and Art [her husband] looked out the window and said, 'There it goes.' It just drifted over the house. It was a big red ball, just like a heartbeat. It was pulsating. It didn't make any sound at all and it was very low. We ran out to the fence and watched it go to the south of us. It was quiet outside, and there was no wind. The thing was silent and seemed to be floating.

"The next night we had just arrived home when it [the object] was moving into the north, higher up this time. A lot of people were outside on the street, so I called to them and they watched it with us." On the following night, she added, "It came again — same time, just farther north of us."

A night later, Frances told me, "Charlie came from the north and headed south over town. The people on the streets around us watched this one, as well. I quickly ran into the house and phoned my daughter [who lived near the centre of town]. Her husband came out and followed it for quite a while. He followed it south for 10 or 15 miles at 60 miles per hour. It was very low and was pacing the car. Finally, he [her daughter's husband] got to the point where he was running out of gas and had to stop, but when he left it, it was going straight south toward Miami. Charlie was low, as low as he'd ever been."

The Staggs saw Charlie more than anyone else in northwest Carman. They figured around 12 times. Most of their sightings occurred in this late May period. Some nights, the Staggs told me, there were "several" UFOs "flying around the edge of town" at one time.

Of all these sightings, the most interesting one was when Art Stagg, Frances's husband, believed he had seen the RCMP chasing one out of town past his house. "Whoever they were," he stated, "they picked it up before I did. They went racing by my place doing at least 80 miles per hour down the back road to the corner. I saw the object they were chasing, and I looked at it with my binoculars. It was close because in the binoculars you'd swear it was going to hit you in the face. It was just like a heartbeat. I wanted to see through the entire glow around it, to see the object, but I couldn't.

"I mentioned the incident to some Mounties a few days later, but they said it wasn't them. They told me they weren't out that night. But it was them. I know because the car had a white door with the emblem. When they got to the corner, they turned out their lights and one guy got out to look at it. He had something he was looking through, but I couldn't tell whether it was a camera or binoculars. They stayed there for 10 minutes watching it because it had landed west of the tower. Then they got back in the car and went flying back toward Britain's airport, looking around, but Anthony said he hadn't seen them."

It wasn't only the Carman area that was visited by UFOs that week. They were seen all through the valley. In Haywood, 12 miles northwest of Carman, there were numerous sightings of a pulsing red object flying around the two Haywood microwave towers.

Ten miles farther north, at Portage la Prairie, a couple of daylight sightings occurred close to Southport Air Base. In the first, a woman who was an instructor on the base left after work to go home. She was driving south down a gravel road near the base when she spotted a saucer-shaped object travelling parallel to the car over the field.

The woman was greatly frightened by the object and became paralyzed with fear when her engine suddenly stopped running. As her car coasted, she glanced at the object and noticed it was rotating slowly. The object appeared to be red, but as the other side spun toward her, she saw that it was green. It seemed to her that it had a rectangular door without hinges or a doorknob.

Her car slowed to a stop between two sets of trees on either side of the road. As she reached the trees that separated her from the object, her car suddenly started again. Without even a second look behind her, the woman put the accelerator to the floor and raced away.

Another "hot area" where numerous sightings were made in the last week of May 1975 was the one between Elie and Marquette. The sightings around Marquette were described to me by one of those involved as "regular — it's not uncommon to see them flying around this area." Close to Brunkild, the sightings centred near the 190-foot microwave tower at the east end of town.

The sightings at the Brunkild tower seemed somehow connected to three major ones at the microwave tower three miles south of Elie, or at least that was what Wilson McKennett thought. He was involved in all three sightings.

"I heard about the ones at Brunkild," McKennett said. "They were around the tower there. My impression was that the tower was the logical place for them to be sighted."

McKennett, his hired hand, and 10 other witnesses had watched a huge UFO appear over the telephone microwave tower at Elie three consecutive nights during the last week in May. Each time four smaller craft emerged, two to sit watch, one on top, and one to fly back to Portage la Prairie and Winnipeg.

It was during that week that I initially became involved as an investigator in researching the numerous UFO sightings. I had heard the news reports that they were being seen throughout southwestern Manitoba like clockwork and figured that if they were actually there, I wanted to see them myself.

On the night of May 29 and into the morning of May 30 some friends and I decided to travel by car to Carman where Charlie Red Star made his regular swing through the valley. None of us had ever seen a UFO before. Therefore, we spent more than an hour driving around Carman searching for something unidentified with no idea what to look for. At 12:55 a.m. it happened. As we journeyed west into Carman, we sighted a red ball advancing northeast over the town, moving fairly slowly in an up-and-down pattern.

We got out of the car and watched it fly by past the tower and off toward Winnipeg. Looking more closely, I noticed it wasn't the simple red ball we had first seen. The outer part of the object was red, but the inner section seemed to consist of a smaller white portion with the white extending vertically up and down from the centre. The object disappeared over the horizon in about three minutes.

Two nights later I returned with one of the friends from the first sighting. Figuring that the object would come over the same area at the same time, we placed ourselves on a dirt road a quarter mile west of Friendship Field.

When we arrived at the spot, we discovered nine parked cars and assumed it was the airport parking lot. That assumption was wrong. As it turned out, the owners of the cars were people from surrounding towns and Winnipeg.

The 25 people, like us, were there hoping to catch a glimpse of the now-famous Charlie Red Star. It was 11:00 p.m. and the majority of people had been there for more than an hour without seeing anything.

Glancing around, we noticed other cars driving along the mile roads surrounding the area. Everyone was trying to get a good spot for the night's

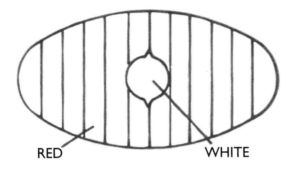

RED   WHITE

Strange lighting on a UFO craft.

air show. Midnight came, and some of those around us became discouraged. They left thinking that as long as they were there nothing would appear. As 1:00 a.m. approached, there were only two cars of hopefuls left. The other car that was there was also preparing to leave when I told them that two nights before a sighting had occurred five minutes before 1:00 a.m., so they decided to wait.

Just before 1:00, Charlie materialized on the western horizon. First came one flash, then another eight inches down in the field of vision. Shortly after, there was another flash over to one side. Whatever was coming appeared to be jumping all over the sky. Minutes passed and the flashes became closer together. Finally, it was near enough that we could recognize it as the same object we saw two nights earlier. It flew straight toward us and looked as if it would fly right over. When it reached within a half mile of us, the object turned northeast toward the CBC tower.

As it crossed our field of vision, the object again seemed to bounce up and down. Once it was downrange, it started to jump all over the sky again. Nine people saw it and all were speechless. What the others thought about their sightings, I don't know. I do know that I told myself that after all these sightings in Carman it was about time someone found out what was going on.

I had two definite sightings in two nights. Little did I know that on my third trip I would have my third sighting in a row. With two good sightings in the week prior to June 4, I and two other friends headed to

Carman early on the fourth to see if we could again see Charlie. The two previous times he had appeared close to 1:00 a.m., so we left Winnipeg shortly before midnight to be just in time.

At 12:25 we passed Sperling and then drove the last dozen or so miles to Carman. Suddenly, I spotted Charlie flying a mile north of the highway above a line of trees parallel to the highway and along a set of power lines running in the same direction.

Of the dozen sightings I had of the mysterious object, this opportunity provided the best view of it. We were well within a mile when we first spotted it, and it gradually moved farther and farther away as it crossed directly north of us. The object was no more than 100 feet in the air, and its size seemed intense compared to the two previous times we had viewed it.

The pulsing of the object was slow and extremely evident. It almost gave the impression that it was changing shape. Because it appeared to be flying the same flight plan reported by Carman residents and because it was the same object we had seen previously, we figured the nightly trip had occurred early and we would see nothing in Carman. Nevertheless, we waited in Carman until 1:10 a.m., but nothing appeared.

Eight miles directly north of us, though, something was happening. Joseph and Anna McCann were returning home at 12:15 a.m. when they spotted a red light to the west of their farm near the Haywood tower.

"We followed it for a ways," Joseph told the *National Enquirer*, "but then we lost it. We kept on going, and all of a sudden, there it was in the field, Abe Trenja's field. It was a huge red thing. The neighbour boy, Alex Dufferin, saw it, too. It was slowly revolving and there was a silvery pink colour around. Suddenly, it disappeared. I don't know how. We didn't see it rise."

"I never saw it disappear," Anna added.

"That's the end of it," Joseph said. "Maybe it was our imagination. I'm going to finish my seeding." At 1:00 a.m. Joseph was planning to head out to finish seeding his fields.

The McCanns then turned their truck around and drove home. Just south of their farm, they spotted the object again in the field northwest of their farmyard. "We thought it was in our field at first," Anna told me. "But when we got to the yard we saw that it was on the other side of the road.

We had about 20 horses around the yard and they were real scared. There were some stallions in the barn, and we swore they were going to knock out the side of the barn."[4]

"There were some horses in the yard," she continued, "and the object wasn't far away. After the horses calmed down, we noticed that the light from the object was shining down on one of the horses and he looked bronze because the light from the object was pink. The object itself was very bright, bright red in colour, and it was revolving very slowly."

Anna McCann told the *Dufferin Leader* that she wasn't sure whether the object had landed or whether it was hovering, but it was close to the ground and sitting on an angle. What caused it, she didn't know, but it appeared to her that there had been some movement of objects that resembled human forms around it.

"The light, it turned slowly, slowly, slowly," she told the *National Enquirer*. "I said to Joseph, 'I think there is someone walking around it.' And then I said, 'No, it must be from the lights.'"

Later I questioned Anna on this point and found that she believed the shadows were caused by large rotating lights on the bottom of the craft, and because of the movement of the high grass around the craft.

Joseph and Anna McCann's barn 35 years later.

The McCanns watched the craft until 3:30 a.m. At no time did they try to get closer. "We were too scared to get closer," Anna said.

When they finally decided to go to bed, Anna covered up the windows on the west side of the house because of the pinkish red light filling the rooms. They had recently built the house and hadn't put up drapes yet.

Randy Neuman, a 17-year-old who lived with the McCanns, was awakened by this red light, as well. He told the *National Enquirer* about one of two encounters he had. "I wouldn't have believed them [the McCanns] when they told me about seeing them, but I saw it myself. I saw it about 4:00 a.m. [after the McCanns had covered the windows and gone to bed] out in the field. I just woke up and saw the red light. It was about a hundred yards off the road. It was huge. Like from that end of the room to over here [30 feet]. It was red, steady red. I watched it for five minutes and then it just took off. It was still red when it took off. All of a sudden I couldn't see it anymore. On the Sunday night I saw the object, it was almost in the same place. It was flashing Sunday night off and on. I thought it was a cop car outside, so I looked and this thing was sitting in the field. It stayed about 20 minutes that time and then it took off."

A little more than four hours later, 55 miles west of Carman, Henri François joined the group who claimed to have seen a UFO close up on that day. "It was daylight, twenty to eight," he told *National Enquirer* reporter Daniel Coleman. "I was going east on the road that passes my house, going toward Route 34 where I turn and go south 30 miles to St. Leon, where I work building houses. About 200 yards from the highway, I saw this flashing light, real bright, on the dirt road directly ahead of me, a half mile or so beyond Route 34. I didn't know what it was. I was looking for a tractor or a car or something, and the closer I got to the highway, I knew right away what it was from reports I'd heard.

"I was a little frightened. You don't see these things every day. The object was right in the middle of the road, but not on the road. It was maybe a foot or two off the road, because I could see a little bit of the road underneath it. The light was on top, just bright flashes, so bright I couldn't see anything in the centre of the object, but I could see the sides and they came out like wedges, like the edges of a disk, out over the sides of the road. The edges were sort of greyish, like the atmosphere."

François rolled down his window but heard nothing. He drove south 100 yards and stopped. The object was still there. He then headed to the nearest farmhouse and brought back a woman as a witness, but when he returned to the scene, the object was gone.

There was another daylight sighting nearby that occurred hours later. The case again involved the McCanns and it happened in their 160-acre pasture about 20 miles north of the main farm. Dr. Hill, a Carman veterinarian, was with the McCanns checking their horses pastured there for swamp fever. It was between 2:00 and 3:00 in the afternoon.

Suddenly, Anna McCann spotted the top of a round silvery object settling behind some trees north of them. She thought it was a weather balloon and put it out of her mind. The "weather balloon," however, was very close to her husband.

The huge craft passed 20 to 25 feet from the truck Joseph was in at treetop level. Joseph described it to me as consisting of two "domes" making up the top and bottom of the craft. In between these two domes there was a section of clear material resembling glass. The top was silver and the bottom was milky white. "Like the belly of a fish," he told me.

Joseph was naturally quite shaken by the unexpected appearance of the object and tried to get the truck home as fast as possible, but it stalled and wouldn't restart. (He had bought it new only the day before.)

"Maybe it stalled because I tried to get away so fast," Joseph told me, "but it wouldn't start." He sat and watched the object as it flew slowly east, finally disappearing behind the treeline.

The object, as described by Joseph to the media, was 80 to 85 feet in length, but that wasn't the actual size. His wife told me, "It was the size of the barn — at least 200 feet."

I asked Anna why her husband had only reported 80 to 85 feet. She explained that Joseph was quite rattled by the sighting. He had had two sightings the previous night and still had one to come later the same night. Joseph figured that with so many close sightings in such a short time nobody would believe him if he told them the thing was 200 feet — and he was right.

The majority of the people in the area didn't believe the McCanns' numerous encounters, even though most of them were seeing the same things. The incident at the pasture became only one more story the family would have to live down.

That sighting wasn't the end of the experience. "About 15 minutes later," Anna told me, "there was a big whirlwind and everything was moving around. The branches were breaking off the trees. There was a rumbling sound, and you could feel the ground shake!"

In addition, ashes from an area that had been burnt a year earlier swirled up about 30 feet into the air. She gazed north toward the trees and saw a large greyish object rising quickly into the sky, which seemed to shrink rapidly as it flew north away from them.

Seeking a witness to this bizarre occurrence, Anna approached Dr. Hill, who was near her. He had seen nothing because he was busy checking a horse. "Had he heard the noise?" she asked.

Anna said to me, "He told me he had heard and felt it but that it was just a bunch of moose moving through the bush. I told him, 'There are no moose around here.' And then he told me it was a lumber wagon going through the bush. 'There hasn't been one of those things around for 20 years,' I said. I told him we don't live in those days anymore."

I was extremely interested in what Dr. Hill really thought of the incident, so I visited him in his Carman office. At this point, to the *National Enquirer*, he had already discounted the incident as anything significant.

After introducing myself, I asked him whether he remembered an incident that occurred while he was working on some horses in the McCanns' north pasture. The McCann sightings were extremely important to me for many reasons — one being that the majority of people didn't believe the couple.

"It wasn't a UFO," Hill told me. He said this despite the fact I hadn't mentioned UFOs yet. "I'll tell you the same thing I told the last guy who was here [Daniel Coleman from the *National Enquirer*]. I don't know what it was, but it wasn't a UFO."

I continued to question him about what the McCanns had told me, and he confirmed all the basic details of the story. Hill had been looking down the whole time and had seen nothing, but he admitted he had heard the strange noise. The doctor also verified he hadn't been glancing up when it happened. Therefore, he hadn't witnessed the debris flying around in the air.

When I asked him what the noise was and what it sounded like, he mentioned a third sound he believed resembled the noise heard in the McCanns' pasture. "Like someone slapping a board against the bottom of a truck," he told me. Hill then raised the possibility of a second unseen truck in the field.

Daniel Coleman and I checked for the possibility of another truck in the McCanns' pasture, but since there were no roads in the surrounding area, chances of a second truck seemed remote. "It's not that I don't believe in UFOs," Hill concluded. "It's just that I don't think there was one in the pasture that afternoon."

For the McCanns, it was only the first of many encounters with UFOs. On that same night as the incident in the pasture, they had one of their most spectacular sightings. Anna was starting to say her prayers when her husband said, "Don't say your nightly prayers. I've said them for you." As Anna laughed, she turned to the west window and spotted a red light.

The object was just south of the Haywood tower, and according to Anna, "I knew it was something because there aren't two towers out there." It was 1:30 a.m. on the morning of the fifth. As the object approached the house from the west, it changed appearance from a light to a two-and-a-half-foot "glowing red ball" to a "huge saucer."

"It was the most beautiful thing I've ever seen," Anna told me. "It was flying at an angle with the top side flying at us. It was a great big thing with a silvery dome and alternating red and green lights all along the edge of the saucer."

I questioned Anna about these sightings on 10 occasions. Each time she described this one as "beautiful," saying, "It was a great big thing with a silvery dome and alternating red and green lights all around it. I couldn't see the bottom. It was just like the whole thing was a tilted top with its top to me and it was flying on its edge."

I asked the McCanns how many times they had seen the object flying at an angle, because this was a peculiar oddity that arose in descriptions of UFOs. The response was immediate. Every time they had seen such things they were on an angle.

"I thought it was going to hit the house," Anna said, "but it made it over and landed behind the set of trees across the road [1,000 feet from the house]."

"It didn't make any noise," she told the *National Enquirer*. She knew there was no sound because when she watched it approach the house she had opened the window. As the object passed over the house, the McCanns rushed to the east window with their three older children — 11-year-old Jerry, nine-year-old Lucy, and eight-year-old Connie — to watch it. "It crossed the road [60 feet from the house] and settled in behind a clump of trees 1,000 feet east of the house," Anna said.

Now there were five witnesses watching the object rise above the trees and drift back and forth for 15 minutes before flying toward Carman.

The most bizarre part of the story was yet to come. In three separate interviews with Joseph, Anna, and the three older children when the parents were absent, I put together the story of the "whitish creamy stuff" given off by the UFO as it travelled over the house.

"It was the colour of mother-of-pearl, like the northern lights, and it was beautiful," Anna told me. "That's the closest colour I can think of. It covered half the sky so thick that you couldn't see the stars. It was very thick and you couldn't see the part of the sky where it had flown. The other half of the sky toward Carman was clear and you could see all the stars. The kids wanted to go out and look because it was so beautiful, but Joseph told them to stay in because it might be dangerous.

"The stuff came out of the craft and swirled around and around in big waves until it covered half the sky. Connie, my youngest daughter, asked me if this was the end of the world. 'Are the heavens going to open and are we going to see God?' she asked. I told her it wasn't, but I didn't know what it was."

All three children told me in a separate interview about their excitement over the object's exhaust.

"I saw the white stuff," Jerry said. "It was like the Milky Way if you were close up to it. It was like the northern lights but brighter. Yet I think it was nicer in a way. It was darker, more together."

Connie described the exhaust as "white foggy stuff." She watched the exhaust for about 10 minutes before going back to bed

"You saw it?" I asked Lucy.

"I wasn't there early enough to see it," she replied, "but I came just after it left. I saw this milky stuff, and it spread out more and more. When I saw it, there was a light blue colour to it."

While all this was going on, Joseph had raced to phone Jeff Bishop, the *Dufferin Leader*'s publisher, for the second time in one day. He had phoned earlier about the incident in the pasture, and Bishop had gone there to search for clues, which he didn't find. Now Bishop jumped out of bed and raced north from Carman toward the McCanns' 1,100-acre farm. Once again he was unlucky and saw nothing.

The craft also had a bizarre lighting pattern to it. "They weren't just ordinary lights," Anna said. "They were huge lights raised right off the saucer. They looked just like the lights they used to have on the 1956 Oldsmobile."

Joseph thought they seemed more like "the clearance lights on the backs of trucks, oval-shaped with alternating red and green lights. They were revolving, and my little girl woke up. She's eight years old, and she said, 'Mom, look at that diamond ring around that silvery thing.' She came and watched. The other little girl woke up and said she saw a big white steam in a circle [the smoky white haze described by Jerry and his mother]."

"It sat across the road for a while," Anna continued. "Then it flew off toward Carman, and when it decided to go, boy, did it go!"

Two nights later the McCanns had their last sighting for a while in what was becoming their own personal UFO flap. We had the baby [a one-year-old toddler] in bed between us," Anna said, "and I was tired of having him kick. I got up to put him in his crib and the house was all lit up red, pinkish red. Everything inside was pinkish red. Joseph was asleep and I said, 'Joseph, the barn is on fire.'"

Anna continued the story at length:

> I went and looked and didn't see anything, but I did see some-
> thing red. It had a tail. It was the longest tail I have ever seen. It

[the object] was an oval-shaped thing, but it disappeared real fast, in a flash.

It went over the house to the east, and what shocked me was when it got on the other side of the road beyond my tree [a tree in the front yard 50 yards away], I thought I saw the *Dufferin Leader* cameramen taking pictures.

I saw great bright lights, like what you see on tow trucks, but bigger, and they were lighting up all my trees all orange. They were turning and turning. I called Joseph and we watched through the garage door [on the south end of the house]. Those big orange lights were lighting up all my trees and then it came completely to a dead stop. That's all there was to it.

I phoned [Jeff] Bishop the next day and he said that neither he nor the RCMP came out, so I wonder what those lights were.

The activity might have continued, but the next sighting report I received wasn't until June 11 and 12, this time by Jennette Frost, south of Sperling. The first was a classic encounter (see the report of this sighting in Chapter 3, "Classics"), the object coming within feet of her and then disappearing. The next sighting was made by Jennette from a greater distance at 12:30 a.m. the next night.

On June 20, the number of sightings again skyrocketed all through the valley. This part of the flap lasted up until July 9, with numerous sightings in Miami, Elm Creek, Sperling, and Carman. With the amount of publicity the whole UFO story had received, the Britains had retreated to UFO watching from Rachael's parents' place high in the Pembina Hills overlooking the valley near Miami.

Charlie seemed to fly after 11:00 p.m. Jennette, who by now carefully recorded all her sightings in a book, reported one on June 20 at 11:00 p.m. and again on June 21 at midnight. The Britains worked until 11:00 p.m. restoring planes and then made the 20-mile trip to Miami.

It was during this period that the Britains spotted UFO after UFO. One period during the flap they made sightings six nights running. Along with Tannis Major, they chased Charlie two nights in a row, the second evening seeing him "blast off into orbit." They spent a night with

CBC-TV personnel who had come out to see whether or not they could get film footage of Charlie as had CKY-TV.

"It came out of the fog bank that night," Anthony said, "right up along the hills. Of the three guys from CBC, only one would believe what he was seeing. The other two didn't want to accept it. They came within two miles of the thing and they didn't even run the camera. Instead, they were interested in taking pictures of us watching the thing. We weren't interested in that, so we got in the car and chased the thing over the hill. We then got a good look at the thing. It was shaped like a football, not flat, and it was pulsing red."

The Britains had another sighting during this period when Martin Rugne, a cameraman for the CTV affiliate, made a second trip to see if he could get any additional film footage. "During this time," Anthony stated, "they were appearing in bunches. We would see four, five, and six a night. One night we saw six on the ground in the Rosebank area."

Numerous people made the trip with the Britains to their lookout over the valley. One gentleman, who brought his girlfriend with him to Miami, later wrote a letter back to Anthony, thanking him for giving him the opportunity to see Charlie: "It was the greatest night I've ever had without pot."

It was also on June 20 at 2:00 a.m. that Myles Lyttle, who was 12 miles east of the Britains' position, looked southwest out of his Roland home and saw "a blue-and-red light that had a slight orange twinge on the top."

He told the newspaper he thought it was similar to a street light until it started to "rise up and then lower again." According to Lyttle, it made "some north and south movements, then rose and went southwest at a fairly slow speed." Only minutes later another resident of Roland reported the object as "a huge fireball" flying north very low along the east side of town.

The next morning Lacy and Toby Christian discovered a clearly burnt cross next to a bush on their front lawn. The evening before, the volunteer fire department in Roland had been called out to fight a blaze. The fire turned out to be a blood-red object flying around town. Two years later the area of dead grass was still visible.

The Christian family lived on the east side of town. They had seen nothing that night, but, as Lacy Christian told me, she and many others in Roland had spotted the objects. The stories of sightings at the end of May and June were therefore no surprise to her.

"If there's a heavy storm, then they'll be out," she told me. "It seems like the 25th to the end of the month — in that cycle." True to Lacy's theory, the sightings continued heavily to the end of June.

July 1 arrived and with it there were two daylight sightings. The first was made by Brendon Eagle, who had built the relay tower in Carman and who had made quite a success with patents he held related to augers.

"It was eight o'clock in the evening," he told me, "and it still wasn't dark. My son, wife, and I were travelling west on Highway 23, coming toward Jordan Corner [one mile west of Roland]. My wife was watching things bobbing up and down out her window. My son, Kelly, saw it and asked, 'Is that a flying saucer?'"

Mrs. Eagle told Kelly to keep quiet as his father drove, but Brendon heard Kelly and glanced out the side window. "Sure enough," he told me, "it was coming in at, I'd say 1,200 feet. We got out of the truck, and watched it. It was coming across from the south-southwest at a 22-degree angle. It was sitting down, lifting up, and then going again. It was going up and down at terrific speeds, and it did this four or five times.

"It passed over the Jordon elevator at about 1,500 feet," Brendon continued, "and it lit up the elevator so bright that you could actually see the nails in the elevator. It was about 85 feet in diameter and perfectly round — so round it was unbelievable. It was saucer-shaped, and what astonished me was that the top and bottom travelled in two different directions.

"The bottom one spun, looking straight up to the right, and the top was spinning to the left. There was a centre section that didn't move, about six to eight feet in width, and there were oval-shaped windows in it. I'd say that there were about 16 windows in the whole circumference, eight looking on the side we were on.

"It went over and landed in the field southwest of the corner where that runway is. He was in behind the bushes, and my wife wanted me to chase across the field after him. I've got a four-wheel drive, so we drove the mile after him. We came to this old hangar about 50 feet wide, but that wasn't big enough, because that thing was three storeys high. We lost him."

Shortly after Brendon Eagle left, a second witness reported that the object reappeared just as the runway lights were turned on. This farmer's runway, which was only a half mile away from where Brendon lost the object, had only gone into operation that night, and this was the first time the lights were being used for night flying.

The object appeared and landed momentarily on the runway. It then rose, hovered, moved a little down the runway, and descended again, only to rise and land farther down. After seven touchdowns and liftoffs, the saucer-shaped object had covered the entire length of the runway. It then took off and flew away.

Between July 1 and 9, the sightings came in a large flurry from Carman. Corporal Glen Toews, the RCMP spokesman for the Carman detachment, told the *Winnipeg Free Press* on July 8 that he had received five reports in seven nights. "And a lot of people just casually mention it to you without filing a report," the corporal added. "There are still a considerable number of sightings, and the people that are seeing them are pretty well reliable people."

Those who had been active watchers in Carman again took up their posts to wait and watch. After a few nights in July, the reports came to me. I was told that it was still Charlie and he was arriving between 10:15 and 11:10 p.m.

Tannis Major still hadn't obtained the clear, convincing photographs she wanted, so when the sightings began once more, she set up her camera in the living room, looking out the front window west toward the Pembina Hills.

It was early in the morning, July 7, when Tannis got her first chance at a good shot. She had gotten up to let her dog out when she noticed an object east of her house over the feedlot. Running back into the house, she retrieved her camera, pointed it out the kitchen window, and took four pictures.

When Tannis developed the pictures, she saw four white bell-shaped entities, with the objects increasing in size with each shot. The one on the final number 4 frame was four times the size of the bell-shaped object in frame 1.

The photographs and sighting report were sent by the RCMP to the National Research Council's (NRC's) Herzberg Institute of Astrophysics in Ottawa where Dr. Ian Halliday in the Planetary Sciences Section analyzed them. Even before Halliday received the photographs, however, the *Brandon Sun* phoned him and asked whether he had seen the pictures yet. Halliday stated he hadn't but that he would let the newspaper know when he had.

When Halliday analyzed the photographs, he concluded that the object was the planet Jupiter, based on time, direction of the camera, and the exposure. The *Brandon Sun* printed a story, discounting the July 7 Major photographs, while a Winnipeg radio station followed suit and did a 15-minute interview with Halliday. Meanwhile, the *Winnipeg Free Press* published the biggest story on what the doctor had said, running the following headline on July 11, 1975: JUMPING JUPITER! IS THIS CARMAN'S UFO?

It appeared that the hundreds of sightings would go down in flames as the planet Jupiter because of one analysis on one set of photographs.

"Those mysterious saucer-shaped objects sighted recently in the skies of southern Manitoba," wrote the *Free Press*, "have been identified as the planet Jupiter." It then quoted Halliday as saying, "There can be little doubt about it … we got the report from the RCMP and we saw the photographs. The sightings were at the right time and in the right part of the sky to be consistent with the planet Jupiter."

The *Free Press* report gave many skeptics reason to say: "I told you so." It also made a great number of people in Carman very angry, and there is little doubt they would have tarred and feathered any NRC scientist if he walked into Carman after the Winnipeg newspaper's story.

I contacted Dr. Halliday by mail for an account of his statement, and he informed me that the *Free Press* story deviated from his actual statement. "At no time," he wrote me back, "did I state that all the reports were caused by Jupiter, although again the newspaper report may tend to generalize too much. Neither was I presenting any formal conclusions based on the Manitoba observations."

These comments by Halliday were contained in a letter addressed to me October 27, 1975. The letter confirmed that the *Free Press* account might have been completely inaccurate, but it was too late. The damage had already been done.

Two days later Tannis shot three more photographs, this time of the famous Charlie.[5] These pictures, like those on July 7, were sent to Dr. Halliday, but this time there were no newspaper banner headlines telling people what was "actually" seen. Other people explained the glowing oval object as a plane, but no newspaper printed that reason, undoubtedly because no one who had seen the pictures believed it.

All through July the sightings continued in a line running east and west from Carman to Sperling. All dozen odd reports involved Charlie Red Star.

During the first three weeks of August, sightings occurred almost nightly in the Starbuck area. Bob Sanderson, who lived just south of Starbuck, provided me with the names of 12 people in the town who had had experienced UFO sightings during the first three weeks.

Sanderson himself was involved in three of them, the only ones of his life, all in this three-week period. The first happened with six friends on the old highway just outside town. A 60-foot craft flew toward the two cars where the six witnesses were. For 20 minutes the object hovered mere feet from the road.

Shortly after that, Sanderson had three encounters in which he heard a beeping noise in a clearing in the woods behind the farm. "At first it was a low beep, but then it would go faster and then real high-pitched. Then it would go low again. Each night the beeping went on for 5 to 20 minutes. The third night there was a brilliant flash, and it looked like it had landed southwest where the bush ends and where the next field begins. I could hear branches breaking on the ground, and as I looked out my second-storey window, I could see this bright orange glow behind the trees."

"Did you check the spot?" I asked.

"No, I told the people in town, but nobody believed me so, I quit telling everybody."

Near the end of the Starbuck flap, sightings started up again in the towns south of Carman. At Carman one of the many people to spot a UFO was Kerry Kaelin, along with his fiancée. Kaelin, a reporter for the *Dufferin Leader*, got a look at Charlie Red Star, who he had seen before.

The reporter and his fiancée spotted Charlie hovering above a field northwest of Carman. In the half-hour they watched, they saw two pairs of white lights rise into the UFO and one pair of red lights emerge from it and descend to the ground. Occasionally, the smaller objects moved around horizontally as they glided under the larger white craft with a red pulsating aura. His fiancée also noticed a beam of light that shone down from the craft that didn't seem to have any particular purpose.

Jennette Frost, who lived directly south of Starbuck, also spotted a UFO the same day Kaelin did and observed another on August 28 after the rash of sightings in the area.

September brought with it numerous UFO reports, especially ones that described landings, chases, and close encounters. That month is harvest time in Manitoba and farmers were in their fields, which might have had something to do with the number and type of sightings reported.

On September 1, 1975, 12 witnesses at the McCann farm watched as a "red fireball" appeared to tail Joseph McCann's truck as he approached his farm from the south. Joseph and his friend, Pete, didn't see the UFO behind the truck. The 12 witnesses on two adjoining farms, however, all told me how the huge object raced after Joseph's truck until he turned into the yard, after which "the object flipped over and zigzagged back into the south."

Two hours following this dusk sighting, the McCann family watched a second triangle-shaped object as it sat in a field across from the farm-yard. When this object finally left, it, too, flew "at a tremendous speed toward Carman."

There were also numerous sightings reported from the Delta area north of Portage la Prairie. In one location 10 miles north of town, dozens of people were involved.

Tony Douthitt and his father, two wheat farmers in the area, became the latest witnesses. Both Tony and his father were harvesting wheat one evening when the former noticed two orange-white lights in the south-eastern sky. "They looked like the old six-volt battery lights that they used on cars years ago."[6]

Thinking little of the lights, Tony made a few more swings around the field, and when he was at the south end of turning north, he gazed at the sky again. There, almost flying directly over him, only a couple of hundred feet in the air, was a 30-foot-diameter, circular-shaped object with two bullet-shaped doors or hatches on the bottom. They were about five feet deep on one end, tapering to nothing on the other end.

Tony described a peculiar set of lights about four feet high set at a 45-degree angle into the craft on the deep end of the opening. These lights, according to Tony, were set so that the light would be projected out of the craft.

"The lights were honeycomb lights," Tony told me. "You could definitely see the dark edges of lights. They were bluish-white, but not too bright."

Tony watched in amazement as the craft flew northwest over his father, who was combining at the other end of the field. "I was too amazed to think anything at first," Tony stated, "but the second I thought *UFO*, the lights were gone. It seemed that it knew what I was thinking."

No longer able to see the craft, Tony scanned the northern sky to relocate it. A couple of minutes later it reappeared a mile northwest as a black silhouette against the setting sun. Now he could see the top part of the craft as it flew away on an angle.

"There were five windows on the side I could see," Tony said, "and there was whitish light coming out of the rectangular windows. The light was brilliant, even though it was far away. The light was as bright as holding a 60-watt light bulb a foot away from your face."

Immediately after the craft flew over the horizon, Tony went to his father and asked if he had seen the craft. His father reported that he had noticed nothing, but at the time Tony had observed the craft, his father was having trouble with the combine. The combine had begun to sputter, and Tony's father figured that a gas line had clogged. Although the combine almost stalled out, Tony's father managed to keep it going, and after a minute or so, the trouble suddenly disappeared.

The next day Mr. McGowan discovered a rash on his left side, which was the same one the craft had passed over. It appeared only on the left side and only on the exposed areas of his face and neck.[7] "It stayed for quite a while," Mrs. McGowan told me. "It was fairly itchy for three or four days and then it went away."

One mile east of the McGowan farm Don Zalusky and his wife, Beverly, had numerous encounters with UFOs but didn't tell anyone about them until March 1, 1978.

"We watched those things fly around here every fall," Don told me. "It was at harvest time in 1975 that I saw it the best. It was a huge saucer-shaped thing with five windows on the side I was looking at. I saw lots but that was the only one during the day."

I showed him a drawing that Tony Douthitt had done for me and asked him if it looked the same. "Yeah," he said, "exactly. That's it."

From his trailer on Portage Creek, Don stated that he spent many nights watching the glowing red UFOs fly around near his place. As in many descriptions of Charlie Red Star, Don told me the craft jumped around in the air, zigzagging as if playing tag with each other.

Like so many who made vain attempts to chase Charlie in Carman, Don said the UFOs seemed to know what he was thinking and played games with people who attempted to chase them. "I tried to race after them," Don told me. "I would drive down the road with my lights off and get fairly close to them. Then, just when we were about to get a good look, the thing would shoot another mile away from me."

Beverly Zalusky had a terrifying experience with a UFO in the fall of 1975. She was one of two people chased north down Highway 240 toward the delta. Driving from Portage la Prairie one night, she noticed a brilliantly lit object right behind the car over the trunk. The huge object lit up the whole area and kept pace with every move she made to lose it.

Her car was going about 80 miles per hour when suddenly the object backed off until it was just a small light down the road. Figuring the object was gone, Beverly slowed to 60 miles per hour and continued down the road. Then, in mere seconds, the dazzling object was again behind the car, following her.

Beverly attempted once more to lose the object, but it remained behind her. Not only could she not shake the object but now she had to make a right turn onto Highway 227.

"I almost didn't make it around the corner," she said, "because of the speed I was going." Nevertheless, she did make it, whereby the object flew away from the car for good. Rattled and shaken, Beverly returned home to tell her husband about her experience with "those UFOs."

In addition to the other person who was chased down Highway 240, there were also people pursued west of Portage la Prairie near Brandon. At Kenton a woman with a van full of children was paced one morning on the way to school. At Carberry, 50 miles west of Portage la Prairie, two women were trailed back to town one night by a brilliant whitish object. The experience, which lasted many minutes, terrified the women to the point where they refused to talk about what they had experienced.

Thirty miles south of Carman, Ralph Driedger, who lived just off the Canada–U.S. border, also reported one of these bizarre close encounters with a low-flying UFO. The Driedger family farm was a large one, and because of the short season, there were harvesting shifts throughout the night.

"It was three or four in the morning," Jacob Driedger told me. "It was a mile and a half from me, but my father was close up."

Jacob was combining in the field when suddenly the object appeared, lighting up the whole countryside. It was so bright, in fact, that Jack stated he could tell where it was even when it was behind him, due to the brilliant light it gave off.

On the mile road west of Jacob, his father, Ralph, was driving a truck loaded with grain. The object, no more than a couple of hundred feet off the ground, darted in front of Ralph's truck.

In the account he gave me of the incident, the object moved northeast very low to the ground. It was cone-shaped and multicoloured, with the major hue being red. He estimated the object was 30 feet in diameter.

"It came fairly close to me," Ralph stated. "It was extremely bright, and yet I couldn't take my eyes off it. In all my years I've never seen anything like it. It was frightening. I hope I never have to see anything like that again. I was watching it so closely that when it disappeared into that big cloud I noticed that I wasn't watching where I was driving. The truck was halfway into the ditch, and I just about tipped the whole load."

In October 1975, there were more landings in the Pembina Valley. One of those, at the farm of Bill Wheatley, was only 24 miles north of the Driedgers' farm. This landing near Roland was the second for the town in four months.[8]

Farther up the valley, 14 miles north of the Wheatley farm, the McCanns notified Rachael Britain that "they were back." The record shows there was a sudden and short score of sightings in the Elm Creek–Carman–Sperling area between October 16 and 22.

The McCann family had sightings on October 16 and 19. Both involved objects looked like Ferris wheels, which mystified the family to no end. The McCanns were so disbelieved by the people of Elm Creek and Carman that a lot of the residents of the farms around them kept quiet about what they had seen. It seemed logical that if the McCanns were actually seeing so many UFOs that the people around them would have witnessed the objects, as well. It took a long time to get the McCanns' neighbours to talk, but eventually in interviews they admitted they, too, had seen these UFOs all along.

One farmer defended the silence of the farmers in the area by stating, "You don't talk about things like that in town. People call you cuckoo. They'll call us another bunch of McCanns."

The initial sightings of the other farmers also occurred in October 1975. Ronald Middleton, for example, was out disking on October 31 at Kitty Corner, only a few miles southwest of the McCann farm and 12 days after the McCanns told me about seeing objects that looked like Ferris wheels.

It was 4:00 a.m. when Ronald first noticed what appeared to be a bright star in the east. He drove in that direction down the field and saw the light get larger and brighter as it came toward him. As he watched the light, it moved until it reached a set of trees a mile east of him where it stopped.

Ronald couldn't see the shape of the orange-white light because of the intensity, but he could plainly see that it was illuminating the entire bush. There was a bright flash radiating from the object and sparks shot off one side of it.

He shut off the tractor and found that the object made no noise. Just then it began to move again, and as he stated, "I decided that it was time to stop for the night."

As quickly as he could, he started the tractor and turned around, but by then the object was only about 500 feet behind him. It was now so bright that he couldn't even look at it. All around him he saw the light being cast by the object on his tail. He drove as fast as the tractor would go, but minutes seemed like hours until he finally reached his farm. Just before he arrived, the object backed off into the east, becoming smaller and smaller as it moved away.

Still, as is the case with everyone who has been chased by UFOs, the shock for Ronald didn't set in until the experience was over. Once in his farmyard, he tried to light a cigarette as he gazed eastward where the object had retreated "but I couldn't because I was shaking that badly."

That November Manitoba took second place for a week due to sightings that happened in the neighbouring provinces of Saskatchewan and Ontario. In Ontario a radar tracking was made from North Bay of two objects moving straight up from 42,000 to 72,000 feet. Jet fighters from U.S. bases were scrambled to check on the radar contacts. After some investigation, the involved parties admitted they had tracked two unidentified objects, and wire services were alerted. Later, after the North American Air Defense Command (NORAD) read all the reviews of the incidents, it explained the whole incident as a mistake. The objects on the radar screens were only ice crystals.

In order to check if this radar sighting was linked to any of the sightings that occurred in Manitoba, I managed to get a friend to question NORAD about its involvement with UFOs. The only positive comment we received was from a member of the organization stationed in North Bay who simply said: "You wouldn't believe what goes on here."

National Enquirer reporter Daniel Coleman tried to confirm the Manitoba sightings with NORAD as part of his paper's investigation of them. He spoke with Lieutenant Doug Caie, information officer at the Canadian Forces Base in Winnipeg.

When Coleman asked Lieutenant Caie if the Canadian Forces had followed the sightings in the Carman area, the officer said they had but that no targets were picked up on radar screens. "I checked about five or six of the different sightings," he told Coleman, "and times with our own radar and with the 24th NORAD region at Minot, North Dakota, and we didn't get any correlation whatsoever."

"There was no correlation at all?" Coleman asked.

"Nope," replied Caie. "No, as far as I know the phenomenon has been reported to us, and we have a research centre in Ottawa. It has been reported to them."

The November sightings started in Manitoba on the 13th when Rachael Britain stepped out of a hangar at Friendship Field to see Charlie come at her on the "beer run" from the west. She called her husband and Sam Brazil from the hangar to see the object, and as the three watched the pulsing red ball, a second one appeared travelling in the same pattern.

Immediately, Anthony Britain phoned the local RCMP detachment, and the office dispatched Constable Wotherspoon to witness the flyby. He made it to the airfield in time to see the third object arrive on the horizon and watched it through binoculars as it passed by. While viewing the object, Wotherspoon doubted it was anything he had ever seen before, but when a newspaper asked for a comment he was less anxious to be definite. He thought the object could have had something to do with a NORAD exercise he had read about.[9]

After the third object flew by, the Britains went to the RCMP office to file a report. They did so not knowing that the Staggs, another family in town, had continued the chase.

Greg Stagg was warming up the family car for a trip to Winnipeg when he, too, spotted the first object as it passed by. He called his parents, Art and Frances, who came out to see the three objects moving northeast toward Winnipeg. They jumped into the car, and the chase was on.

Frances described the objects as doing a docking manoeuvre. The Britains had explained the strange actions as "appearing to jockey for position." The two outside objects around the main one made big loops just before linking with the opposite side of the centre object.

"The distance was as though they were measured," the Staggs told me. "Before the outside objects moved, they were white, and then one at a time they would link up. 'A' would make a loop and come together with the centre object and then turn red [the one in the centre was always red]. Then, after a few minutes, it would loop back to where it was and turn white. Then 'B' would do the same thing. It was kind of queer."[10]

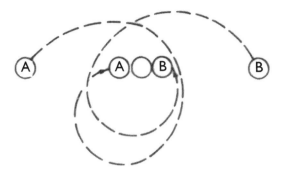

Strange action of smaller satellite objects.

"After losing them again, we picked them up again [east] at the Starbuck tower," Art Stagg said. "One was just along the ground and the other was hanging over the Winnipeg airport runway. It was about 1,500 feet up and was glowing red. Every time a jet took off it would go up until it looked like a star. When the jet would make its turn, the object would drop back down again. When he was up he was white, and when he was low he was glowing red."

The Staggs were in a hurry to make it to Winnipeg for an appointment, so they left the two objects flying around in the west end of the city.

Later, while the Britains were still at the RCMP detachment office, Wayne Teal, who had remained at Friendship Field, witnessed the three objects flying west in formation past the airport and back to wherever they had come from.

November also brought with it by far the most controversial report of the entire flap. This was the disappearance of 32 registered horses from the herd owned by Joseph McCann. Combined with the many UFOs the family was reporting, this dynamic new development spread like wildfire and included a daylight sighting of a UFO in the pasture where the horses were located.

Days after Joseph reported the loss of his horses he appeared on CBC-TV in Winnipeg. His story was short and simple. His father had been checking the herd in the north pasture one day when he noticed that the best horse was gone. When he and Joseph tallied the 200 head, they discovered they were 32 short.

The loss was reported to the RCMP, which investigated the possibility that the horses had been stolen. Its report came up negative. The RCMP found no broken fences and or evidence of tire tracks other than from the McCanns' half ton.

"The interviewer at CBC wanted me to say that the UFOs had stolen my horses," Joseph told me, "but I never said it. I stated that they were missing. They taped that section three times, but I wouldn't say it."

Rumours spread throughout the towns surrounding the McCanns' farm about what had actually happened to the horses, but none of them stood up. One account suggested that Joseph had sold the animals and was trying to collect the insurance, but that story didn't stick because there had to be corpses to qualify for insurance. In fact, Joseph never did file a claim. The most he ever did was to list the missing horses as a loss on his income tax.

The only other explanation worth considering involved the possibility that Joseph never had the horses to begin with, but this again was without factual backing. All the horses were registered. Therefore, Joseph had to produce the papers to the RCMP. Second, the six McCann family members I talked to were all able to tell me the names of at least five horses that were gone.

Even with all the scorn surrounding the family, their story never changed. The ridicule was more than anyone should have had to live with. Frances told me that people she had known for years were suddenly not quite as friendly as before. At the post office, for example, people acted as if they hadn't seen her and walked the other way. She swore to me that she would never report another UFO sighting publicly.

I questioned the three older Stagg children and found they, too, had been mocked because of the sightings their parents had reported. "Some kids said that there was no such thing as UFOs," Connie, the youngest, told me. "I said that I know there are UFOs. I'm sorry. They then said, 'You don't really see UFOs. You're just making it up.' When my father was on television, they said it was all baloney."

"When my dad was on television," nine-year-old Lucy said to me, "some of my classmates asked me whether it was really true, and I said, 'We didn't say that the UFOs took them. That's an assumption.'"

"All I said," Jerry, the oldest, insisted, "is that Dad never said the UFOs took the horses. He's just assuming because there's no tracks around there. Dad didn't think it could be horse rustlers, but they're good at covering their tracks, but we couldn't find any tracks. When my dad was on TV, the kids at school asked me whether our horses were at the Big Dipper drinking out of it. Then would they be let loose."

Joseph himself took some criticism from friends in town, but he, like the other members of his family, refused to back down. It was lucky for him that he was in business for himself because otherwise he would have probably become unemployed.

I talked to the members of the family for countless hours together and separately. As was the case with all their UFO encounters, they never changed the story — not then and not two years later when I talked to them again.

It seemed then that they were indeed telling the truth about what had happened to them during the flap. Maybe, as some people still contend, the horses were just stolen. In the end, I told the McCanns that if someone was able to steal 32 horses without a trace, "it became easier to believe that UFOs had done it."[11]

December brought two more flaps of sightings in southwestern Manitoba, but they were small in comparison to those in the rest of 1975. One of these sightings, however, is worth noting. It was December 22, mid-afternoon, and two government pilots were westbound into Winnipeg at 14,000 feet. One of them was my father, Robert Cameron, who told me the story. They were 20 miles north of Portage la Prairie.

My father, the flight's captain, was glancing out the window and saw a DC-9 outbound from Winnipeg at 15,000 feet above his plane. Then he noticed off the contrail of the jet a circular metallic object, which he estimated was 100 feet across. It was pacing the jet.

"I sat there watching it for about a minute," he told me, "and then I got the attention of the co-pilot. His first comment was 'That must be one of those UFOs.'"

My father radioed the Winnipeg tower to confirm the visual object on radar. "What have you got?" he asked.

"I've got you, the plane behind you, and the DC-9 above you," came the reply.

"What's behind the DC-9?" my father asked next.

"Nothing," the tower replied.

"There's got to be something," radioed my father. "We're sitting here looking at it."

"I still have nothing."

The tower radioed the crew of the DC-9, but they couldn't see anything from their position. (There are, after all, no rearview mirrors on planes.)

"We had the object for two minutes," my father told me. "One minute I watched and the other minute both of us watched. We took our eyes off it for a second to look down, and when we looked up the thing was gone." He didn't dare file an official report of what he had seen.

The sightings continued into 1976, but the reported number was nothing compared to those in 1975. The other thing that differed with the 1976 sightings was that they had spread all over Manitoba along a 200-mile line. The sighting numbers tended to be about 50 percent of those in 1975, and there were only 50 percent of the 1976 sightings in 1977.

The 1975 sightings were the ones that were unsurpassed, especially those involving Charlie Red Star. Sightings continued into the summer of 1978, and they were numerous in contrast to any other part of the world. Yet, relative to Charlie Red Star, the rest of the sightings seemed dull.

CLASSICS

When you hear someone else, you think, oh, well, it might have been someone else. But after I saw this, nobody is going to convince me it was anything else.

— Michael Perreault

During the two years I spent covering the Charlie Red Star flap in Manitoba full-time, I heard literally hundreds of stories and met an equal number of people. However, my research method was different from the one employed by most UFO groups.

Instead of waiting for sightings to be reported to me, I set up a system of sources, one or two in each of the small towns involved in UFO sightings in Manitoba. Each of these people had experienced sightings themselves and had come into contact with the stories of others. Their ears were always open when the topic of UFOs was discussed.

This system worked extremely well.

Every month I made a trip to my sources in the various towns to find out what the latest incidents were. In this way, I was able to actually follow the flap as it moved from municipality to municipality. In exchange for their help, I had to share last month's most spectacular sightings with them. So I would sit back and, like a grandfather with his grandchildren, amaze them with the reports of sightings that had occurred elsewhere in Manitoba.

Near the end of the second year I discovered that storytelling had become a major part of the job, so I decided to write down some of the better accounts in a book so that everyone could read them. Telling the stories to four or five people at a time had become costly; there were many days when I told them for six hours at a time when I should have been collecting them.

When I was putting this book together at the University of Manitoba in the late 1970s, I wrote only at night to avoid meeting with friends who might force me to accept cups of coffee for the latest tidbits in the "saucer world," for which I had become known. Not being able to resist telling a story, I sometimes killed an entire night of work telling them. My accounts became known as "classics" — stories with a new twist, or ones in which there was little doubt about what had been seen.

Never did these story seekers ask for the latest graphs related to the number of sightings, or data about who saw what. What they wanted to hear was something weird enough to test their sense of believability. Then they were satisfied.

About 20 of the following stories can now be considered classics and were the most popular. Each contains unique characteristics that bring them to the forefront of my mind when I am asked to share my experiences in the 1970s.

I have let the persons involved tell the stories to keep them as close as possible to the original telling. They are accounts that were told to the *National Enquirer* and me. The *Enquirer* took a special interest in them because, as a tabloid publication, it deals in sensationalism.

The Bobby Baker Case

Ufologists are influenced by many factors in their efforts to evaluate the evidence related to the phenomena they study. Two of these factors are sightings they experience personally and the people they interview who have had dramatic UFO encounters. In connection with the second one, the Bobby Baker case stands out heads above most of the other incidents in the Manitoba UFO flap.

Much of the story's power lies in the way a timid eight-year-old boy, Bobby Baker, told me about the UFO he had seen. If it hadn't been for his father's questions and prodding, he probably would never have related it.

In a field as questionable as ufology, one wouldn't normally rely on an eight-year-old boy's word, particularly if he was the only witness, but Bobby's case was different. I can say with certainty that out of the hundreds of witnesses I have talked to, no one gave me more confidence of truthfulness than he did.

The entire interview session with Bobby was done in co-operation with Lloyd Baker, whose concern for his son's well-being caused him to report the sighting to Anthony Britain in Carman. Anthony in turn told me about the incident and suggested we talk to Bobby.

The boy was present for the entire 30-minute interview but seemed detached from it as well as from the world. He looked as if he had been haunted ever since he had seen the object, even though it had occurred two weeks prior to our arrival.

I received word from Anthony that the event had happened on February 6, 1976. Anthony simply told me that there had been a close encounter at a farm north of Carman. Two weeks after the sighting John Losics from Winnipeg and I arrived at the Baker farm to find out what had transpired.

Bobby and his father met us at their farm. The boy was thin and frail-looking. His father appeared to be in his early thirties. It was a very small white house with a south-facing open deck. Lloyd escorted us to the living room where John and I sat by the front window. Then he went into the kitchen to get a chair, placed it in the centre of the room, and asked Bobby to sit. "Tell the men what you saw," he told Bobby.

Lloyd was eager to get to the bottom of what his son had experienced. Bobby, on the other hand, wasn't. Instead, he chose to withdraw and sit on the floor at the far end of the room near the kitchen, hiding behind a chair.

In response to my first question, Bobby peered out from the chair and merely nodded. The look in his eyes and the fact that he was trying to hide sent chills up my spine. I had a distinct feeling that for some reason he expected me to attack him.

"Bobby had me kind of scared," Lloyd began, "so I phoned Britain and said to him, 'Before I say anything to you, tell me what they look like.' [He was aware through the local newspaper that Anthony had had numerous sightings in the previous year.] Anthony told me, and it was as if it was coming out of Bobby's mouth. Well, I pumped him several times to see whether he was fibbing me or not. He kept telling me the same thing."

While his father talked, Bobby remained on the floor behind the chair, peeking out. He continued to stare at me but said nothing. He appeared not even to be listening. There was no expression on his face. His mind seemed somewhere else.

"You see the next-door neighbour's lights?" Lloyd asked me.

Both John and I glanced out the window.

"It was just over the bushes there … two hundred yards, I guess."

Looking out the window, we saw that the view to the set of trees was unobstructed.

"Where was Bobby?" I asked.

"On the front step," Lloyd said. "Our girl, she's 10 … I wish he'd have called her in time [to see the object]. She said his face was pure white. My wife and I were away at the time. So was the neighbour." By the time Bobby's sister found out what was happening, the object had disappeared.

At this point in the conversation I asked Bobby about the colour of the object. He didn't answer. He merely sat and stared.

"You just tell him what you saw," Lloyd urged, but Bobby said nothing.

"How big was it?" questioned John.

"It was big," Bobby finally responded, his face still blank.

"Sit up," his father said. "Don't be shy."

"How big was it?" repeated John. "Was it as big as a truck or as big as a car?"

"It was as big as a house."

I produced a UFO shape chart produced by the International UFO Registry and placed it on the floor in front of me. "Did it look like any of these? Can you come and take a look?"

Bobby gazed out from behind the chair, his curiosity captured. He crawled slowly across the floor on his hands and knees and glanced at the chart of sketches. His review of the objects was quick. He pointed at a simple saucer with a rounded dome top. "It looked like this one. It had lights all over it."

He had finally decided to talk but volunteered very little. His father told most of the story.

The boy had been on the front steps of his house facing south. He happened to turn west and saw a huge saucer sitting over the bushes at the neighbour's house.

When I asked him about the colour of the object he said, "First it was green all over. Then there were all kinds of lights [separate lights, not flashing], and when it took off, it turned like blood. Then it went straight up [about 50 feet]. It turned solid yellow and stopped. Then it moved over the road [100 feet south] and disappeared."

"Did it disappear or did it fly away?" I asked.

"It just disappeared."

"Did it fade away?"

"No, it just disappeared," he insisted.

"Did it happen instantly?"

"Yeah, it just took off."

"Like turning off a light?"

"Yeah, like turning off a light."

The only noise, according to Bobby, was the sound of a branch cracking and falling, just as the blood-red object took off. Lloyd had checked the area the next morning and stated there appeared to be a depression in the snow, but no one had bothered to verify the part of the story involving the branch.

By the way Bobby was acting, I was convinced he had actually seen this bizarre sight, but he capped the story when he related an animal reaction to the incident.

"You forgot to tell him what the pony was doing," his father prompted.

"I called him and he came around," Bobby said, "and then … then he looked up at it, and then I said, 'You see that, Sonny?' Then he kicked up his heels and ran to his house [small shed]."

According to Bobby's father, just after the encounter, his son had constant headaches and the first nosebleed of his life.

Concerned over this turn of events, the Bakers took their son to doctors in Carman, but none could account for either of the symptoms. Bobby missed school for the first couple of days, but the strange symptoms seemed to fade after the initial week. Upon returning to school, Bobby told his story to his friends. When they started to ridicule him, the teacher defended, explaining that the things Bobby had described could exist.

I asked Bobby if he had experienced any nightmares about the event, but he didn't answer. Later, from his father, I learned that after John and I left, Bobby told his father that he had had "dreams about them."

The Bakers were deeply worried about what had happened, but because his mother believed these things "to be of the devil," we didn't bother to confirming the medical symptoms incurred.

"One thing for sure," Lloyd told us, "he was scared. In fact, Bobby had been so petrified [while it was happening that] he was going to shoot the saucer" — with his father's 30.6 rifle that was in the house.

"The gun's probably as big as he is," Lloyd added. Then he addressed Bobby. "You're lucky you didn't try that. The rifle would have laid you right on your back end."

Bobby didn't look at his father. He sat there quietly. There was no response, verbal or otherwise.

Crashing Plane or UFO?

While tracing some stories in the Carman area, I was told that Jennette Frost had experienced a sighting that was unquestionable. Checking with the *Dufferin Leader*, I found that the reason it had never been printed was because her son was the editor of the paper, and for reasons of objectivity in reporting, the story had been dropped.

In talking with the white-haired but active Jennette, I discovered that the report was indeed a classic. In interviews, first with Daniel Coleman at the *National Enquirer* and then in a second one with Roger Timlick — a science student at the University of Manitoba — and me in March 1977, I got the whole story.

Sitting in the living room of her home, Jennette located the incident in the first of two notebooks she used to keep track of the sightings of the past two years, the same period as the rest of the UFO incidents in Manitoba.

As recorded in her book, the sighting occurred at 1:15 a.m., June 11, 1975, at the height of the first Carman flap. Because of a sick horse, Jennette had been up. Shep, her dog, had alerted her that something was nearby.

"Even before you see the light," Jennette said, "you know Charlie's around because Shep growls in his throat. He always looks around when there's something that he hears, and he cries and whines, a very high-pitched whine."

Jennette was on the back landing of her two-storey house when she gazed up at the western sky and the object suddenly appeared. The bottom of the object was lit up, but the top was against the night sky. It was some 40 feet away, flying about 15 feet in the air just north of the house.

"Well, I couldn't believe it, Jennette said. "I thought that it was a plane going down backward. I was holding my breath because I thought it was going to crash into the trees. It went behind the trees over the field that low. There was no danger at any time of it hitting the house. It was over the garden. It must have come over the wires. There was no noise … the only noise that I heard at the time was the hydro wires and they were really humming.

"This thing was big. Well, it looked as big as the granary out back [18 by 20 feet]. That's how big it looked. You could tell just from the width. You could see along the back of it, and I think it extended farther along the side, but that is what I could see.

"There was a little light and that thing flashed. It was sort of yellowish-orange. The big ones were more like car lights, the old types of cars like the old Model Ts. They sort of had yellow in them, an orange glow to them. The big ones were about two feet across and the little one was about a foot across and there were three or four feet between the lights.

"The thing in the middle was a brassy gold colour. It was shaped like a bullet and there were these black stripes, which I could see real well. They looked about an inch broad, looking from the back step.

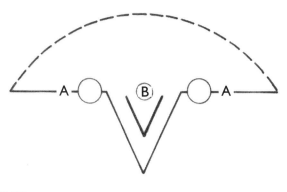

The "Model T" UFO.

"I ran off the steps after it cleared the trees," Jennette continued, "to see where it was going to land and there was nothing there. It was just gone. It sounds crazy. I guess if I hadn't seen it and someone came and told me that they had seen this, I would tell them that they were crazy. Anyone would because it sounds so stupid."

Three Pilots "Just Astounded"

"Well, it seems to me that he had seen them before," Mrs. Roger Pitts told me, "but I don't think that they impressed him as much as this one. They could have been this or they could have been that. But this one I really think shook him up. He kept hearing about them, but to actually experience one that closely, to see the shape."

That, in short, is what was told to me by the wife of Roger Pitts, a pilot for Ontario Central Airways, 27 years in the air with 17,000 hours flying time in all types of airplanes from small aircraft on floats right up to Boeing 737 jets.

The incident took place on May 6, 1975, only seven days before the famous CKY film was shot in Carman, and during the period of the heaviest flap in Manitoba history. Instead of the sighting taking place over the flat wheat fields of Southern Manitoba, Pitts's encounter took place at Berens River, 200 miles northeast of Carman. Here, bush country and lakes extended for hundreds of miles. Only the odd isolated settlement gave indications of any people inhabiting the area.

The three pilots, Roger Pitts, Ralph Dickenson, and Manuel Hernandez, were bound for Aspen Air Base in Gimli from the port of Churchill on Hudson Bay. As Pitts described the weather and time, "It was about noon. It was clear and there was very little cloud, scarcely any cirrus. It was a clear day."

Pitts continued: "There were three of us. We were southbound with a DC-3 at 6,000 feet and we were coming up on Lake Winnipeg. Over to our right we spotted an aircraft, or what appeared to be an aircraft, coming toward us at quite a distance. It drew closer and we [Pitts and Dickenson] were both watching it, trying to determine what it was. We noticed then that it wasn't flying straight and level. It was flying at an angle of 45-degree bank, but it was still coming straight toward us.

"It didn't turn around. It just went directly in the other direction, straight away from us. Without changing its angle of bank or anything else, it went away off into the distance away from us, and a puff of smoke appeared. An odd shape, like a small cloud. And it disappeared in that.

"Then another one appeared over toward our right, approximately 20 miles farther over to our right, and all we got out of it was a dot and a puff of smoke. It disappeared. Then the one that we previously watched reappeared and came back toward us and did the same thing — disappeared again. There's just no way that anything I know of could come directly toward us and not turn around to retreat.

"The first and third ones, 10 degrees off their track, were the best ones to get a look at. Dickenson and I watched the first one. We drew Hernandez's attention to it, and he came from the back to look at it. By this time it was receding and he couldn't see it as well as we could. We yelled at him, but he took his time coming up. It was slanted down to our right."

Asked if he got a good look at the shape, he said, "Actually, yes, well, I would say just a flat cylindrical shape. I didn't get a real good look at it to see if it had any windows. I couldn't distinguish colour [except to say it was dark]. All I could see was the form at that distance." When he was asked about the size, he said, "There was really nothing to gauge any size to it, but we could plainly see that it was coming toward us."

Pitts was asked by the *National Enquirer* to comment on the whole affair in light of his experience in the air. "We'd just heard rumours of some sightings in the Sioux Lookout and Thunder Bay, Ontario, area the previous day. It's a few hundred miles to the southwest of where we saw the sighting. I thought to myself that in view of the rumours I'd actually say that I felt that I had seen something that I couldn't describe, that I could say that that was a UFO. This is what my thought was.

"I've never gone out of my way deliberately to look for them, but we've had some reports from some of our airline pilots on Transair. We've had some people who have seen them. I felt at that point that mine was an actual sighting, something that I couldn't explain in any other way than that it could have been a UFO. I've wished ever since I saw it that I had gotten a better look at it, but certainly what we saw was something that I couldn't explain in any other way."

A Disk Visits Friendship Field

Jackie Answers, an audiovisual technician at the University of Manitoba, and I were driving into Carman on July 23, 1976, in an attempt to film the ground lights. It was about a half-hour before sunset. Jackie and I had hoped to be in position eight miles north of Carman before the sun set so that we could watch exactly how the "ground lights" at that particular location appeared.

Coming up to Haywood, about eight miles east of Carman on Highway 3, we both noticed an egg-shaped cloud south of our position in a line that placed it near Roland, Manitoba.

"What's that out there?" asked Jackie, who was driving.

"I've been watching it for a while," I responded. "It looks funny, but it's probably just a cloud."

Jackie retorted that there were no clouds in sight, and when I glanced around, I could see that he was right. He wanted to stop to shoot some film, but I insisted that we keep on driving so we could arrive at our appointed spot by sundown. "We can watch while we drive," I added.

It was a solidly outlined object sitting 15 to 20 degrees off the horizon. It was quite dark, almost black, but I attributed that to the angle of the sun. We watched it for about five minutes during which it never changed shape. Suddenly, at a point when neither of us was looking, it disappeared. We continued on to Friendship Field without stopping.

Two nights later I walked into Anthony Britain's main hangar and found a crowd of people talking. Anthony spotted me and said, "Boy, did you miss a beauty!"

Hunter Ames, one of Anthony's assistants, had seen a UFO during the day, his boss told me. "He was always telling us we were seeing things," Anthony said, laughing, "and now he says that anything we've seen is a wheelbarrow compared to the thing he saw."

When I was told that it had appeared like a cloud and that the cloud "was the only one in the sky," I cut Anthony off and asked if Hunter had seen the cloud in the south.

"Yeah," Anthony said, "how did you know that?"

"I saw it," I replied.

I checked the time of the sighting and found that Hunter had seen the object 15 minutes after we had. A couple of days later I met Hunter, who told me the whole story, including references to "wheelbarrows" and "hanging pictures."

"You never seen anything like it," Hunter told me.

As he said this, Anthony chided him about his former skepticism. The criticism didn't bother Hunter in the least. He simply continued with his story until he was finished.

When the *National Enquirer*'s Daniel Coleman was in Carman, I suggested that he talk to Hunter. We taped the interview in the Carman Motel. "The sun was just setting," Ames began. "I was out at the airport. I go there quite often to visit. I never noticed anything until I walked out into the field. While he [Anthony Britain] was taxiing down the runway [toward the south], I noticed this grey cloud above him. It was a long way away and egg-shaped. The first thing that I thought was, *Gee, that's a funny-looking cloud.*

"Britain took off, and as soon as he took off, this grey thing was underneath him. He made a circuit east, and I could see this grey thing again. I was standing there looking right at the cloud, never turning my head. My eyes subconsciously followed this grey streak in the air and my eyes were looking at a saucer right over the sunflower field [halfway down the runway]. That's how fast it moved, you know. My head was still facing where I was watching [the cloud], and my eyes were on the saucer [overhead].

"So I looked at the saucer, and it hung there perfectly stationary for about 10 seconds. It hung there like a picture hanging on the wall. You could actually see it spinning. You could see the streaks where the portholes would be. It was spinning clockwise, I'm sure.

"There was a purple halo around it, and the saucer itself was the same colour as the sky. Like if it hadn't been for the halo, and if it hadn't been stopped, I wouldn't have seen it, because it came up so fast. All around was this halo, the perfect shape of the saucer. The saucer was the same colour as the sky — invisible. You'd never see anything in the day. They go so damn fast."

"Was it right side up?" asked Coleman.

"Oh, no," shot back Hunter. "It was hanging with the bubble down. Well, actually, what it looked like was one of those kids' toys, but it's got this extra bubble on the bottom." Later the spin was estimated to be 1,000 revolutions per minute.

"It was a lot deeper than the pictures I've seen," Hunter continued. I guess it could be 80 feet in diameter, anyway … and I couldn't get over the depth of it. I'd say it would be 60 feet between the top and the bottom of the bubble. I never realized it, but that thing … I'm sure it saw me watching it. As soon as it noticed I was watching it, it just backed off. It faded back into that same cloud formation, then all of a sudden, you could actually see the arc of it. It left black stuff, like the colour of the cloud part, just left behind little tinsels in the air.

"And fast! You never saw anything so fast in your life. It was just remarkable. It went away just as fast as it came. From the time I started looking at it, for about four or five seconds, it was only about another five seconds before it made this arc in the sky and was gone. Those things seem to take off from scratch. I imagine it was going 1,000 miles per hour, just like that. They really poured the coal to it when they took off. It was half a mile away before I even realized that it had started to move."

Anthony Britain, who was flying the four-seat Mooney plane, saw nothing. "I was climbing at the time," he told me. "Your nose is up and you're lucky if you can see over the nose. It just knew where the blind spot was."

Someone else, however, had seen it. Three days later Kip Faux, a carpenter in Carman, came up to Hunter Ames and told him he and his son had seen the whole thing from Stephenfield, eight miles west of Carman. He told Hunter, "You remember the night you saw that thing? My boy and I were looking at it, and we saw this grey cloud moving along the horizon. I told my son, 'There's a flying saucer,' and as soon as I said that, it made this arc in the sky and was gone."

It was a classic case: two witnesses eight miles west of Carman, two witnesses eight miles east of Carman, and one witness right under it, also in Carman. It would have been a much better case, however, if I had followed the rule I had laid down to all photographers I took out: "Shoot first, ask questions later." Had I followed this rule, I would be showing a film instead of telling the story with words, which does the report no justice.

Charlie Goes to School

While I was a guest on the biggest radio talk show in Winnipeg — CJOB's *Action Line* — a call came in from a woman in Kenton, Manitoba. She told us that she had had an unidentified object trail her during the day. I asked Peter Warren, host of the program, to get her number. After the show ended, I checked to see where Kenton was and discovered that it was 170 miles west of Winnipeg, where there had been a fair amount of UFO activity from August 1975 through August 1976.

The *Enquirer's* Daniel Coleman was with me on the talk show. When I arrived at his motel room, I told him the case seemed good enough to investigate, so together we taped a phone interview with the woman, who refused to give her name for publication.

The woman was a housewife on a farm, and she had a part-time job driving children to school in a small van. It was the fall of 1975 at 8:30 a.m., and the woman was driving with three of her own children as well as other kids. The van was travelling south toward Kenton when one of her children suddenly cried, "Mom, look at the sun!"

"I looked," she told us. "Then I looked again and told them, 'Kids, that's not the sun.' It was fiery red and was in the shape of an ice-cream sundae. That's what it looked like, like it had a cherry on top of it. We really couldn't distinguish any marks on it except for a couple of strips around the top. We could see it rotating around, and it kept ahead of us a wee bit."

It wasn't very high in the sky because the bottom part of the object became blocked out when they passed behind some high trees. The trees, however, gave her an idea of the size. "To me it looked as high as an elevator," she said. "It was enormous. It really was."

"As high as an elevator?" Coleman asked in surprise. A grain elevator is 70 to 80 feet high.

"Well, I would say about as high," she said. "You know that's approximate because it was unbelievable, unbelievable ... period. You could look at that thing, and when you turned your eyes around, you couldn't see it at all. You were blinded for a minute or two."

She told us that the object was flying along beside them on the east side, so Coleman asked her whether or not what she had seen might have been the sun.

"No way!" she shot back. "In my own mind, I'm positive that it was not. It wasn't shaped that way, and we couldn't see it rotate if it had been the sun."

In addition to these items, the woman mentioned actions of the object that I was to find in other independent cases. "I stopped the van twice," she stated, "and each time I stopped the van and backed up ... I got a funny feeling when that thing stopped ... and then when I moved it would move on."

After about five miles, they turned west. Again she described a weird phenomenon that was common to other cases. "When we got to the corner where we turned off to Kenton to go west, we could see it a bit ... it was still going south ... the kids could hardly wait to get to school. After that the object had simply vanished."

The effect upon the woman in this case was interesting. "I really didn't believe in the darn things," she told us, "but I'm so positive that it had to be something like that. I mean, seeing is believing. I was so excited. I didn't know how to describe it. I was shook up. I had two girls in the van who were really terrified by this thing. They turned white and didn't say a word. The boys were just the opposite. They were excited."

This case is a good one — daylight, numerous witnesses, and small but important parallels to other encounters in Manitoba. It was referenced on an open-line show in Brandon that there were similar sightings the same day, but we were unable to verify those ones.

Seeing Them in Bunches

The following classic story is actually the account of a two-day rash of sightings that occurred in and around Starbuck, Elie, and Portage la Prairie. They happened during the first week of August 1976. The importance lies in the fact that more than one UFO was seen on each occasion and that all of them were travelling to the same point north of Portage la Prairie. In addition, all the witnesses described objects moving at high speed, which was rarely reported during the Manitoba flap.

First to spot the objects was a group of people who operated the Frontier Portage Motel on the east side of Portage la Prairie. Those involved were Mickey, Spencer, and Chad Watt, as well as Debbie Sanu and Dorothy Sanu. Debbie, a middle-aged woman, was the one who made everyone aware that a UFO would be around in August.

"I read everything I could get my hands on [UFO material]," Debbie said to me. "I've told the kids about them and gotten them interested. I told them about the August flaps around here. They're supposed to be quite prominent in this district of Manitoba. The kids were looking for them and they found them.

"Mickey, the oldest, got to see them first. 'For most of the night,' he told me. 'I noticed that there were about five lights in the eastern sky and that they were standing still. When it got dark, you could see them better, so I went and got my binoculars and looked at them. I asked Debbie what she thought they were, and she said they were UFOs, so we went into the house and got everyone out. They were there about two hours steady. Not moving. Then they started to move and they disappeared across the sky.'"

The five objects were stacked in the sky in the east over Elie. A common element to everyone's story was that once the objects started to move, they began to multiply. Everyone told me that when the objects disappeared in the northwest there were nine.

"I was watching them when they got north of us," Debbie said. "I noticed all of a sudden that there seemed to be all kinds of them. They were in a nice little formation. They were all individual. They weren't captive or anything. They were all individual blobs."

Mickey, who had the binoculars for the longest time, saw the "objects go into formation" and drew exactly how it happened. He was "amazed at how quickly they go into formation and with such precision." The drawing he made had seven objects as they were lining up and nine when they assumed the tight formation. He, like everyone else, stuck to the story that the objects multiplied out of nowhere.

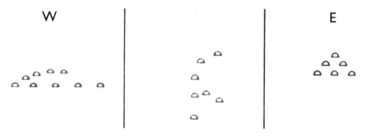

UFOs flying in formation.

Another element agreed on by everyone I talked to was that the objects didn't accelerate, a common facet in other cases such as the Hunter Ames one. They were just suddenly going at an incredible speed.

"They picked up speed real quick after sitting there for two hours," Dorothy Sanu told me. "Then they went *voom!*"

"Boy, they could go," added Debbie Sanu. "When they wanted to go, there was no gaining speed. They just went."

The formation was described by Mickey as "like a horseshoe with one side longer" and by others as sort of a rounded V. Concerning the drawing Mickey made, he stated that he could see the shapes of the craft and that he could distinguish that each had three lights on it.

As to the colour and position of the lights, Mickey didn't want to say, since he wasn't too sure. "It all happened so fast," he said.

Chad and Spencer Watt were very skeptical of Debbie's tales before they made the sighting, but they had both turned 180 degrees in their thinking.

"Mickey, the oldest boy, came in and drew them right away," Debbie said. "Then he phoned Allen [an announcer] at CFRY [in Portage la Prairie]. He phoned because he had always scoffed at me. He said, 'I've seen them. I can't believe it.' So he was really enthused, and he phoned the radio station."

I checked with Allen at CFRY, who confirmed the bizarre account of being flooded with phone calls. He didn't recall exactly how many came in during the two- to three-minute period, but it was a lot. He thought perhaps 10 to 12.

"They were all describing the same thing," the radio announcer told me. There was no place to file the reports, so he simply phoned the Portage Air Force Base tower to confirm if they had seen anything. The answer was no. Allen then sent out someone to the area where everyone was describing the objects, but it was long over and the fellow returned empty-handed. The announcer hadn't recorded the names of any of the people who had phoned. As he told me, "There was no need to."

Allen's involvement with UFOs, however, wasn't over. The next night he received another call, this time from Ben Dyck, who was a resident of Starbuck and a third-year agriculture student at the University of Manitoba. Coleman and I happened to stumble onto Dyck when we were in Starbuck looking for directions to the farm of Wilson McKennett.

We went to the restaurant to ask directions, and as we were leaving, I mentioned to the men there that we were trying to locate McKennett regarding a UFO sighting he'd had. The flap was heavy in this area, and I thought perhaps these people had been involved. Two of them jumped up from their table and told us about their involvement. Ben Dyck was the one we became interested in.

"My friend, Karl Bandeau, and I had been painting his car," Ben told us. "We got thirsty and decided to go for some beer. We pulled out about 15 minutes before dusk. We just pulled out and had driven about half a mile when all of a sudden I saw a small bright cloud about to the northeast, and it was about 10,000 feet [in] altitude, 10 times the height of the Starbuck tower, which is 1,000 feet.

"I said to Karl, 'Hey, look at that weird cloud. Have you ever seen anything like that?' He said, 'Yeah, that is weird.' And I said to him, 'I've never seen a cloud separate from the pack like that. That's no cloud. Put down the throttle and go after it!' So we went after it. It was a small cloud, and if you looked at it long enough, like maybe five to six seconds, you'd see that it was almost changing shape. It was pulsating. I don't know, like a small pulsating cloud.

"We started following it. We couldn't gain on it. We were heading west, and it was over to the northwest of us. We were doing about 60 miles per hour and we'd gone for two minutes. By that time it was 30 miles away. We stopped two miles from the La Salle River and got out to watch it.

"I was going about 90 miles per hour, as I calculated it. It was effort-lessly gliding across the sky, and it was just going … no noise, no sound, no vapour trails, nothing. It just glided and then it went right past Elie, and I thought it was somewhere between Elie and Portage la Prairie. All of a sudden another one came up. Out of the horizon to the right of this object at about half the altitude of the first object, say, 5,000 feet, another one comes gliding out. By the sun's rays, it looked like a small red cloud. It came up, this small object, and they sat there and maintained their position relative to each other."

After flagging down Allen and Dell Shade from Starbuck, they contin-ued to watch the "second one." Ben explained: "It was like it just faded into the sunset. It just moved quickly right into the sunset and was gone. The other one stayed for about 20 seconds and then took off. It seemed like it probably veered off north of Portage la Prairie. We followed it until it was just a pinpoint in the sky, and then it was gone.

"Allen said that it was a plane, but where was the vapour trail, where was the noise, why was it moving at 900 miles per hour? I didn't say anything. I didn't want to argue. Dell said, 'Yeah, it looks like a small cloud,' the same thing I described it as, and she said it was right over Starbuck and then it started to move."

At about 9:30 Allen got to a phone, called CFRY in Portage la Prairie, and told his story. "He told the same thing I described now," Ben said to us, "and he says before you go any further, that's pretty well the same thing a dozen people described last night." Just after making the call, Ben told us a jet came over, leaving a vapour trail. The plane was about 2,000 to 3,000 feet lower.

"The object took off northwest and the jet was going west?" Coleman asked.

"No, the object was gone," Ben replied. "The jet came over about 30 minutes later."

"There was no comparison between this thing and the jet?" Coleman pressed.

"Absolutely not. I would say the jet was 10 times the size of this thing."

Beams and Circles

After investigating hundreds of sightings in the two-year Manitoba flap, such stories as the previous one became a dime a dozen. Then there is the following bizarre case related to me by Chris Sedaris, a prominent UFO researcher in Winnipeg who spent hours tracing some of the hundreds if not thousands of sightings.

The incident, Chris told me, happened in October 1976 on a farm south of Austin, Manitoba. It was a pleasant fall day, and the farmer involved was out disking at about 2:00 p.m. There were no clouds in the sky. Suddenly, as the farmer was driving along, it started to rain. Perplexed, the farmer glanced up and confirmed to his startled mind that there were no clouds, yet lukewarm rain was falling in a circle in a radius of about 20 feet from his tractor.

He got off the tractor, walked to where it wasn't raining, and felt the ground. It was dry. Then he went back into the rain and touched the earth. It was damp. Not knowing what to do to correct the situation, he got on his tractor and drove out of the circle, at which point the rain stopped. The farmer told Chris that the rain lasted three to four minutes.

While lecturing at Starbuck Junior High School, I ran across a very similar case. Completing my lecture, I answered questions for about 30 minutes. Then, after five attempts, the principal finally got the students back into their classrooms. One small, timid boy remained behind. "Can I talk to you?" he asked.

He told me that he and his family had been driving at night on the highway outside Starbuck when they suddenly found themselves surrounded by a circle of green light that extended beyond the edges of the two-lane highway. The family, quite astonished by the turn of events, got out to see where the green light was coming from.

"It didn't come from anywhere," he told me.

"You looked above you?" I asked.

"Yeah, there was nothing there."

"And yet this light extended all the way around the car? Was it bright? Could you see the road easily? Could you read a newspaper by the light?"

"Oh, yeah, it was really bright."

As with the farmer south of Austin, the whole affair lasted three to four minutes. Then the lights went out, the family got back in their car, and drove off, probably wondering what the world was coming to.

Then there was Michael Perreault's case at West Hawk Lake east of Winnipeg. This area, as opposed to the flat farmlands of Austin and Starbuck, is on the Canadian Shield and is hilly and forested. It was the fall of 1974, about the same time as the famous UFO landings at the Edwin Fuhr farm in Langenburg, Saskatchewan (see beginning of Chapter 6, "Landings," for a more detailed description of these incidents).

"There was a light hovering above me and Brock Taveras," Michael told me. "There was a low cloud ceiling and the object was in the clouds."

Both had the impression there was a light revolving around a circular object in the clouds and that the light projected down a beam fixed on some point on the cliff.

"It seemed like some guy on the ground with a flashlight, a high, intense flashlight, which he was rotating in the air," Michael continued. "The round object was in the clouds, and it was moving around in a circle. I figure the beam would be about a foot and a half across. It was a very strong light. It lit up everything. You could really see the light. Boy, Brock and I were just vibrating. We were shaking."

The object followed the car for a while, rotating, and when they stopped, the beam suddenly appeared on the cliff beside them. "People are always talking about UFOs," Michael told Brock. "If there's one up there, I want to see the cotton-pickin' thing."

Michael told me: "The point was no more than 200 yards away from us, 100 to 200 yards. Brock left the car running and we headed up the cliff. When we were on our way up, the thing took off. It didn't make any sound, really. It just took off like a shot. I've seen some fast things, but that was the fastest. We watched it disappear. As we were on our way up to it, it sort of shut the light off, but there was still a light in the clouds, whatever it was. You could still see a light in the clouds. It sure was something that would put a spooking into a guy. It was something else!"

"It took off like a flash," Brock told me in a separate interview. "All you could see was this spark that went down the road along the bush line. It was above the trees on my side. I was even scared to come back."

Although this case was similar to the previous two, it acquired its bizarre quality from what happened to Michael Perreault a few months later at his home in Winnipeg Beach.

"It was just after Christmas, January 1975," Michael began. "I was sound asleep in my bed, and I couldn't get out of my bed. It was as if you were to get this intense electric shock and you can't let go. It was that feeling that I had. I couldn't let go. In fact, I did smash my right wrist against my desk when I did break free of it. I was conscious while this whole thing was going on. I ripped the whole bed apart — everything. I thought to myself for damn sure those Martians are coming to get me, and I told that to the guys at work. They told me, 'Now you're really cracking up.'"

Charlie Goes Sightseeing

Anthony Britain was a prominent citizen in southwestern Manitoba, and as a public figure related to the UFO flap, he received a lot of calls from around the province telling him about UFO sightings in other towns. One such case phoned in to Anthony was a classic one told by a woman who had trailed a Greyhound bus driving down Highway 2, heading for Winnipeg. The date was January 21, 1976. The bus was just west of St. Claude when the woman said it stopped right on the highway.

The woman told Anthony that all the people suddenly got off the bus and looked north. She stopped her car, as well, to see what the commotion was about. There, in plain daylight, was a huge metallic disk flying along the treeline.

On the other side of the object, the woman further reported, a group of snowmobilers also halted their machines to watch the silver disk. That was the story that was given to Anthony.

I talked to Chris Sedaris, who worked on a lot of sightings in Haywood and St. Claude where the incident occurred. He told me the account had even captured a few lines in the district's French newspaper. "I talked to the Ski-Dooers," he stated, "but couldn't get a straight story. Some said that they had seen it, but some said they didn't see anything."

We had been told the bus was a Greyhound, but that company denied being involved. The same disavowal came from the other two bus lines that travelled along the highway. The woman who phoned Anthony hadn't left her name, so the story, though a classic tale, was a dead end.

Estimates of the number of people who experienced the sighting ran as high as 40. Two ufologists, Chris Sedaris, and I followed every lead we had. Although we could confirm the whole affair, we couldn't obtain enough statements to complete the report of what had happened and who was involved.

Charlie Powers Up

Then there was the case of the two brothers, Jerry and Tracy Moore, in Dunleath on the Manitoba-Saskatchewan border. The object was sighted first by Jerry's sister, Leslie, who saw the object hovering above high-voltage lines south of the farm. "It then headed for the power line that feeds our farmhouse, and while it hovered over the lines, it shot two rays to the line," Leslie told the local newspaper. "When the rays touched the lines, they turned red, and the yard light dimmed."

The object, described as red on top and bottom with a silver section in the centre, then headed north of the farm where Jerry was working in a stubble field. Jerry told the paper that he saw it coming from the south: "It moved so fast, it was just a streak with no sound at all."

Over the three power lines at Highway 10, the craft again shot beams at them. "The beams were thin at first," Jerry said, "but they got bigger when they touched the lines. The beams didn't retract into the UFO. They just disappeared in about five seconds."

From there the UFO took off at high speed and a sharp angle into the northern sky. Leslie was now on her bike, headed into the field to tell her brother what she had seen, but her brother had spotted the same thing. The kids remained in the house until their parents arrived. "After that," said Joe Moore, their father, "they wouldn't go into the field again."

Joseph McCann at his farm north of Carman told a similar story. The McCann family had countless experiences with UFOs in the air and on the ground. It was one of the stories that Joseph took a lot of criticism for telling.

The McCann farm used a lot of power, but as Joseph told me during the Manitoba flap period, it started using a lot more. He fought the hydroelectric supplier but found it hard to convince the company that they should lower his bill because a flying saucer was stealing power when no one was watching.

And Yet More Cases

After two years investigating these classic cases, I found that they occurred in front of crowds of people more often than might be expected. Asked a thousand times to account for why UFOs were seen where they were, I usually responded that the sparse population of the area was a major factor.

Here, however, the opposite situation arose. Instead of an object doing its tricks in front of one or two persons, it performed its "thing" in front of huge groups, which only helped to confuse the situation.

Consider, for example, the case of seven junior high students in Starbuck who got the scare of their lives during a heavy flap of sightings in the area during the first three weeks of August 1975. The leader of the group, Bob Sanderson, told me the story. Later, while lecturing at the school, I was able to confirm the account with the others who were involved.

"They — Cathy Wall and three of her friends — were driving right behind me," Bob said. "They were following me because my transmission was gone and all I had was reverse. I was driving backward down the old highway outside Starbuck. It was about a mile [west] down the road. I was backing up down the road when I saw this blue light. I thought that it was an airplane or something. It went over Starbuck where it circled and turned around. I could see that it was now a red light, and I noticed that it started to come toward me. It was pretty big. The length of it was maybe 60 feet. It came about 150 feet away."

Bob recalled: "This was at night. I opened my window to see if I could hear anything, but all I could hear was a sort of rushing sound. It was moving back and forth, and I shut my lights off when it came back on again."

He told me that it had been rotating. It was shaped like two plates together — no dome. There was a blue light on one side and a red light on the other side. Other than the two lights, the craft wasn't lit up. "It was dark," Bob said. "All I could see was the outline against the sky."

All five were now petrified, and Bob got in Cathy Wall's car and they raced back to Starbuck to get two friends to witness this. "When we came back," Bob stated, "it had started to leave. It was a bit in the distance. It always sat level, about 10 feet off the ground. When it left, it was gone. Just like one minute it was there and the next minute it was not there. While the whole thing was going on, I didn't believe it. When it started in closer, it scared the hell out of me. That's why I turned my lights off."

In another case related to the *Enquirer*'s Daniel Coleman and myself, 11 people were involved. The incident occurred on July 23, 1976, in Arborg, Manitoba. Gary Maturchuk, a youth counsellor in Winnipeg and a third-year student at the University of Winnipeg, who related the story to us, led a group of teenagers to the area for a weekend of camping.

It was about 11:00 p.m. on a Thursday night. The group had just arrived from Nasa Beach, and most of the kids had gone to bed. Some of them, including Gary, had remained up and were talking in the van.

At about 3:30 a.m. one of the kids saw a very bright light above them. The people in the van got out and climbed on top to get a better view. After a few minutes, the object started to make erratic movements as it dropped into the south. Apparently, the kids made a lot of noise, because now everyone was out watching it.

In a jerking motion, the object plunged below the trees east of them.[1] By now, according to Gary, everyone was staring. When the object disappeared, some of the kids returned to bed, but others remained, hoping to get another glimpse of the spectacular light display.

Five minutes later, in the same spot where the object had vanished, an incredible sight was revealed, and the few observing it got the fright of their lives. They now saw the object moving south through the trees.

The object was fairly close to them, and the five witnesses got three good views as it travelled behind the trees surrounding the camp on the east side. It appeared only when it entered the clearings in the forest, and according to Gary, everyone described seeing only parts of it. The object then projected a bright light onto the ground, which they described as simply white and quite intense.

Reactions to the sightings, according to Gary, varied. Seeing was, of course, believing, and the yells of the lucky five again woke up the rest of the campers, who didn't see the second part of the sighting because it all happened too quickly. "Some," Gary told Coleman and me, "couldn't believe what they had seen, and some were quite terrified by the whole thing."

IT'S FUNNY
THEY SHOULD
BE THE SAME

It is not reasonable to assume that hundreds of ordinary normal people whose words we would readily accept under more mundane circumstances, for instance as witness to an automobile accident, should suddenly become liars, fools, neurotics, and otherwise quite incompetent observers. I have interviewed many of these people myself and am convinced that they are sane, sober, honest folk who are reporting to the best they can something that they really did witness. I will concede that maybe some of these people did not do a good job of observing as someone who was better trained might have done, but within limits I believe they did honestly report what they saw.

— Wilbert B. Smith, Head of the Canadian Government
Investigation of Flying Saucers, 1950–54

In the late 1970s when I was first putting together the manuscript for this book, a movement away from the extraterrestrial theory as the most logical answer to the UFO mystery began. The theory that came into

vogue was the inter-dimensional one. It proposed that UFOs might orig-
inate in some other dimension and that they were merely popping in and
out of ours.

Those supporting the inter-dimensional theory pointed out there
were many paranormal events occurring around UFOs sightings. They
referenced cases in which UFOs disappeared into thin air, people near
craft being cured of illnesses, and persons who claimed they were receiving telepathic messages from UFOs.

One of the main reasons for the withdrawal of the extraterrestrial
theory was the wide variety of craft and beings being seen. It was as if
no two UFOs were ever the same. Was it possible, critics of the extraterrestrial theory questioned, that so many different races of beings would
suddenly appear at one time?

Jacques Vallée, one of the key proponents of this new paranormal
theory, theorized: "UFOs exist in some other reality; that at least in part,
its manifestations are shaped in the contents of the human mind. This
is what we call the 'reflective factor,' which is the central tenet of the
para-ufological hypothesis."

There is no doubt this theory has a lot of evidence to back it up, and
there are many cases during the Manitoba flap that can be used to bolster
the multi-dimensional theory, or a theory that involves the human mind
being a key factor in UFO sightings.

Like any coin, however, there is always another side. The Manitoba
UFO flap evidence supports a theory that there is a common technolog-
ical component at work.

In opposition to Vallée's idea of a "reflective factor" are the many interviews with witnesses who exhibited "common factors" in their stories
during the Manitoba flap. These shared aspects completely contradict a
reflective factor as the core of UFO phenomena, and they also support
the accurate reporting of what witnesses experienced.

Important to the "common factor" is that some of the elements
described were very unusual facets that wouldn't be expected to pop
out of the minds of multiple people. It is for that reason that I chose to
include this chapter on things characterized by "it's funny they should be
the same."

Many witnesses, for example, told me that when a low-flying UFO passed over them or their houses it lit up the countryside. Such experiences are totally unknown in the everyday world. Such a description is common only to UFO-sighting reports.

Now if I had heard the "lit up the countryside" story only once, I could go along with the notion that it arose from the mind of the viewer. The description, however, was actually quite common and supports the hypothesis that UFOs brightening the countryside as they appear is a real event supported by a collective reality.

One man told me that a UFO a mile away was "so bright that you could only look at it for a few seconds before your eyes started to water." Again, it was a tale that sounded far-fetched until the fact is raised that I heard five other people give the same account.

In Manitoba in the 1970s, many witnesses described saucer-shaped craft with small windows around the middle. This sounds like something people might make up, even though more than 40 years later observers still report windows in UFOs.

The most frequent oddities reported by Carman witnesses were triangular disks. "It's not what everyone else saw," I was told, "but I'm sure it was a triangle shape." I myself saw this object a number of times, including once close up. In 2014, triangle sightings were the most commonly reported UFO shape, but in 1975 accounts of triangle UFOs were almost unheard of. The peculiar shape being described seemed again to point to a collective reality.[1]

What I hope to convey in this chapter are the "common factors" in the southern Manitoba sightings during 1975 and 1976. Taken on their own, they made no sense. They were unusual things not seen in daily life.

If the human mind was the key factor in UFO sightings as maintained in the inter-dimensional theory, then cross-indexing the sightings should show very few mutual elements. Moreover, the reported events should be related to everyday human experience or to the modern understanding of technology.

In many cases in Manitoba, this expected situation didn't dominate. Instead of people, for example, telling me the object flew in a straight line (based on the common knowledge that the shortest distance between two points is a straight line), they said it bounced up and down or zigzagged all over the place. Instead of people saying the saucer flew straight and level like all flying machines in the modern world, they insisted it flew at an angle of 20 to 45 degrees.

The people who shared their sightings with me had usually done very little reading about UFOs. The weird "it's funny they should be the same" items they told me about were typically referred to in passing. Witnesses often said, "You know one funny thing I noticed was ..."

What arose from the various UFO sighting reports was a series of common occurrences that made no sense. They were things as distinctive and odd as a bank robber with red nail polish on his fingernails, or a man wearing glasses with no lenses. They became collective reality observations that represented events that probably happened as described.

The Small Disks

> Keith Chester was describing to us what they looked like. We were looking and he said, "Holy Moses, there they go now!" There were three of them in formation and they were all wobbling. They were wobbling and were deep red or blood-red.
>
> — Mick Yexley

Of all the collective reality oddities reported in Manitoba, the most impressive took place in the summer of 1975. In 10 independent observations, witnesses recounted seeing a large craft drop off and later pick up smaller vehicles. As usual most of the sightings were never reported to authorities, and it was only after extensive interviewing in the area that the similarity became evident.[2]

The first person who spotted the small disks was Jennette Frost, who lived south of Sperling, Manitoba. The sighting occurred on May 12, 1975, just as the Charlie Red Star flap was starting up.

On the same night that Jennette said she saw the craft and smaller objects, numerous people were with a Winnipeg television crew in

Carman trying to film Charlie Red Star. They sighted Charlie but didn't get any film. Had they been in Sperling 11 miles away they might have got the movie of the century.

"I rubbed my eyes a couple of times," Jennette explained. "I couldn't believe what I was seeing."

Gazing north toward the town, she watched a red disk approach from the direction of Carman. Reading from one of her notebooks, in which she filed the many sightings she had during the 1975–76 UFO flap, Jennette described the beginning of the bizarre experience:

> There was a red light the size of the rising moon. Sighted about one and a quarter miles west of Sperling travelling in a bobbing undulating fashion as it approached the grain towers [in Sperling] where it suddenly glowed a bright red and increased in speed terrifically. Then the light disappeared into space, and as I looked for it, it reappeared in the near vicinity north of town.

As she watched the object, she noticed that its east side (right) suddenly glowed brilliant red. "There was a short interval and then this thing glowed and the disks came out."

She pointed at the diagram in her notebook as I looked on. "They came out this side. All four came out there, and as they did, the east side of the craft glowed. It would really glow when the disks would come out. Then when the disk would come down [toward the ground] it would glow at the top."

Jennette continued. "As I sat rubbing my eyes a couple of times, I couldn't believe what I was seeing. Then the next one came out, so I kept looking and looking. There was an interval of about five minutes. Then it glowed on the east side and the next one came out. There were four of them, and they came in intervals of about five minutes [each]."

She wrote that the small disks came out at a 45-degree angle, west-ward toward the ground. "They were not quite as big as the big saucer, but you could definitely see that the smaller ones were saucer-shaped on top, like a saucer upside down. It wasn't a flat disk. They were a metallic colour, sort of metallic blue, a bright metallic blue or bluish-green. I looked out that window many times after that to see it again, but I didn't."

During the same month, the exact thing was seen in two more towns in the area. One of them, Elie, is 37 miles directly north of Sperling; the other, Carman, is 11 miles west of it.

The witness in Elie was Wilson McKennett. Again, like most of the sightings that were made, it wasn't discussed with anyone outside a small group of friends. In August 1976, Daniel Coleman from the *National Enquirer* came to the area to interview witnesses. Together Coleman and I went out to talk to Wilson.

When we arrived at his place, we were under the impression that he had been the only witness, but when we spoke with him we discovered a dozen others had experienced the event, which occurred near the end of May 1975, a couple of weeks after Jennette Frost's sighting.

"It happened about 11:00 p.m. or midnight," Wilson began. "We saw it three nights in a row. We were seeding. We were going around the field, eh? So one time we got around there's nothing, and the next time we turn the corner, there it is."

Just as in Jennette's sighting in the south, the Elie witnesses stated there were four smaller objects. "It was west of here," Wilson said, "close to the [telephone] microwave tower. The mother ship seemed to be close to the tower."

"How long did you watch it before you saw the smaller ones?" Coleman asked him.

"Oh, not even five minutes. The four small ones came out of it. When they first came out, they seemed to be in position, you know, four even positions. There were two above and two below. The two below were explorers. The other two above it just stayed on guard above it. From there one of the explorers headed toward Winnipeg [east] and one headed toward Portage la Prairie [west]."

Wilson reported that when the two explorers flew away and returned they travelled in an up-and-down motion "just like little waves." This would be something many people seeing Charlie Red Star described as one of his main characteristics.

Immediately, I realized how close Wilson's account was to the story told by Jennette, so I asked Wilson about the colour of the objects.

"All pretty much the same colour," he replied. "They were brighter than a star but the same colour. The mother ship was real bright. It was the brightest and the biggest. It's hard to tell how much bigger than the small ones it was, but it was so bright that if you watched it for a couple of minutes, it would make your eyes water."

According to Wilson, the small objects that flew toward Winnipeg and Portage la Prairie seemed to get where they were going in two to three minutes. After about 30 minutes, they returned, gathered themselves around the glow of the larger bright craft, and then the whole army of objects moved west toward Portage la Prairie. At that point Wilson said "it seemed to move quite fast." The whole event had taken about 45 minutes during which Wilson stopped his tractor and watched.

Other witnesses to the incident were Wilson's father and mother, who lived a mile east, his two brothers, and a hired hand who was so upset over the sighting that he refused to leave the tractor during the entire affair.

The next two nights Wilson and many of his witnesses watched exactly the same objects do the very same thing.

Meanwhile, in Carman, Freda Waterman stated that she had seen something quite similar in the spring of 1975. She lived on the Boyne River, which ran through Carman, so she had seen Charlie many times, because the river was on Charlie's beer run. During an interview with me in May 1976, she related that one night Charlie wasn't alone.

"There were three objects. There were two red and one big silver one The big silver one used to hover over my house every night. You could hear it. It made noise, something like a tea kettle. The two red ones were always around when we heard this big silver one. You'd go out and look, and they would be around, except they were flying lower down along the treeline. Sometimes we would see the small red ones dock up with the big silver one."

Freda described the complex docking manoeuvre in which the small UFOs took turns linking to the big silver object. "The middle one was always the silver one," she said, "and the red ones always linked to the top, never to the bottom."[3]

The final reference to the small disk stories came from Kerry Kaelin, a reporter for the *Dufferin Leader*. This incident took place in August 1975 during a brief flurry of sighting activity along Highway 13 between August 11 and 21. Kaelin and his fiancée, Janet Robertson, spotted Charlie Red Star as he hovered over a field northwest of Carman.

The *Dufferin Leader* reporter wrote: "We saw two pairs of lights rise up into the UFO and one pair of red lights come out of it. They descended to the ground in the half-hour that we watched the object."

He estimated the time they first noticed the craft to be about 12:35 a.m. on a Sunday evening. "The movements of Charlie were erratic in that it would drop to the ground and rise up again moving occasionally horizontally, but remained in the same general area. The UFO was a small white light with a pulsating red area. At times the whole craft would just about disappear and then the light would brighten." He said there was a tail of light that shone down from it. Eventually, the UFO disappeared to the northwest.

Triangles

If I were asked to design the classic model of a UFO, I would undoubtedly base it on the many reports since 1947 that describe a disk-shaped object with a cupola on it. It was for this reason that I was confused when I first heard Joseph and Anna McCann tell me they were seeing triangle-shaped UFOs. I hardly knew what to think. Looking back more than 40 years, it might have been the beginning of something new, since triangles are now reported much more frequently than saucer shapes.

The McCanns, more than any other witnesses in the entire flap area, were met with scorn and disbelief for their numerous and sometimes bizarre UFO sighting reports. I had talked to them and their children many times, so I knew they were probably telling the truth. I also knew that their farm north of Carman was in the general direction where many Carman citizens said they saw the object going when it left town.

Anthony Britain is the one who ignited the UFO fire with his high-profile sightings, but it was the McCanns who poured fuel on the flames and took the UFO stories beyond run-of-the-mill tales. As many of their accounts were controversial, it was perhaps only appropriate that the McCanns should have started the triangle stories. Yet, in the end, I only filed their stories and waited.

In the spring of 1976, I began to get other reports that indicated the McCanns weren't alone in their triangle sightings. In May 1976, I spoke with Freda Waterman, who had been one of the many witnesses to the 1975 Charlie Red Star flybys. She told me Charlie was only one of two craft that flew at low altitude through the valley back then. "There was a big silver craft that used to drop off smaller red craft," she said. "The silver craft used to sit right above the house every night and you could hear something like a tea kettle. On the top of this silver craft were two red lights and a green one which rotated like beacons."

In our conversation, Freda stated that the silver craft with the triangle light pattern on it stationed itself over her house in Carman from April 10 to 30, 1975, so she was the first to mention triangles. The McCanns didn't report seeing them until the last week in May. The family's full UFO story included five separate triangle sightings between May and October 1975.

The McCanns reported that their first encounter with a triangle occurred when they saw an object with a solid yellow line forming the three sides of a triangle. They stated that there didn't appear to be anything inside or outside the lines.

At the time the McCanns were returning to their farm a mile west of the main highway they were travelling on. They turned onto the mile road that went to their house when suddenly a huge yellow triangle flew over their truck. The triangle was on an angle and moved at high speed.

Joseph quickly slowed down and turned off the truck's lights. Immediately, the triangle reversed direction rapidly and then remained stationary down the road. Joseph switched the truck lights back on and continued down the road. Instantly, the triangle raced toward him at a terrific speed, so he turned off the lights once more. The triangle reversed itself away from the truck and hovered over the road some distance away.

Totally unaware of what this might be and why it was happening, Joseph left the truck lights off and made the remaining trip to the farm in the dark. Upon reaching the McCann place, Joseph and Anna hurried

Road where Charlie Red Star was attracted to Joseph McCann's truck.

into the house where they remained with the lights off and the doors locked.

"It moved at a speed you couldn't imagine," Anna told me more than once. "It moved so fast back and forth. We kept the lights off in the house because we were afraid it would come to the house."

Jerry, their son, stated that the triangle was still sitting in the field after the truck arrived home. "I watched it just sitting in the northeast field," he said.

The second triangle witnessed by the McCanns happened not too long after the first. Similar to the first sighting, the border edges on this one consisted of a solid lighting pattern. This time the light was white as opposed to the yellow of the first triangle. The triangle flew at a very steep angle and travelled in a northwest direction from Carman. According to Anna, the triangle was very low and moved at a very high rate of speed.

Young Lucy McCann sighted the third triangle on Labour Day 1975. The McCann children were sitting on the front lawn with three cousins visiting from Winnipeg. Anna was in the trailer next door, and Joseph and a friend, Pete, were approaching the farm on a gravel road from the south.

In March 1976, I went to talk with the McCanns only to find they weren't home. The children told me their parents would return soon, so I sat with them to wait. I used the opportunity to question the kids about what they had seen without any influence from their parents.

It was during this interview that I discovered that only Lucy had seen the Labour Day triangle. The other children thought she was talking about the first one that had followed the parents to the house in May. Lucy insisted this was a distinct sighting. Here is a section of that interview:

> **Lucy:** Yeah, I saw it over there [south]. I can't describe the yellow. It's a yellow, but it flipped over, and I never knew how a triangle could turn into a red ball.
>
> **Grant:** The triangle flipped?
>
> **Lucy:** Yeah, and it turned into a red ball. It started to bounce up and down, and then it chased the truck. We thought it was chasing the truck.
>
> **Grant:** Were the lights on the triangle connected or were they just spots of light?
>
> **Lucy:** It was like a solid triangle. Not like the one across the road [referring to the first triangle seen by her parents]. It seemed to be coming slant down. Then it sort of flipped while it was coming, and then it was coming backward. It seemed to go behind the bushes at the Corans' and then it popped up again. Then it zigzagged all over the place and left.

The fourth triangle the McCanns witnessed was seen east across the road from their farmhouse, sitting in a field. This triangle had red, green, and white lights forming the corners of the triangle instead of solid lines. In an area around the triangle, a red light bounced around.

Jerry McCann, who saw it, believed he remembered it the best and described it this way:

> **Jerry:** The one across the road had red, green, and red lights on it.
>
> **Grant:** Were the lights separate or connected?

Jerry: No, they were separate. There was a red light that was sort of revolving around it. It would go to different spots, but it would stay near the triangle.

In the spring of 1976, other people, including me, began to see triangles. The objects were definite triangle shapes, unexplainable as such things as planes, weather balloons, or other natural phenomena used by skeptics to talk themselves out of tight corners.

In 1976 it wasn't the McCanns who were reporting triangles, because the sightings being made had shifted to the Carman-Brunkild area. Before the year was over, there were 15 sightings of triangles by 38 witnesses. No matter how unorthodox they were the sightings indicated there was something real that had invaded Manitoba's skies.

Common to all the 1976 sightings was the fact that the triangles flew at very low altitudes. The triangles in 1975 were reported moving quite fast, while the 1976 ones filed featured extremely slow-moving objects.

Barbara Pelletier, who had a triangle fly right over her and her boyfriend near Brunkild, described her experience this way: "It moved our way and came right over the car, and it was shaped like a triangle. It wasn't that high. You could see the shape of it. I could see how high it was. There were big lights in the corner of the triangle. There was a red one in the one corner and two blue ones on the other sides. There were a couple of lights forming the sides of the triangle. They were white, about four or five forming the sides of the triangle."

In the spring of 1976, I was lucky enough to be present at five sightings in which triangles were seen. This is because various cameramen were out in the flap area trying to photograph UFOs.

I noticed during my observations that other high-flying UFOs accompanied each low-flying triangle. The triangles were just as others had described them: low at less than 1,000 feet.

The simultaneous appearance of a triangle and a bouncing light was an unusual combination, but important in the entire UFO mystery because Manitoba wasn't the only place to experience such a phenomenon. Dr. Harley D. Rutledge, chairman of the Physics Department at Southwest Missouri State University, researched identical incidents.[4] Because of

Rutledge's position he was very hesitant to talk about his discoveries. He told me in a letter dated March 24, 1977: "We value our reputations more than life itself."

Rutledge and his team of researchers had more than 70 experiences with the bouncing lights. He estimated the speed at over 5,000 miles per hour and reported: "Detecting unusual radio waves which he believed were being emitted by the objects."

According to Wendelle Stevens, it was on May 25, 1975, during his research on the bouncing lights, that Rutledge reported "watching a large triangle over the Farmington area at an altitude of 2,000 feet."

Although there were descriptions of low-flying triangles in Missouri, Minnesota,[5] and Manitoba during 1976, the colouring of the objects varied considerably. The most prevalent triangle report was of an object with a light at each corner. In Manitoba where triangles were sighted all over the southern part of the province, the most common colour combination was red, red, and green. Twenty people in eight incidents saw this object, and in these sightings it was flying with the blunt end of the triangle forward.

When the object maintained a stable altitude, only two of the lights could be seen. As soon as the green light appeared, the object rose in altitude until it could no longer be distinguished. During all this, the triangle travelled very slowly.

I was with three other people when we spotted a couple of triangles, including a dramatic one close up.[6] It was 9:16 p.m., according to notes I took that night. Danny Penner yelled to me that he saw something flying off near the Brunkild microwave tower. The object with two distinct red lights just cleared the tower and continued its slow flight southwest.

Just after the object passed the tower, a green light suddenly became visible as it began a slow ascent into the sky. During the next 14 minutes, I watched as the object moved higher and higher until it was a small red light among the stars.

An hour later the same triangle dramatically reappeared and flew over the front of our car only a couple of hundred feet up as we sat on Highway 205 East, eight miles south of the microwave tower.

Small ground light shows the same colour pattern as Charlie Red Star.

"I figured it might have been the same craft I saw go over the tower," Danny stated.

It came back in the same direction as the other one had vanished (southwest) and looked identical from what I could see. "It could have been the same craft," I told Danny.

When the triangle reappeared and approached our car, I gazed up at it with my binoculars and noticed an interesting characteristic described by many other witnesses. Through the binoculars, the object covered my entire field of vision. The three lights forming the corners of the triangle seemed to be five or 10 feet across. Yet for such large lights they weren't illuminating anything in the centre of the triangle. This same phenomenon had been reported about the triangle on March 19, so I made an effort to peer at the middle of the triangle at its closest point. There was nothing there, just three well-shaped lights forming a triangle. (See photograph on page 186, which was taken with my camera in Sperling, Manitoba, in 1976. The front two lights of the triangles are visible as the object moves up and down in its flight path.)

The sightings of the triangles continued right into 1977. On March 6, 1977, for example, David Rosenfield, a pilot who flew out of Friendship Field, phoned Anthony Britain and reported that there was a UFO on the western horizon. Anthony and his wife, Rachael, hurried to glance out the west window on the second floor of their house.

The scene was described by Anthony: "The thing was real close, no more than two miles away. Through the binoculars, I got a real good look at the thing. I had the object in view for five minutes. Just as it was dropping behind the trees along Highway 245, I could see that the corners of this object had definite red lights. In between the lights there was what looked like red neon lights.

"Now that V-shape or triangle is not a guess at the shape of the thing. Rosenfield saw it, too. There was definite spacing between the three lights. The neon structure reminded me of heated metal. We had a real good look at it. It was there for five minutes."

Rosenfield, meanwhile, followed the object eight miles west to Stephenfield and stated that it spent its entire time flying back and forth between the Haywood tower and the lights at Stephenfield. He had it in sight for 30 minutes. Rosenfield's impression of the triangle is that there "were lights on the bottom of the saucer."[7]

Towers

During 1975 and 1976, the sightings of UFOs in Manitoba were almost a daily occurrence. The province had become one of the areas of the world with the highest number of sightings, if not the highest. What attracted these objects to Manitoba? No one theory seems to provide even part of the answer. Nevertheless, whatever attracted Charlie and his friends, one thing can be said for sure: they were often spotted around the many microwave, radio, and television relay towers in the province.

Sprinkled across the Manitoba prairie, these towers range from the 190-foot one at Brunkild to the 1,400-foot structure at Pembina, North Dakota, near the U.S.-Canada border. They might have provided some form of visual guidance for the objects, or they might have been important because they were the source of large volumes of communication.

From the reports I saw, it appeared that if there was a UFO sighting, there was often a microwave or other tower nearby. This, of course, might have been a coincidence because the towers were visible from long distances.

Many accounts had UFOs travelling from tower to tower. For example, in a case at Sanford, Manitoba, two women were confronted by a UFO that hovered over their car. In their story, the Brunkild tower, 10 miles away, was a key part.

"Then it lifted and headed for the tower at Brunkild," Phyllis Johnson, one of the women, stated. "We could see it all the way over to the tower and back. There was just this one light. It went straight over."

In the car with Phyllis was her friend, Marnie Herb, who told her, "That's what they do, you know."

In 1975 when the UFO flap was in full swing, there were many articles in magazines and journals about the attraction UFOs seemed to have to power lines, military installations, the space program, and new weapons tests. The microwave tower theory hadn't gotten any press as far as I could tell. So when I learned that in some towns people went to their local towers to watch UFOs I paid attention.

In April, May, and June 1975, for example, the CBC tower just north of Carman became a regular meeting place for those trying to see Charlie Red Star. Rachael Britain told me it was such a popular place that "You'd go out to see people you hadn't seen for months. We'd bring along coffee and sandwiches and have a real get-together."

At a lecture in Starbuck, Manitoba, I mentioned that microwave towers might have something to do with where UFOs were going. After the lecture, many of the students came up and said they knew this already. Apparently, in August 1975, a number of the students had seen an object around the 1,066-foot tower just outside Starbuck.

Sitting by the towers paid off many times for those who went out to spot UFOs. The famous CKY film clip was taken at the Carman CBC tower. The TV camera was stationed at the tower and was pointed west. There was an alleyway between the lights at Stephenfield and the

Haywood tower, and the UFO seemed to fly between them and the CBC tower.

Three photographers who had come out a number of times with me had a dramatic close encounter at the same tower. Two others and I had a vivid sighting that involved a UFO that flew past the Brunkild tower twice.

Jennette Frost lived 12 miles east of the CBC tower at Sperling. In her description of the numerous times she saw Charlie, she mentioned not only that the UFO had visited the tower but had also affected it. "Whenever I saw it [Charlie] coming from Carman that tower would just glow! Oh, it would look about that broad [indicating a couple of inches] from here. It always seemed to affect the tower. It didn't always come from the same place, but you often saw it coming from Carman and just north of the tower."

Even Brendon Eagle, who constructed the Carman CBC tower, spotted a UFO there. "I saw one at the 4,000- to 5,000-foot level over the radio tower at Carman," he told me. "It hovered there. I wonder if they're using that tower. They might be using the beam of frequency for guidance."

The Carman tower was the main one where people observed UFOs, but they popped up at other towers, as well. Jennette recorded everything in her diary:

> One night Doug [her son] and I were pumping water into the cistern. You have to stay with it till it's done. At 11:30, as a severe thunderstorm approached, I saw Charlie sitting and pulsating in the sky straight north of Brunkild, not too high up. It stayed there stationary for some time and then approached the Brunkild tower very slowly. It then dropped down on the east side of the tower below the top red light. It hovered there for a few seconds and then moved in an easterly direction.

I received reports from UFO researcher Chris Sedaris that there were numerous sightings at the two towers on the edge of Haywood, northwest of Carman. As for my own reports, I could only find a half dozen that happened near the Haywood tower. One came from Marcel Viugnier in Rathwell, Manitoba. "I saw something out this way [east] one night," he told me. "I said, 'There's a UFO over by the Haywood tower.' Later, people said that they were coming to the power station at Haywood."

Many sightings occurred near the Elie telephone tower. In one, Wilson McKennett and a dozen other people watched five UFOs, one big and four small, come to the tower three nights in a row. "It was west of here," Wilson said. "Close to the microwave tower and the mother ship seemed to be close to the tower."

There were trips being made to the Starbuck tower as early as May and June 1975. Tannis Major in Carman was already aware from circulating stories that UFOs had been seen around the tower. Working from her own reports, she visited Starbuck on many occasions, hoping she might snap a photo of one of them. "We went to the CBWT tower at Starbuck," she told me. "I took a whole slew of pictures there because there were quite a few of them there."

Even on the last day of the long two-year flap a Mrs. Krutcher experienced a sighting on September 29, 1976, of an object that flew past the Manitoba Telephone System tower in Morden.

Ferris Wheel

The community of Carman provided good evidence for the objective existence of UFOs because most people there reported the same red pulsating object, with Charlie Red Star being the most documented one. However, the accounts were so numerous that skeptics started insisting that all the witnesses were telling identical stories regardless of what they saw.

In the Carman area, there was also a second major UFO type — a "Ferris wheel" shape. The descriptions of this object were very similar but were never publicized. In 1975 alone, a dozen witnesses told me they saw a "giant red Ferris wheel" fly through the sky.

The first person to catch a glimpse of this unusual sight was the late Carl Major from Carman. The incident occurred on May 12 and was related to me by his wife, Tannis. "He was going south," she said, "the day before CKY took that film. He was going south to see what's what. He joined us later on and he said, 'I'm pretty darn sure I saw one because it was the shape of a Ferris wheel, lights all around.'"

The next witnesses to report the Ferris wheel shape were the McCanns, who had observed the giant object moving toward Carman. "It was just like a Ferris wheel at the fair," Joseph McCann told me, "except it was ten times the size."

Anna McCann told me the same thing as her husband in another interview.

"Was it on the ground?" I asked her.

"No, no!" she insisted. "It was in the sky and it was rotating as it moved toward Carman. There were spokes just like a Ferris wheel."

"Was it at an angle?"

"No," Anna McCann replied. "It was on its side, slowly rotating."

Most witnesses living near the McCanns' farm failed to report their sightings for fear of being associated with the McCanns and the family's little green men friends. However, a majority of the neighbours *were* quietly seeing the Ferris wheel. These neighbours' stories became known to me when one witness pointed out others who hadn't come forward. Once it became established that other people were seeing something, witnesses began ending their accounts by saying, "I wasn't the only one who saw it, you know." Two of the neighbours I approached stated they had, indeed, seen the red Ferris wheel but pleaded with me to keep their identities secret. They didn't want to experience the ridicule the McCanns knew so well.

The last witnesses to see the Ferris wheel were a group of five who had gathered at the CBC tower north of Carman to watch for Charlie. Anthony Britain, one of those present, described the sighting. "I had the 7x50 binoculars and it got in close enough so that I could see it. It was about one to one and a half inches across in the glasses. It looked like a huge flaming Ferris wheel, with the whole outside flaming hot, with the reflection on the inside of glinting metal. It had a very pronounced halo on the bottom corner with actual little fingers licking out.

"Then it came up to us. It was flying a bit higher that night. It was 2,000 to 2,500 feet up.[8] I searched behind me for the movie camera when someone said, 'Hey! It's going the other way!' It backed out of there, exact reverse course — 180 degrees and at about 300 to 400 miles per hour. It's hard, however, to estimate speeds at night."

Getting Rid of a UFO

Any ufologist who files reports continuously runs up against stories in which people are chased down highways by low-flying UFOs. Manitoba was no exception. In filing such cases, however, I discovered a second bizarre yet common occurrence that people described: on numerous occasions they reported being chased down roads by UFOs that "flew off" when they made 90-degree turns onto other highways or into their yards.

In one case, two girls were heading southwest from Winnipeg to Manitou. It was near sunset when a huge flaming object appeared on the driver's side and followed the car for many miles. They reported that there were now two red objects in the sky, one in the east and the sun in the west. According to the two girls, there was a considerable difference between the two. Coming up to Highway 3, the girls turned west. At this point the object vanished. Mystified by this event, the girls drove around, searching for the object, but saw nothing.

In another case, an unidentified woman from Kenton, Manitoba, told me that a blood-coloured object paced her car as she drove six children to school in Kenton. "Well, when we got to the corner where we turn off to go west toward Kenton," she said, "the kids could hardly wait to get to school. We turned west and the darn thing just vanished. We don't know where it vanished or anything."

This case, as bizarre as it might seem, occurred in broad daylight. Daylight close encounters are few and far between.

Perhaps the best example of this phenomenon was the one involving two school principals who were chased down the road by a UFO. The two, Marnie Herb and Phyllis Johnson, had a saucer hover only a few feet above their car as they returned home to Sanford, 15 miles west of Winnipeg.

The two were so petrified by what was happening that Marnie, who was driving, decided to turn into a farmhouse yard along the road. At the precise moment the car made the turn, the object shot away.

"It just lifted," Marnie said. "That made me wonder. The house is right close to the road. It just disappeared immediately at that lane."

The craft headed west to the Brunkild microwave tower, and the two women could see it clearly sitting near the structure. It appeared to be finished with them, so Marnie pulled the car back onto the road and continued north toward Sanford.

Within seconds the object was back over their car. "It came back," Marnie stated. "We saw it put its lights on and it came back, sat above us, and followed along with us."

At the main highway Marnie sped across the intersection right through a stop sign and into town. As for the object, it lifted and accelerated northeast toward Winnipeg.

Beams

One of the odd similarities that became apparent after studying hundreds of UFO reports across Manitoba was that in a significant number of cases the UFO reportedly projected one or more beams onto the ground for one purpose or another.

This phenomena, it should be noted, has been mentioned in other cases around the world. In the famous Travis Walton abduction in November 1975, the five witnesses near Travis stated that he was hit and lifted from the ground by a blue-green beam projected by a saucer-shaped object just off in a forest clearing.

At the same time the Manitoba flap was starting in April 1975, John Womack told his own story about a UFO contact he had in the Tennessee Valley:

> The most incredible thing happened. From the bottom of the machine, a beam of light several feet thick began moving slowly toward the ground. After a few seconds had passed, the column of intense light reached the ground. I couldn't believe my eyes when the light, instead of stopping at the ground, continued to spread out over the meadow. The light flowed over the area like some sort of foggy spirit until it almost reached the road.[9]

After Womack's experience, beams of light were reported in connection with Manitoba's sightings. It was mid-May 1975 when Anthony Britain, Martin Rugne, and 12 other witnesses watched from the Pembina Hills as Charlie projected a triangle-shaped beam of light onto the ground before dropping into the trees.

"We were looking toward Morden," Anthony said, "and it was moving slowly south toward the U.S. border. Suddenly, it started zigzagging across the bush, lower and lower with every zigzag. It got down over the bush and stopped. It stopped pulsing red and turned solid red and then there was that beam that came out from it. It was like a triangle, but it had definite edges. It wasn't a light. It was a definite beam. The beam was so intense that it took on a reddish-white tinge."

In August 1975, more witnesses five miles east of Carman saw the same thing. Larry First, one of the people, described the zigzagging, the beam, and the sudden vertical descent. The only variation from the object seen from the Pembina Hills was that this time the beam was blue.

On July 13, 1976, Anton Olson and Hubert Drosen were just about to turn into Cardinal, Manitoba, when they noticed a peculiar light in the northeast. "It had form," Anton commented. "It wasn't just a light. It was an object. It was peculiar. It was red — mostly red with some blue lights. It was moving west toward Elm Creek. It was swerving back and forth at a very high rate of speed, stopped, then started pulsing in the sky. They were bluish-white [pulses] and it started to drop down."

"It would move down," Hubert said, "and then stop. Then it would move down a bit farther and stop. All the time it moved down, there was a beam of light projected down to the ground. The beam was moving around. It looked like it was trying to find a good place to land."

"It came down about Elm Creek," Anton added, "and we watched it until it was down."

In another August 1975 case, *Dufferin Leader* reporter Kerry Kaelin reported seeing Charlie on the morning of the 17th at 12:35 a.m. "The movements of Charlie were erratic. It would drop down to the ground quickly and rise up again, moving occasionally horizontally but remaining in the same general area."

In connection with two smaller objects that had left the craft and descended to the ground, there was, as Kaelin reported, "a tail of light that shone down from it."

There were other cases in which beams were reported being emitted from craft. In the dramatic triangle case I was involved in (see the "Triangles" section earlier in this chapter and "Charlie Fights Back" in Chapter 7), Danny Penner reported that the object in the air projected a beam of light down onto (or close to) two ground lights we had been annoying with flashlights a half mile south of our position on Highway 205 East, south of Morden.

Finally, in a case that occurred in Riding Mountain National Park northwest of Carman, Carl Bachmanek and Paul Dawkins reported to me that they were standing on the edge of a lake one night when they noticed a peculiar light on the opposite shore. The object moved toward them to the centre of the lake where it projected a beam of light into the water. The beam, according to Carl, penetrated the lake right to the bottom. Slowly, the beam started moving toward them. Both Carl and Ron watched as it travelled up onto the shore and right onto the two men. "I knew the beam was on us," Carl told me, "but I couldn't feel anything."

The beam began to retreat after a few moments onto the ground at their feet and again into the water. Where it went next, neither man could tell me, because they had long since turned and run from the area.

Animal Reactions

Just outside Ottawa there is a government communication station called Shirleys Bay, where in 1953–54 the Canadian government gave authorization for a bizarre experiment. A small hut supplied by the Defence Research Board (DRB) was moved onto the property. It was known as the "flying saucer observatory." Its purpose was to detect "flying saucers."

Five different monitoring systems were set up to detect (1) change in the gravitational field; (2) change in noise; (3) change in magnetic field; (4) change in gamma ray background; and (5) mass changes in the atmosphere.

Likewise today small companies in Canada and the United States put out a vast array of "UFO detectors" designed so that UFO investigators are alerted when a UFO flies by. Most of these detectors work on the principle of change in magnetic fields.

It was found through cases such as the one at Falcon Lake, Manitoba, on May 20, 1967, where a UFO landed that magnetic fields could be affected by the presence of a UFO. In the Falcon Lake incident, Stefan Michalak, a geologist, discovered that the needle on his compass spun erratically when he was in the forest opening where the UFO had landed. As well, a former member of the DRB told me that animals were used in the 1950s in Canada to detect the presence of UFOs.

The sighting reports of the Manitoba flap reveal a similar ability of animals to sense UFOs. The reactions of animals seem particularly strong when UFOs land. The evidence both from Manitoba cases and from former government work show that animals are somehow capable of detecting sounds humans can't distinguish.

In the Falcon Lake case, the animal response that alerted Stefan Michalak was the "frightened cries of a flock of geese." When the geese reacted, he looked up in time to notice the object landing 50 yards from his position.

Probably one of the most dramatic animal reaction cases in the 1975 Manitoba sightings occurred when a glowing red craft settled down in a field a half mile northwest of the McCann farm, north of Carman. Present at the farm were 20 of the 200 horses owned by Joseph McCann.

"We thought it was in our field at first," Anna McCann told the *National Enquirer*. "We had about 20 head there. The horses were real scared. It was hovering not far from the horses. They stampeded, but later settled down."

Months later I questioned the McCanns about the reactions of the horses and discovered something quite interesting. On their farm is a 200-foot-long barn where the horses were kept. Of the 20 horses present at the time, only a couple were in the pasture west of the house and south of the object. The remainder were in the barn and had no visual contact with the object. According to Anna, these horses were unable to see the object, yet were the ones that had the most severe reactions to the hovering object.

"They really went wild," she told me. "Joseph and I thought that they were going to pull the barn down. This lasted only for a minute and then everything stopped. No more than a minute, then dead silence. You could hear a pin drop."

The horses couldn't see from inside the barn, so most likely they heard the object. This noise had to be outside the human audible frequency because the McCanns reported hearing nothing from the object when they were only 500 feet away.

The McCanns' account of the short period during which the horses reacted and the unusual silence are observations common to other landings. Consider, for example, Mary Berezuik who sighted two objects with four windows in each that settled in a swamp three-quarters of a mile north of her home in Sundown, Manitoba, just north of the U.S. border.

At 3:15 a.m. on February 15, 1977, Mary heard her dogs howl and hurried out of the house with a .22 calibre rifle in anticipation of finding a stray dog attacking her cows. Arriving outside, she fired two shots into the air to scare away whatever was bothering the animals. Then she looked at the cows and noticed they appeared to be extremely frightened by something. "Their eyes," Mary stated, "were glaring bright red, like flashlights."

She added that suddenly it became "quiet" and "unnaturally still," so much so, in fact, that she became alarmed and hurried into the house. Seconds later, through the north window, Mary saw two objects slowly drop into the swamp.

The third case I recorded that dealt with this curious silence was a similar event experienced by Anna McCann. She was awakened early in the morning by the barking of her two dogs. Getting up, she went outside, fearing that someone was stealing gas.

Once outside, she spotted an object in the direction of the Haywood tower but figured that a second one was down the road behind a line of trees. She was quite frightened because the dogs were still barking and the birds were making a racket as well. Suddenly, all the animals stopped making noise, and for the second time in a year, Anna experienced a peculiar eerie silence.

"There was absolutely no sound at all," she told me. "I thought that that thing had landed again, so I started to walk out to the road to see past the set of trees in front of the house."

As she strode down the driveway to the road, the larger of the two dogs placed himself in her way. He pulled at Anna's legs and wouldn't allow her to go out to the road. After a few minutes of struggling to get past the dog, she gave up and returned to the house.

A year before the Manitoba UFO flap began there was a famous landing case at Langenburg, Saskatchewan, a couple of miles from the Manitoba–North Dakota border. The farmer was Edwin Fuhr. His animals exhibited actions indicating they knew long before Edwin that something odd was at the farm. The reactions came from cattle that broke through a fence during the events as well as barking by neighbourhood dogs.

Edwin's sightings involved seeing "five small metallic domes" in his farm field. The incident occurred on Sunday, September 1, 1974, at about 10:45 a.m. An interview with Ted Phillips at the Center for UFO Studies reveals, however, that the object might have been in the field all night.[10]

"Well, he [the dog] barked, when was it?" Edwin told Phillips. "Saturday night, they barked. The neighbours' dogs barked, too. They all barked at the same time Saturday night, about midnight [the night before the reported event]. Then they barked at about 3:00 in the morning. Jack, our neighbour had a babysitter who was frightened because the dogs were barking, and when Jack came home, he said the dogs were still barking.

"On Monday night about 10:30, the dogs were barking. My dog had been out in the field and he had backed up to the house. He wouldn't go into the field. He usually follows me, but this time he wouldn't go out there. On Tuesday morning, I found the ring there. When I heard the dogs barking Monday night, I thought, *It could be out there again, but even if it is, no way am I going out there.*"

Phillips asked Edwin if the neighbours' cattle were disturbed.

"Yes," said Edwin, "the cattle were making a lot of noise that Sunday morning. The fence was broken in four places. The Saturday night after [September 7] the dogs were barking again and we found that one [UFO]."

An interesting point to consider is the type of barking done by the dogs. Usually, they bark to protect their property or the property of their masters. They will charge a mailman and come as close to him as is safe. Here, however, we find barking that exhibited fear.

"My dog had been out in the field," said Edwin. "He backed up to the house." The dog wouldn't go out into the field again, though in the past he usually did. This reaction is hardly one of a dog protecting his master. It seems more out of fear or an irritation caused by some unusual noise.

A very similar event happened at the farm of Howard Rempel, south of Carman. It was 4:15 a.m. on May 2, 1975, eight months after Edwin Fuhr's experience. This time all the animals in the valley were affected.

The Rempel farm lay at the base of a valley high in the Pembina Hills. The reported craft passed low over two farms before it finally settled on Howard's front lawn. The other farms belonged to Mr. Wheeler and Mr. Stevens.

"The two dogs at Wheeler's farm and my dog started howling long before the object appeared," Stevens told me.

It was Tina, his wife, however, who first became aware that something strange was occurring. She awoke to find that it was suddenly daylight, even though it was only 4:00 a.m. The light seemed to fade, and Tina realized something quite out of the ordinary was travelling over the house. Her husband didn't wake up in time to see the object, but though it was gone, he, too, had a weird feeling. "By the way my wife was reacting, and by the funny feeling I had, I figured that something must have been in the yard."

Tina continued. "The dog was howling outside, and our two cats were at the window screaming. Not meowing, or crying, but screaming. I've never heard anything like it before. I went to the door to go out and see what was going on, but with the reactions of the animals and the weird feeling I had, I never did."

Moments later, the object landed a mile south in Howard Rempel's farmyard. There, both the chickens and dogs were spooked by the object. The chickens raced around the yard, then gathered in bunches, while the dogs hid under the steps of the house.

"The dogs woke us up with their barking," Howard told the *National Enquirer*. "This usually means the horses are out or something. We looked out the window and immediately noticed that there was a light in the corner of the driveway out there. I was really tempted to go outside, but the dogs wouldn't go down there. They stayed right by the house barking. I figured if they weren't going out there, I wasn't, either."

At Carman there was an interesting reaction from a horse involved in a close encounter north of town. Eight-year-old Bobby Baker stood on the deck on the south side of his house when a large saucer descended and sat inches above the neighbour's tree, perhaps 50 yards away.

Standing next to him as the saucer appeared was Bobby's pet stallion, Sonny. Just as the child noticed the craft, he drew the horse's attention to the object. "When he saw it," Bobby told me, "he kicked up his heels and ran to his house."

In the summer of 1975 and April 1978, there were numerous UFO sightings and landings, as well as reports of Sasquatches near the former Southport Air Force Base, south of Portage la Prairie. It was the same area where 32 horses from the pasture of Joseph McCann had disappeared in 1975.

Two Sasquatches were observed close to houses on a road south of the base fence, and there were strong indications that UFOs were involved. At both Sasquatch sightings the dogs in the area reacted strangely. One of them near the base perimeter was a vicious Great Dane and was therefore chained to the house at all times. Yet, when a Sasquatch was spotted peering in the kitchen window only a few feet away, the dog froze and didn't even growl. It was a canine response similar to a reaction to the presence of a UFO.

During 1975, Sasquatches were seen at the Native reserve southwest of Portage la Prairie and a dog there also froze. However, when the first Sasquatch was spotted near the air base at a house across the street, I was told the larger of two chained dogs tried to take a run at it. The animal lurched across the length of his chain, attempting to get to the road. The dog's owner reported that the creature almost choked to death, straining against his leash. When the owner let the dog go, he immediately headed toward the bush where 18-inch footprints were later found running along the creek and up into a clearing.

Shortly before 6:00 a.m. on January 19, 1978, Mike Ryshytylo, his wife, and his son, Tony, watched eight small UFOs and two large ones hover over their farmyard in Rossburn. The objects were so close that they covered 30 degrees of the horizon. Because it was so early in the morning, the family would probably never have seen anything had they not been awakened by the barking of their dogs.

And so, perhaps in the future, researchers will find a way to employ animals as their UFO detectors and discover what it is the animals pick up and react so strongly to. Such a method might allow researchers to arrive at a sighting while it happens rather than days or weeks after it occurs.

Jennette Frost experienced many sightings during the two-year Manitoba UFO flap and used an animal detection method with her dog, Shep, to help her know when it was time to watch the skies.

When you enter the Frost farmyard, there is a sign that reads DO NOT LEAVE YOUR CAR UNTIL THE DOG IS CHAINED. Shep wasn't the sort of dog to be frightened by anyone or anything. When UFOs were around, however, the aggressive nature of the dog changed to cringing fear.

"That dog always growls when things are around," Jennette said. "He always gets excited. He'll look up into the sky. He looks around. There's something that he hears, and he'll cry or whine deep down — a very high-pitched whine."

During the 1975–76 flap, Jennette spotted many UFOs thanks to Shep's reactions. "Every time the dog acted up, I'd check the sky, and on every occasion, there'd be something flying around," she maintained.

Humming Hydro and Telephone Wires

In the countless tales of UFOs that fill book after book, there are references made to UFOs being attracted to power lines. In Manitoba we had many similar cases not only with hydro lines but even more frequently with telephone wires. Just before the first sighting occurred in the valley near Carman, Mr. Hay, who lived in Starbuck, witnessed a saucer-shaped craft fly low along a string of hydro lines north of town — the first of many such cases.

As mentioned previously, brothers Jerry and Tracy Moore witnessed a UFO as it hovered over the lines near their farm close to the border with Saskatchewan. "It shot down two rays to the lines," stated Leslie, the brothers' sister. "Where the rays touched the lines, the lines turned red."

It remained there for a few seconds after which it then travelled north to a second set of power lines near Jerry, who was working in the field. This time the red-and-silver craft shot eight beams onto the hydro lines.

"The beams were thin at first," Jerry told the local newspaper, "but got bigger when they touched the lines. The beams didn't retract. They just disappeared after five seconds."

Ufologists generally keep an eye out for this particular type of sighting report because it shows how the object might get its power or how it works.

As well as stories of UFOs being attracted to hydro lines there are accounts of them hovering around telephone wires. These stories aren't researched as much because there are no known effects such as the blackouts often attributed to UFOs and their attraction to hydro lines.[11]

Because I actually heard noise during a sighting and taped it, I think there is relevance to examine similar incidents to get an idea why UFOs sit above hydro and telephone wires. My own particular case involved telephone lines rather than hydro wires. That might seem unusual, but in Manitoba there appeared to be as many reports concerning UFOs and telephone lines as there were for hydro wires and UFOs, which led me at the time to believe communications might be just as important as power to the visiting craft.

In late July 1976, I was driving to the abandoned road south of Sperling where the ground light called Little Charlie was usually found. Danny and Toby Penner and Rob Wheeler were with me. It was just after dark, and there was nothing on the road except the two tiny green lights that were present when Little Charlie wasn't flaring. After unsuccessfully trying to get the object to flare, we continued west toward the Pembina Hills to see if we could spot anything flying around the valley.

We returned at 2:30 a.m. and discovered Little Charlie sitting on the road at a point where the telephone lines end going south. After taking five pictures, we moved to the next mile road east and watched another ball come down the road and collide with Little Charlie.

Because my only success getting near ground lights was to follow them on foot, we decided to take the movie camera and hike the mile across the field to see if we could get close to the lights. Danny explained what happened next.

> We kept on coming closer and closer and shooting some more film. When we got to the road, they seemed as far as when we had started after it, and that's after walking a mile across a farmer's field. Then we heard what we thought to be hydro lines, but they actually were the telephone lines humming really loud. We looked around and came to the conclusion that maybe the object was taking power, but it couldn't take power from a telephone line.

We then saw these two objects that we knew as "the objects at the end of the road" right on top of the telephone lines. "I don't know why," said Danny, "but we saw so many objects that night. They were all over the place."

Asked what the appearance of the two objects was over the lines, Danny responded, "The ones that were sitting over the telephone lines were both an orangey colour and further down the road you could see the green ones that we had seen earlier. They were bright orange lights, but they were so bright that they looked white — close to white."

"When we first went after them, it was close to 2:30 in the morning," Danny explained. "It took us 15 minutes to walk down there, and we spent about five minutes trying to figure out what was causing the noise."

Later calculations at the sight placed the objects 13 telephone poles south down the road. Danny shot some film. "I finished the roll off," he stated. "There really wasn't much film left, so I finished it off. Through the lens you couldn't see them too bright, but I could see the outline of the poles, and you could see them changing their intensity of light and colour — brightening and dimming."

Later in the summer of 1976 I was just south of Elm Creek with some university students when I heard a strange noise. This time I had my tape recorder and taped 30 seconds of the sound. The next day the sound was put on an oscilloscope to see what the wave pattern was. There, on the scope, was a double-wave pattern, one high-frequency and one quite low.[12]

At one of the main hydroelectric developments at Kettle Rapids in northern Manitoba I was told that workers had reported numerous UFOs. During construction, they said sightings of mysterious lights flying up and down the river occurred almost daily.

Two Manitoba hydro employees also let me in on the fact that during the long Carman flap of 1975 a major drain happened on the line heading to Winnipeg. However, a hydro spokesman who answered my questions about this report failed to confirm there was a heavy drain off the lines.

A few of the landings that took place in Manitoba also seemed to indicate that high-tension lines played a central role in at least some of them. Mike Pomehichuk of Rossburn found 14 swirled spots in his grain field. Many were near a high-tension line running past his farm and one was directly under it.

North of Portage la Prairie, Betsy Clinton and I discovered 12 horseshoe-shaped areas in a pasture where the grass was burnt out and refused to grow again. Many of these were close to high-tension lines following an east-west direction along the south side of the pasture.

The next day Betsy and her son found a new horseshoe mark that had just been made where the grass was burnt and pushed down. This was also right under a hydro line.

Finally, Jennette Frost reported that when she saw the large craft that nearly hit her house there was a noise associated with it. Roger Timlick, who participated in the interview, asked her what sound the craft had made.

"None at all," replied Jennette. "The only noise I heard at the time was the hydro wires. They were really humming. That thing always affects the hydro lines. You can pretty well tell when it's coming. It [the object] must have come over the wires."

A Peculiar Form of Light

There are many different types of lights found in the sky on a clear night. Those of identifiable origin give off a light with a repeatable and well-known nature.

Stars in the evening sky twinkle with a white to yellow-white colour. Planets, on the other hand, appear larger and glow rather than twinkle. While elevated high over the horizon, their colour is basically the same as a star's, but when their nightly course brings them close to the horizon, they appear reddish-orange because of the amount of atmosphere the observer looks through.

Planes, though, exhibit a series of lights to tell others in nearby airspace they are there. These are called navigation lights and are the same for all planes. The right wing tip has a small green light, the left wing tip a red one. In the middle, on the bottom of the fuselage, there is a larger red beacon that rotates once per second. On the tail a zenon strobe light can be seen. It looks like the flash of a camera and also repeats its cycle once per second.

The only time these navigation lights aren't visible is when the plane has its landing lights on. These resemble car headlights except they are much brighter. Some of the larger commercial jets have three landing lights.

This list of lights, when compared to the numerous reports of nocturnal lights or nighttime UFOs, leaves a lot of lighting formations and types unexplained. They seem simply enough not to be products of our technology unless government bureaucracy has secretly sanctioned a second group of flyers to travel at night with whatever lights they please.

Yet, what if these unidentified lights belong to alien technology? If the aliens wish to remain hidden, why do they place lights around their craft for all to see? Are they afraid of a mid-air collision? Are these lights indicators that they want to land at our airports?

These simple lights therefore pose a problem and deserve a much more important place in history than ufologists have been willing to give them. The majority of UFO reports involve light of one type or another. That is how they are detected. But what is the light's source and why is it there?

Of all the thousands of reports in Manitoba concerning light of one type or another, the most famous involved Charlie Red Star's lighting. The object seemed to emanate red light from its entire surface. Those who saw Charlie close up weren't even sure of his shape because of the great amount of light. "It looked," many people said, "like a great big fireball."

Like most odd similarities found in UFO reports, the lighting formations seemed to have a purpose. Most people who had time to consider the problem related the light to the propulsion of the craft. Different formations and colours were translated into different manoeuvres and speeds. Red was slow and low; white was high and fast.

Two lighting similarities arose, however, that appear rather unconnected to anything. They were *daytime light* and *dead light*.

Time and time again, witnesses reported experiences to me in which UFOs they saw lit up the entire countryside. They stumbled around trying to express the unbelievable, but rarely did they find words to adequately describe the amount of light coming off the objects they observed.

Usually, they explained it as daylight at night. "It came down the river," Marnie Herb told the *National Enquirer*'s Daniel Coleman and me, "and it was just like the sun had come out. It was just as bright as the brightest day in summer. You could see the shadow of every tree in the bush."

"It was 500 to 1,000 feet in front of the tractor over the bushes," witness Ron Middleton told me, "and it was so bright it lit up the entire bush." Not only did it light up the bush, it illuminated the entire field Ron was working in. It was so intense a light that he couldn't look at it without hurting his eyes, and at that point he decided to turn around and go home.

"When I saw it," Frederick Clinton told me, "it was just off our yard behind a set of bushes. There were four of five bright lights that lit up the entire bush. It was terribly bright. I woke up. It must have flown right over the house."

Tina Stevens also awakened one night in the spring to find that it was suddenly as bright as day at 4:00 a.m. "I didn't see the object," she stated. "I was much too scared to go to the window, but I did see the light. I tried to get my husband up, but by the time he got up, whatever it was, was gone."

In a landing in Letellier, Manitoba, near the U.S. border, a farm family was alerted to the fact that something was happening when in the middle of the night it suddenly became daylight. The next day a huge circle of young sunflower plants was found dead in a field a half mile west of the house.

Finally, Brendon Eagle, a successful inventor, saw the brilliant light one evening at dusk. Watching it closely, he calculated what might be causing such a light. "It was at about the 1,500-foot level," he said, "and it passed over the Jordan, Manitoba, grain elevator. It was so bright you could see every nail in the elevator. It had arc ray lighting on it. That's what it was. It was arc ray lighting. It's one of those arc welder's lights. We're starting to get lights somewhat like them now."

In addition to these daytime lights, the accounts revealed a type of light reported as dead light, which failed to illuminate anything around it. For the main example of this phenomenon, I will draw from my own experience while researching ground lights in April 1976. Standing 100 to 150 feet from a ground light that was a couple of feet in diameter, I noticed it was sitting low between two dikes in a drainage ditch. It was also touching a white-painted bridge crossing the ditch. Even though the extremely bright object brushed the bridge, it threw no more illumination on the structure than two candles would.

From this the "internal light hypothesis" was developed, which seemed best at describing what numerous witnesses and I had seen. Most, like me, reported that the *entire* object produced this light. In other words, it wasn't a light *on* the object; it was actually the object *itself*.

Thus many Charlie Red Star witnesses reported the light was "a terrific glow" or like "heated metal." Again, as with the ground lights, accounts indicated that this glow all over the surface of the object made it hard to determine its exact shape.

This characteristic is crucial, and many people have attempted to link this type of light to the propulsion system of the craft they observe.[13] More important, the dead light phenomenon is significant because ufologists constantly confuse the distinction between "light" and a "glowing light" when filing reports. The light is thrown off; the glow just spills over. The difference between a dead and glowing light is vital because it eliminates almost all the natural light forms known to humans.

Flying on an Angle

Nearly all the hundreds of UFO books published include sections of pictures showing the vast array of unidentified objects people have been lucky enough to photograph. The majority of these reveal an object tilted to one side or the other, or in other words, an object flying on an angle.

Logically, such a strange flying angle must represent an important purpose because it is uncommon in current aviation technology. Planes today are still basically designed on the principle of throwing a smooth rock and are therefore built to cut through the air as cleanly as possible.

The strange reported flying angle is also of consequence because it rules out hallucinations and hoaxes as possible explanations of the Manitoba UFO flap. Those whose reports were hoaxes would be expected to describe well-known normal flying characteristics, and hallucinations would produce descriptions that would be all over the map without any common elements.

For such a glaring characteristic about UFO flight, it is odd that little has been written concerning why saucers should be tilted in flight.

In the Manitoba UFO flap experience, reports of angled flight were extremely common. In fact, of those people who saw UFOs during the day or were close enough at night to see them clearly, the observation of horizontal flight almost never occurred. However, a tilt was nearly always described in these accounts. Manitoba researchers whose interest it was to discover how UFOs are powered gave numerous explanations of this peculiar angle. Of these, only one hypothesis has promise.

Regardless of why UFOs appear to fly on their "edges," the fact remains that countless reports describe this phenomenon. Because of the scarce mention of the phenomenon in UFO literature, I am still able to use this oddity to validate the reliability of each account in Manitoba.

It is very unlikely that any of the witnesses could have read about the angle feature, so they must have experienced the phenomenon. Such was the case with the UFO reports given to me by the five members of the McCann family. Because the family members had so many close encounters with UFOs, very few people chose to believe anything they said.

I talked to Anna McCann about the half-dozen times she witnessed UFOs flying in and around the family's farm in late May 1975. "It was a great big thing," Anna told me concerning one UFO that almost hit the house. "It had a silvery dome on it with red and green lights around it. I couldn't see the bottom. It was just like the whole thing was tilted up with its top to me, and it was flying on its edge."

"What do you mean 'on its edge'?" I asked.

"It was flying sideways. It was sort of on an angle."

"Just this one?"

"Oh, no! All of the ones we saw did that. They all flew on an angle."

Statements like that convinced me the McCanns were telling the truth despite the disbelief they incurred in Carman. I was one of the few people who knew the object was flying on an angle, and I kept that to myself.

It seemed to me that Anna and Joseph McCann were having actual experiences, but I wondered about their children. Would they report the same odd flying tilt described by their parents?

In the spring of 1976, I got to talk to the McCann children without their parents present. Sure enough, the three kids told me that on four separate occasions they, too, had observed the particular tilt. Given their very limited life experience, this element common to their accounts appeared to back up their stories. The children also stuck to their stories despite the tremendous criticism they received from their peers at school.

The degree of the tilt angle recounted by witnesses does vary from one report to another, rising from a low of 20 to a very commonly cited 45-degree angle. The leading edge being up and the bottom of the saucer facing the direction of motion were the most frequent descriptions of the angle.

Mrs. Krutcher, who watched a UFO make four passes over Morden, told me the object travelled with its bottom side forward. Such a motion, she told me, reminded her very much of how a Frisbee flies.

She was quite accurate in her description. A spinning Frisbee can be made to fly with its leading edge up from a horizontal axis. The similarity between a Frisbee and a UFO might mean more than we think.

Perhaps the most dramatic example of the angle factor is found in a report that was part of the CKY film. The angle was even given a name — "the unloading position" — when Jeff Bishop, the *Dufferin Leader's* publisher, spotted Charlie Red Star on the ground. He stated, "It was sitting at an angle of 45 degrees … much like seeing a drive-in movie screen from the side." Bishop's story, though unusual, shows that this tilt might have more to do with UFOs than in just the way they fly.

Other Common Elements

As well as the numerous similarities in Manitoba UFO reports already mentioned, there were many other shared characteristics in the accounts. These, too, were just as hard to explain and therefore equally as indicative of an actual reality.

Take, for example, the numerous stories of UFOs flying at a car, beside it, over it, or close behind it. During a three-year period in Manitoba, there were at least 17 such accounts. All those questioned referred to other peculiar similarities that seemed directly linked to their experiences. In every case, their cars were the only ones around, as if every other vehicle usually on the road had disappeared.

In almost all of the incidents, the driver either tried to catch up to the UFO in front, or away from the UFO beside, over, or behind. It was no surprise to hear of frightened drivers racing down a dirt road at 80 or more miles per hour.

Witnesses in all the cases failed to catch up or get away. They reported that if they stopped, so would the UFOs, and if they sped up, the UFOs did the same. In the five cases in which witnesses chased UFOs, everyone reported: "It knew what I was thinking." The common opinion was that the UFOs were playing with them, letting them catch up, and then pulling away.

Another major parallel that surfaced in cases in which trailing UFOs were involved is that the incidents occurred at night. Four witnesses reported that it seemed to be the lights of their cars that attracted the UFOs. Twice during the 1975 flap Joseph and Anna McCann mentioned a UFO that flew directly at their truck at tremendous speed. When Joseph turned off the car lights, the object halted and backed up down the road.

A couple of months later a group of seven teenagers reported exactly the same phenomenon. They were travelling down an abandoned highway when a huge saucer-shaped object flew to within 100 feet of them. "It was moving back and forth," Bob Sanderson told me. "When I shut my lights out, it started to leave. When I turned my lights back on, it would come toward us again. So I left the lights out."

Nine months after that Linda Chociemski sat with her husband watching a saucer hover near their car on Highway 8, north of Gimli. "We were watching it," she said, "and it seemed that every time lights would come down the highway, it would back up. When there were no lights, it would come closer to us."

Ufologists have always questioned why a UFO would travel from another solar system simply to chase cars around. In the 1990s, Dr. Steven Greer, who founded the Center for the Study of Extraterrestrial Intelligence (CSETI), received endless criticism for leading groups of people to various U.S. locations to attempt contacts with UFOs. One of the key elements employed to communicate was to flash lights at the objects.

Greer had no support in the world's UFO community, but in Manitoba, witnesses who had close encounters with UFOs would have likely approved of him. There was a clear link in Manitoba sightings between light and UFOs.[14]

Finally, oddities arising from the Manitoba reports include the fact that UFOs flew within an inch or two of houses, trees or hydro lines. UFOs reported at night were almost always described as moving very slowly, between 10 and 80 miles per hour. Numerous times words such as *crawling* and *floating* were used to explain the snail's pace made by nocturnal craft.

On the other hand, UFOs spotted during the day were portrayed as hovering or moving extremely fast. Independent witnesses told me there were likely many daylight UFOs, but they were hard to distinguish because of their high speed. *Luck* was a word usually equated with seeing a daylight disk.

CAMERAS, PHOTOGRAPHERS, AND CHARLIE RED STAR

That's the best [photography] you can do at night. You can't do any better unless the thing ends up in my own backyard at noon hour, but that's a different story. Then I'll give them lunch, too.

— Tannis Major, Carman Professional Photographer

It had a pattern to it that wouldn't have been any meteor or comet or anything like that. It changed. It moved so quickly across the screen. It was calculated by NASA, and NBC also looked at it, and about 20 scientists in the United States at the time it was hot. They estimated it to be going 32,000 miles per hour. My calculation was 120,000 miles per hour. I was plotting coordinates as the thing moves across the screen, and you'll never get a picture like that again. There's no way that you can try. There it is. Get it. It just went right across the camera while it was running, which was something else. A fluke.

— Dustin Hope, CKY-TV Producer

We always conjured up new and different thoughts that someone was playing tricks on us ... we didn't know where we were going to get on it. I think it was 100 percent luck because that was Martin's [the cameraman's] first filming.

— Dorsey Roberts, Former CKY-TV Reporter

One of the most important aspects of the Manitoba UFO flap was its great regularity. In early and mid-1975, Charlie Red Star flew low over the same general areas of the province, and many photographers took time from their lives to be present.

As I discovered in the photographs I took, it wasn't a simple matter of going out, getting pictures, and publishing them around the world. In fact, looking back, the problems greatly outweighed the fact that Charlie was around.

In the mid-1970s, there were no digital cameras, video cameras, or VCRs. All we had at our disposal were 35 mm cameras and 8 mm movie cameras. Television stations such as CKY and CBC from Winnipeg had 16 mm television cameras, but their interest in filming Charlie always centred on a crew getting paid to film. Those who tried to photograph Charlie knew that was a lost cause, since a lot of waiting was required and a great deal of luck was needed to be in the right place at the right time.

Taking pictures at night in an almost pitch-black countryside was an art in itself. The camera required a tripod and a cable release to achieve the necessary time exposures. Moving a tripod around and then getting a camera set up on it quickly if something was seen often proved comical. A tripod also cut down on mobility, since the camera had to be moved from one place to another and had to be focused on different parts of the sky.

It was hard to take notes describing each photo while working in the dark. It was also difficult to keep track of exactly where in the large valley you were at any one point because of the dark and because there were few landmarks. There were often no trees, farmyards, or anything else.

My personal experience is that it was essential to know the camera as if you were blind. Light couldn't be used to set up because night vision always seemed to fail when it was most needed. When things started to happen, they occurred terribly fast, leaving no time to fiddle with dials and focus settings.

No one can better attest to the problems shooting UFOs than Tannis Major, a professional photographer in Carman who spent every night for a month outdoors to get the one picture of Charlie that would prove he wasn't a figment of the imagination.

"I saw the darn thing," she said. "I was at Anthony Britain's airfield and saw it there at a distance. Low and behold, he [a CBC cameraman] had to put his bright spotlights on me. Well, you don't see anything for a long time. So finally they shut them off and I got my night vision back.

"[Then] I saw it again. Bingo, on went the lights again. Three times they pulled that stunt. I told them that if they didn't get lost with that thing I would knock the spotlight right out of their hands. I said, 'Get lost. I don't want you here.' But they wanted news. I told them they were going to get news."

Another of the major difficulties that arose attempting to film Charlie Red Star was putting up with the paranormal occurrences that took place, an aspect every photographer in the area would swear to.

A good number of the films and pictures didn't turn out, and no one was ever able to answer why. It seemed that if a situation could go wrong, it did. It was safe to say that those who tried to take photos often spent more time trying to figure out why they failed than shooting them.

Tannis, the most active photographer in the early days of the UFO flap in the Carman area, spent four to five hours each day for 27 nights in May 1975 in the countryside waiting for a chance to take one photo that would pay off. "I was out there all the time with my camera," she told me, "because I just didn't believe … well, first of all, I was a little skeptical till I saw it. It's the same as a chair. You have to believe it because you see it. It's just there."

She felt that if she could photograph the object, the result would show the true nature of the phenomenon. "There will be a number of non-believers, you might as well say. To make sure of it, I was going to put it on film," she told me, sitting in her kitchen. "That was my aim — to put it on film in case it's a phenomenon — but then it wouldn't show up."

When I first met Tannis, I was taken by a story she told that outlined her experience with the paranormal aspect of catching Charlie on film. "Wherever you go to film it," she said, "make sure that there is a piece of glass between you and the object."

I stared at her in disbelief, but it was apparent she was serious.

"There must be something with glass," she continued. "It might work in the same way as radar and tinfoil. If you don't shoot behind glass, you aren't going to get a picture. Charlie knows what you're thinking."

This whole idea of glass, thought waves, cameras, and flying saucers sounded insane at best, but I realized Tannis had something going for her. She had (and still has) the best UFO photos out of the many pictures that were taken. I, too, took photographs and brought with me nine different photographers at one time or another, but we got nothing as good as Tannis did.

To back up her contention that glass was a necessary component for successful photos, she told me a story I eventually heard many times — the tale of Charlie "taking off" on the second night.[1]

The people present on the evening in question were Tannis, Anthony and Rachael Britain, and Sam Brazil. The car they were in was just north of Morden when Charlie appeared to fly right at them. "It was coming lower and lower," Tannis recounted. "I said to Anthony, 'If I can get a darn good shot that's clear and we can see the shape of it, then I'm going to get myself a nice silver-coloured station wagon.' Everything was ready. I had it in the viewfinder when Anthony says, 'Tannis, here comes your station wagon.' But when I was ready to shoot it was lights out."

"Lights out," as Tannis described, was an event most Carman witnesses had experienced. It had happened to Tannis many times, and it was experienced by me and to the photographers who accompanied me.

"One time I went out sighting with Mrs. Frost," Tannis said. "We stayed in the car because the mosquitoes were waiting for a good banquet. Then we saw the darn thing. I had it in the viewfinder and I shot a picture of it through the windshield. I said to Mrs. Frost, 'I wonder if that theory is correct? I'm going to get out. I'm going to find out.'" As she went to take another photo, the object disappeared.

A couple of months later I experienced the same thing. During the spring of 1976, I had mentioned to people in Winnipeg that UFO sightings were so heavy in the Carman-Sperling area that I could take them out and show them a UFO every night.

Carl Bachmanek, owner of a camera repair shop in Winnipeg, and his assistant, Paul Dawkins, took me up on my offer. They quickly gathered their high-speed film and telephoto lens and picked up a third photographer, John Losics, and were ready to go. In turn, I called Robin Davies, who at the time was a student at the University of Manitoba. I told him tonight was the night, since he had expressed an interest in photographing the phenomenon.

Robin and I were driving out of the city when we noticed Karl standing at the side of the highway. He flagged us over and said they had brought the wrong telephoto lens and had to go back to the city to get the right one. Since it was almost dusk, we agreed to meet up at the Fireside Inn in Carman.

As Robin and I passed Sperling on our way to Carman, I noticed a blinking light in a field and asked Robin to stop and get out his camera just in case. We pulled off Highway 3 onto Highway 205 East, and Robin began to set up his camera. After shooting 20 pictures, he commented, "That's the most unbelievable thing I've ever seen in my life. I hope this film picked it up."

The photo session had taken quite a while, and we suddenly realized the other car with Karl Bachmanek, John Losics, and Paul Dawkins was now probably way ahead of us. We jumped into our car and raced to Carman. When we arrived, we discovered that not only were they ahead of us but they had been to the Fireside Inn and had already left.

John had been out with me before at the CBC radio tower just north of Carman. I figured that was where he'd gone, so we headed north out of Carman for the tower.

Soon after we started off, we spotted the red pulse of Charlie flying low along the treeline east of the tower. "If those guys went where I think they are," I told Robin, "that thing is going to fly right over them!"

We pulled off the highway, and I asked Robin to take a picture quickly. He set up his tripod and prepared to photograph the bright orange-red object as it moved along the treeline, but milliseconds before he pushed the cable release, the object dropped below the trees. "It's gone," he said. "I don't think I got it in time."

Robin wasn't able to get a picture at all, and as we discovered later, the other car of photographers didn't, either. They had been in the place I thought they had gone and got a good look at the object, but no pictures.

John Losics and the others had been parked on a bit of a hill facing north. The object approached the car from behind. John saw it first. "Boy, it was close," he said to me later. "I told the others, 'There it is,' but they asked, 'Where?'"

Carl and Paul were in the front of the two-door car, while John was in the back when he spotted the object. He struggled to get out of the vehicle so he could get a better look. During all the commotion, though, Carl and Paul failed to take any of their equipment with them when they left the car.

"They stood there and just looked at it," John told me. "Those skeptics had to convince themselves what it was before they would get out their cameras. When they realized what it was, they ran to the car to get their cameras, but before they could get a picture, it dropped below the trees. It was right there, half a mile away, maybe."

After John told me about the object dropping out of sight before they could shoot it, I reflected on Tannis's words when she told me Charlie knew what you were thinking and that you should try to have a piece of glass in the way when trying to photograph him. Charlie's "disappearance," she told me, had happened to her many times. Now we had experienced it, Anthony Britain was subjected to the same treatment, too, when he was at the CBC tower with his movie camera. It had occurred one other time for me when I spotted Charlie with my movie camera in hand at Elm Creek, north of Carman. Perhaps the elusive Charlie did know when to vanish.

This lights-out situation became so common and disturbing that those involved in photographing in the area did whatever they could think of to counteract the disappearing phenomenon. Anthony told me one day about his attempt with four other witnesses to shoot Charlie. "The thing is that those rascals, whoever they are, have a way of being known when they're being watched because it didn't change course until we jumped out of the car and were watching it. It suddenly reversed direction and sped away. I don't imagine it was any more than about 30 seconds to a minute at the most when it stopped and went backward.

"In fact, we've gotten to the point when we see the thing we'll think of how the weather is … everything but concentrate on it, which is impossible to do. If they were receiving thought waves, it doesn't work when you're sitting in a car, because you're shielded. This has been our experience, anyway."

Another bizarre occurrence was the relationship between the distance of the object and the number of things that went wrong with the photograph. It appeared from the experience of the photographers that the closer the object came, the greater the chance something would go wrong with the film, or the lens wouldn't be set properly.

As with the lights-out phenomenon, all the photographers in the area experienced this close-distance tendency, too. Tannis had it happen to her, as well, but not knowing that other shutterbugs were in the same company as she was, she blamed the film processor.

"Mrs. Frost and I took a whole lot of pictures at the Starbuck tower because there were quite a few of them there," Tannis told me. "It was processed and turned up nothing. I gave them a piece of my mind. They told me that it had been underexposed and I told them that it hadn't been underexposed. I said that it hadn't been because I used the same ASA as I used for the black and white and I knew that the black and white could take it."

Tannis had processed the black and white herself, and therefore, she told the film processor, "You just messed it up yourself."

Regardless of who was to blame, future experiences by other people demonstrated that blank negatives weren't a rare phenomenon. Take, for example, the experience of John Losics and two straight rolls of film that the processor told him: "Didn't even go through the camera."

I had been present while these 40 200 ASA colour slides were taken, and neither John nor I could believe the explanation for the lack of pictures. Both of us felt the tension on the film advance when we shot the photos. The first roll had to be loaded at John's home, and therefore with ample light to see that the film was on the spool.[2] Neither of us recalled ever not getting the film on the spool.

The objects were closer when Robin Davies and I went out that early spring night in 1976 than they had ever been before — under a mile away. We used time exposures up to 30 seconds long and therefore felt they couldn't be underexposed. Nevertheless, when the two films were put on microfiche readers there was nothing there.

The next night, March 29, Robin took 60 photos of which only six turned out. Of those half dozen only two corresponded to anything we had seen. The other four were good photos, but we had no idea what objects we had shot. The Winnipeg planetarium had three printed, and I sent the originals to researcher Wendelle Stevens, who was one of the foremost UFO photograph experts. They never arrived.

The first time I tried to photograph Charlie I had a similar experience when I was shooting two miles west of Elm Creek. The object over the field north of me was extremely close, and I used an entire roll of film on one-second exposures.

The object appeared to be only a few feet off the ground and was flying back and forth like a typewriter carriage. It travelled slowly east pulsing red, then stopped and turned green. After that it shot back across the field in a few seconds or so, reverted to a pulsing red, and once more headed slowly across the field.

I had heard the stories of photo troubles but felt it wasn't all that hard and my film would prove it, certain that I had succeeded my first time out. When I got home, though, I discovered just how wrong I was.

A bit before dusk I had taken a picture in Carman, and driving out to Elm Creek I had left the aperture at F5.6, which wasn't correct for shooting in pitch-black conditions, so I didn't get any photos.

Bad pictures as well as no photos were common. Tannis reported taking 60 photographs in one good session with only seven that were worth printing. Robin shot 80 in one session with only 10 good enough to print. John Losics had a single session with 50 photos of which none were usable. Photographer Jonathan Black took 20 photos and got two worth printing. I fired off 100 and got two somewhat decent ones. It was something we all hated to admit, but it happened and we couldn't explain it.

The type of equipment the photographers were using didn't seem to matter, either. We used film from 25 ASA colour up through 500 ASA.

We used lenses from 50 mm to 3000 mm, and exposures from 1/30 a second up to a minute.

There were disagreements among photographers concerning what should be used. Some suggested a short lens and high-speed film because they believed exposure was the problem. Others, however, insisted the power of the telephoto lens was the problem. Should we go for exposure or close-up detail? Neither really worked, and the mystery was never solved.

The Tannis Major Photographs

I have to admit my personal attitude has been to look for some natural phenomena, but Mrs. Major's photographs have triggered my interest. I'm inclined to ask — "What is it we've got here?"

— B. Franklyn Shinn, Former Director of the
Winnipeg Planetarium

The Tannis Major photographs are without question the best taken during the entire UFO flap. Not only did she get hundreds of UFO pictures, she captured clear shots of Charlie Red Star, which meant a lot to town people because it confirmed the reality of what they all had seen. It was then a surprise to me that when the *National Enquirer's* Daniel Coleman came to Manitoba to do a story on the long and prolonged flap of sightings, he had heard nothing about these photos.

However, Coleman had talked to Tannis during his first trip to Manitoba in June 1975. In his report to the *National Enquirer*, he wrote:

Perhaps the record for UFO watching was set by Mrs. Tannis Major, the freelance photographer who was determined to get a good picture of a UFO. Sometimes accompanied by her husband, she went out for 26 days in May and June watching for UFOs before rain forced her to stay in on the 27th day in order to keep her camera dry.[3]

Tannis told Coleman in a June 4 interview that she was out to get a picture of "Charlie Boy." It wasn't until a month later, on July 9, that her dream was realized.

Just south of Carman, Tannis's house faced the Britains' airstrip across the road to the west. Consequently, when Charlie flew the "beer run," most of the path was visible through Tannis's front window. Therefore it was no surprise to anyone visiting the Major house to discover a camera with a long telephoto lens on a tripod in the living room pointed out the window.

"I figured if he ever showed up," Tannis told me, "I would be ready for him. You haven't got time to set up the camera when it happens. This way I'm shooting with everything I've got and I'm also shooting through glass. That's important."

It was July 9 at almost 11:20 p.m. when Tannis happened to look out the front window and spotted Charlie west of Carman near Stephenfield. The object appeared to be flying just above the treeline, moving from south to north and therefore from left to right in the window.

"I knew it was a UFO right off the bat," she said to me. "If you've seen a number of them already, you know right away it's a UFO. I didn't waste any time. I had everything set up already. This was the time to shoot and fast."

The object, according to Tannis, was moving rather slowly, so she set her shutter speed for one second. The camera, a Canon VLB, had a Vivitar lens with a 3x telephoto extender that brought the lens up to 615 mm. The lens was wide open, giving it a T-stop of about 3.5–3.8.

The film used was a surplus Hollywood movie film, type 5247, which has a very fine grain. Tannis shot her pictures at 200 ASA and had it pushed to 400 at developing (the film allows for varying ASAs to be used). Multiple Color Systems in Portland, Oregon, developed the pictures. The blow-ups were done by Winnipeg Planetarium artist Elliot Slater.

All three photos in the series were taken with one-second time exposures. The only movement of the camera was made by Tannis between shots to keep the object in the field of vision of the powerful telephoto lens and to follow the object as it moved to the right in the window.

Estimating the object to be six miles away, Tannis took her first photo. The time was 11:20 p.m. The developed shot showed a pulsing object travelling from left to right with a definite trail left by a one-second exposure indicating motion. The picture reveals an apparent change in the angle of the object. Tannis said it seemed to bank east toward her.

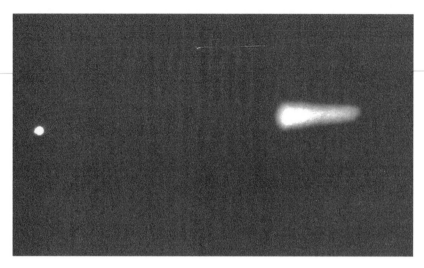

The first Tannis Major photo of Charlie Red Star, with the planet Venus in the background.

In the second photograph taken a minute later, the object is still moving but now appears tilted on its side.

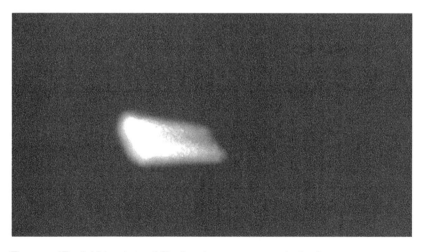

The second Tannis Major photo of Charlie as he appears to turn in the sky.

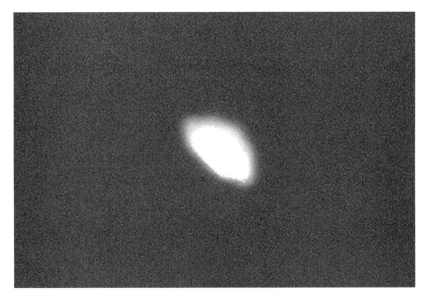

The third Tannis Major photo of Charlie in which he seems to hover in one position.

The third and last picture in the series was taken a minute after the second one and best illustrates what Charlie actually looked like to people such as myself who were lucky enough to see it. Just before the object disappears, the one-second exposure indicates no movement from it. This is still the depiction of Charlie most familiar to residents of the area.

No horizontal motion is apparent in the third picture and therefore the object appears to hover motionless in the sky. The coloration is similar to that in the accounts given by people who saw it — white with a red corona. Two photos taken elsewhere in the world — one from a Concorde jet in France and the other snapped by Ralph Mayher — feature comparable object images.[4]

Just after shooting the third picture, Tannis told me it was lights-out time again — the object suddenly disappeared.

After receiving the developed pictures, Tannis said during our interview that the RCMP came to get copies of them. This shocked me, since I had heard the RCMP story but a different version. I thought Tannis had gone to the local RCMP office and offered them copies of the photos. However, she insisted that the officers had come to her to request them.[5]

After Canada's Department of National Defence dropped its official investigation into UFOs, the National Research Council's Institute for Astrophysics, Planetary Sciences Section, was charged with receiving and evaluating UFO reports filed by the RCMP, the Department of Transport, the military, and any other federal organization approached with UFO sightings. So copies of the pictures were sent to Ottawa.

Some of the Manitoba UFO accounts submitted were briefly analyzed by two of the chief scientists in the Planetary Sciences Section: Dr. A.G. McNamara, head of the section, and Dr. Ian Halliday. McNamara, who did much of the investigation of the Manitoba reports, made his position on UFOs public in an article he wrote entitled "UFOs: What Are They?"

In the summary of the paper, McNamara laid out his personal belief: "Two thousand years of observation and thirty years of rather intensive collection (15,000 reports in the USAF Project Bluebook and 1,500 in Canada) and examination of reports have not yielded any positive sighting or artifact of extra-terrestrial origin."[6]

McNamara wrote the above despite the fact that he and his colleagues did almost no proper examination of cases sent to their office. "It's a matter of priority," McNamara told the *National Enquirer*. "We've got a lot more important areas to investigate and we can't put a lot of effort into chasing down these things which, in general, lead to naught."[7]

Therefore not many researchers took the opinions of the National Research Council very seriously. The analysis done by McNamara on a sighting report was usually a guess made off the top of his head after a brief glance at the accounts, which prompted some investigators to wonder: *If this is the quality of the research at the National Research Council, what about the rest of their research in other areas being paid for by taxpayers?*

In one Manitoba case, for example, a handwritten notation at the bottom of the report suggested the sighting might have been caused by a Frontier Airline flight from Winnipeg to Las Vegas. This was absolute nonsense to anyone who had done UFO research in the area. We had all clearly heard the Frontier flight pass over every night. It was so high that it wasn't visible beyond a faint view of the plane's strobe light. What's more, it went in the opposite direction of Charlie Red Star's beer run and happened only once every night for a couple of minutes.

Furthermore, I visited the Planetary Sciences Section twice to inspect sighting reports. They were kept by a secretary in a filing cabinet in her office, and the analysis was done on Friday afternoons when there was spare time.

While there I interviewed Dr. McNamara and was impressed with his sincerity about the whole UFO thing. He gave me the distinct impression he was a UFO disbeliever and seemed to be someone who wasn't very knowledgeable about the subject. McNamara wasn't even familiar with the material in the filing cabinet that he was supposed to study for the public.

When I brought back the NRC analysis in which McNamara had determined the Charlie Red Star sightings were the nightly Frontier Airlines flight, most of the people who had taken photographs of Charlie laughed. Tannis Major, however, was quite upset. "What makes me so mad," she said, "[is that] Ottawa has the gall to say it's an airplane. I wish they would get smart enough to say either they don't know what it is or that it's a UFO and they don't know where it comes from instead of making up a fairy tale. Unless I'm still living in the era of the Wright brothers, to call that a plane, that's idiotic."

In August 1976, I showed my prints of the three best Major photographs to the *National Enquirer*'s Daniel Coleman. He was interested in using them in a story about the Manitoba UFO flap, so we got together with Tannis to discuss the present state of UFO affairs and Tannis's photographs with her.

I brought out my prints, which were 16x enlargements, but discovered that Tannis had obtained some 64x blow-ups. These showed very clear images, and in Tannis's third picture there was a small bluish field on the lower edge of the object.

Coleman got prints from Tannis and took them back to Florida with him, but in September he phoned me and outlined a problem that had come up with the pictures. He had taken them to various photographic people in Florida and everyone had confirmed that the object was indeed unidentified. However, none of the experts would put their names behind their analyses, so Coleman and I discussed what we were going to do.

It was apparent the object wasn't an airplane as had been stated by the RCMP and the NRC. The difficulty was to get someone with a qualified background to go on record and declare that Charlie wasn't a plane.

I talked with about 30 people, ranging in background from someone with a PhD in astronomy to a nature photographer. Once they heard they were dealing with UFO photographs, they usually insisted they weren't qualified to make an assessment, even before they saw the pictures. Finally, after two days of phoning, I found two people willing to cover the various aspects requested by the *National Enquirer* editors. The editors wanted me to get someone to verify that the three Tannis photos weren't pictures of a meteorite, fireball, or plane.

To deal with the plane aspect, I asked for the opinion of Murray Sutherland, chief of the tower and head of air traffic control in Winnipeg. I showed him Tannis's shots and provided him with a two-page summary of how the photographs had been taken, the weather conditions, and the photographic equipment that had been used to snap the pictures. Sutherland read the report carefully, studied the photos, and then asked, "What do you want me to do?"

"In your opinion, could this be a plane, if what Mrs. Major says is true?"

Sutherland remained silent for a moment, then said, "In my opinion, it looks like no plane I'm familiar with. Just to be sure, I'll call in one of my supervisors, Dick Cowan, and get a second opinion."

When Cowan arrived in the tower, he, too, read over the report and examined the photos.

"In your opinion," I repeated, "if what Mrs. Major says is true, could this be an airplane?"

It took Cowan a long time to answer the question, and when he did, he held up Tannis's third picture and said, "The only thing this might be is the back end of an F-104. This, of course, would mean that, one, an F-104 was flying around Carman without anyone reporting the sound of a jet; two, it would mean that the jet was moving away from Mrs. Major when she clearly remembered it coming toward her; three, the central colour of an F-104 would be bluish; and, four, a jet wouldn't account for the first two photos in the series."

The analyses from these two men, who I was told "knew airplanes better than anyone in the city," was an emphatic no to the object being a plane.

Next I took the pictures to Robert Millar, who had a master of science and was head of the planetarium at the University of Manitoba. He read over the report and looked at the photographs.

When he was done, I asked, "In your opinion, could this be a meteorite or fireball, or any other astronomical phenomena you're familiar with?"

He glanced up as if I had just tried to tell him that one and one was six. "Not if what she says is true. No way." The only thing close he told me was a fireball. Walking over to a photo filer, Millar pulled out a number of pictures and said, "Look at this. This is a fireball."

I gazed at the three photos he presented.

"See how it breaks up," he told me. "It's much different than those photos." He added that fireballs took a long time to cross the sky and were usually well tracked. Tannis's photos, on the other hand, were all shot within two minutes.

Now that the authenticity of the photos had been backed up, I called Daniel Coleman and told him what the three men had said. It appeared that Tannis Major's photos had gained credibility.

Caught, Then Lost Again

During the two years I spent investigating the Manitoba UFO flap, I was always told how much photographs would mean toward solving the mystery. After examining Tannis Major's photos as well as other cases in which people tried to get UFOs on film, I had to reconsider how important any one picture of a UFO was. In Manitoba, for every shot that turned out well, there were 100 that didn't and numerous ones that were just too poor.

Many other photographers and I started to believe that a good photo was "usually an accident." Not only that, but in a couple of cases the pictures came up out of order or didn't correspond to anything we had seen all night.

For me the sighting that brought the issue to a head occurred on July 27, 1976, and concerned a roll of film I shot that night. This incident turned out to be the best and most bizarre, and the pictures I took were also the last of the ones I snapped in 1976.

On that July 27, I left Anthony Britain's house at about 10:15 p.m. and headed eight miles north of Carman, which brought me to a road across from the McCann farm where there was a ground light I wanted to photograph. After shooting a few pictures, I moved southeast onto Highway 305 East where there were two other ground light positions.

When I was positioned on Highway 305, I noticed a light in the sky directly east and at about a 40-degree angle. Its appearance was similar to a landing light on an aircraft about to land but instead of three lights there seemed to be only one. There were no other lights on the object such as a strobe, and it appeared to be flying southwest away from Winnipeg's international airport.

My camera was set up with 500 ASA colour film, a 50 mm lens, and a cable release. I prepared to take a shot even though the sky was overcast, the clouds were low, and there were sounds of thunder both north and south of where I was. But the object was travelling with incredible slowness toward Carman to the south, and I had plenty of time to shoot. The first time exposure was a minute, the second 10 seconds, and the third three minutes. I was hoping the last photo would provide the most information, thanks to the low cloud ceiling and high humidity.

As the object travelled closer to Carman, it suddenly started to pulse. I now had to consider that it might be a plane landing at Carman, but that idea was ruled out for a number of reasons.

1. If the object was a plane landing at Carman, it would have been a small one and wouldn't have had such a strong landing light on it.
2. There was no strobe at any time visible on the object.
3. The object moved from my left to right, which meant there should have been a green navigation light visible if it was a plane. There was none.

4. The speed seemed much too slow for a plane.
5. To land at Carman the object would have had to be a small plane. In that case, it wouldn't have been flying in thunderstorms.

Nevertheless, at 11:25 p.m., I raced back to Carman to see if the runway lights were on at either of the two airports. Not surprising, both airstrips were shut down for the night. I checked the sky and saw nothing, so I headed for home driving east on Highway 3.

At Homewood, Manitoba, nine miles east of Carman, I spotted a brilliant light. The orange crystal light hovered just over the horizon as I grabbed my camera to take a photo. I released the shutter and caught it, believing it would be a good one, because of all the UFOs I had ever seen, this was the biggest. The object seemed to continue its movement toward me and at the same time got brighter.

Mysterious orange glow and small orange object.

I gave the first two shots (frames 10 and 11) a 10-second exposure. Worried that the film might be overexposed, I pushed back the exposure to one second for frames 12, 13, and 14. I didn't aim the camera, since I was watching as the shape of the object began to form. Then, with a brief glance at my camera, I looked up and the object was gone.

Taking out my notepad, I copied the exposures of the five photos I had just shot. Then, when I panned the horizon with my binoculars, I noticed the object was still there — now a small white ball against a black overcast sky. It was higher on the horizon and was moving east about 10 degrees from its previous position. The object then turned red without a flash or pulsation. It wasn't very bright, so I shot a 60-second exposure (frame 15), hoping to pick it up.

As I watched the object, I noticed it was about to cross behind a telephone pole on the highway. Figuring I could get a good point of reference, I shifted to the next frame and snapped a 30-second time exposure.[8]

By this time, the object had moved quite far down the road. I quickly put the camera in my car and sped after the UFO. At Highway 248 I turned south for a half mile and set up my camera again. The object turned once more and headed back toward the highway in the direction of Sperling (four miles from my position). I shot a 40-second time exposure and then a 60-second one. The object changed from solid red, to a pulse every two seconds, and then to a brilliant crystal-white light. When I studied the shot later, the transformation in the object was very apparent.

The UFO then turned north at Sperling, and I snapped frame 19, which was a 15-second exposure. It was now 12:20; the major part of the sighting had taken 20 minutes. I had shot 13 pictures of the two objects in the sky and felt they were good, perhaps even better than Tannis's photos.

I delivered the film to a photo shop in downtown Winnipeg and requested that it be left uncut. In this way, no one could claim the photos had been assembled from a number of different pictures. All the frames would be numbered, and I had a history of exactly what had occurred on each frame, which would provide evidence of an hour of UFO sightings in the main flap area.

When I got the developed film back, I rushed home to view it. Placing it near a light and using a magnifying glass, I could see the prints quite clearly. The lights of the towns showed up well and there had been enough time for the film to pick up the horizon, as well. Second, the film showed that the object had only trailed across three-quarters of the frame during the three-minute exposure. Here was proof of just how slowly it had been travelling.

Nine of the 13 prints were good, the best I had taken up to that date. The five of the brilliant crystal light were very clear, and the differences in the time exposures between frames 10 and 11 and frames 12, 13, and 14 were obvious.

Four of the pictures had horizons because of the high humidity that night. The surrounding towns had cast up round circles of light into the night sky. That, combined with the other things in the picture, gave me excellent points of reference.

In my eagerness to get backup support for the pictures, I immediately mailed them to Wendelle Stevens in Tucson, Arizona, for analysis. It was said that Wendelle had perhaps the best UFO picture collection in the world. What's more, he had published several UFO books and written articles for many publications in the field.

Later, through the *National Enquirer*, I learned that the photos never arrived at Wendelle's place. I wrote him to find out if that was true, and he replied in a letter: "Pictures lost in the mail is a maddening situation. No other mail gets lost, but when you send a new and sensitive picture through the mail the chance is high that it will never reach its destination."

Then, in reference to a possible "men-in-black" connection, he added, "I have a case now where pictures were separated and mailed in separate envelopes from different mailboxes, and neither reached me. How do you account for that? Also at the time when these photos should have arrived, my house was searched professionally from top to bottom, completely, and nothing was taken. I was told that four conservatively dressed men were seen in front of my house during the one and a half hours I was gone. Nobody ever saw them before or has seen them since."[9]

The CKY-TV Movie

We just wanted to go out because this intrigued us. Wednesday we got the film, and the next night we had to beat people off with sticks, the ones who wanted to come out.

— Dorsey Roberts

The story of the CKY-TV movie was probably the biggest and strangest one of the entire Manitoba UFO flap. Once the film was taken on May 13, 1975, and was aired to Winnipeg's nearly 600,000 residents, it caused a deluge of people and cars to appear on back roads around Carman, searching for the object.

The CKY film was a mixture of peculiar occurrences, faith, perseverance, and luck. It was one of those times when everyone and everything worked to create a nearly perfect state of being. Those involved had their own spin on capturing Charlie Red Star on film. Martin Rugne, who took the footage, said, "The film was a disaster for me from start to finish." Dustin Hope, a former producer at CKY who was involved in the filming, called the movie of Charlie "a fluke."

At the time of the CKY filming there were probably only about three dozen UFO movies around. It was in the days before video cameras and cellphones revolutionized UFO filming. Now there are thousands of UFO movies. In 1975–76 you either talked a TV station into shooting footage or you used an 8 mm camera with a small three-minute roll that wasn't good for nighttime filming and was very expensive.

The CKY movie is one of two taken during the Manitoba UFO flap. The other features one of the ground lights in the spring of 1976. Both are unique because the cameramen went out specifically to shoot UFOs and weren't reacting to random events.

Opinions of the CKY film vary. The most quoted one was expressed by J. Allen Hynek of the Center for UFO Studies when he was in Winnipeg on February 7, 1976, to give a lecture at the University of Manitoba's Festival of Life and Learning. CKY and the Winnipeg Planetarium went out of their way to screen the footage for Hynek, who commented after seeing it that it was "the best nocturnal light film he had ever seen."

Hynek asked for and received two copies of the movie. He was supposed to make an announcement about the film later, but he never did. It is doubtful if any investigation took place, because Hynek didn't interview any of the witnesses involved in the shooting of the footage.

People who participated in the shooting contacted Hynek to obtain his analysis of the film but were unable to get a reply. The Winnipeg Planetarium and I also attempted to reach Hynek concerning the movie, but we, too, came up empty.

In March 1976, I spoke to Dustin Hope on this matter. "I think that's almost rude of the professor," he said, "because that's his forte. I know he's a busy man, but not too busy to answer. I waited for him, too. He promised to send back his hypothesis but never did."[10]

Martin Rugne had a similar comment: "I don't know if he [Hynek] was serious about the whole thing. I never heard from him again."

The film itself got little play when it was first shot. CKY aired it for two days and did an 11-minute special on it. They then forgot about it. The *Dufferin Leader*, which had one of its reporters as part of the team that did the filming, only gave the movie 21 lines. The *National Enquirer* heard the whole story but only referred to the footage in passing when it published an article on the landing radiation patches found where Charlie had sat.

Those who were present for the actual shooting were: Martin Rugne, a CKY cameraman and film editor; Dorsey Roberts, a CKY television reporter, and his wife; Jeff Bishop, the publisher of the *Dufferin Leader*; Kerry Kaelin, a *Dufferin Leader* reporter; Anthony Britain, the Friendship Field's owner, and his wife, Rachael; and Al Harpley, another newspaper reporter.

Although many people saw the film, the full story of how it was shot was never released. What follows is the whole account of exactly what occurred.

In April and May 1975, Charlie Red Star was flying his famous "beer runs" out of the Roseisle hills west of Carman toward town and then turned around to the northwest side of town. Anthony Britain and his wife knew more than anyone about Charlie's pattern and were acting as tour guides, leading teams of people around Carman to watch for a Charlie flyby.

Anthony contacted CKY and assured the station that if it sent out a camera crew, he would show them Charlie Red Star. CKY took up the offer and dispatched four reporters to Carman on Monday, May 12. Dorsey Roberts, then a reporter for CKY, later CBC-TV where I interviewed him, was one of the few to spend four consecutive nights on the back roads around Carman. "We were out two nights prior to the filming," Roberts told me, "the night of the filming and the night after. So I was out there a total of four nights. Monday night we saw nothing. Tuesday night we went out, and that's when we saw the thing down at the end of the roadway. The people who had seen this thing before said, 'That's it!'

"There was a fellow with us by the name of Eddie Griffin. He was another reporter from the station who was out on his own. He got his car and went flying down the road toward it. We saw the thing and kept our eye on it, but then it disappeared. We never saw it again that night, but I understand someone else saw it in a different location, but still around Carman."[11]

On the evening of the filming, 10 people showed up, hoping this would be the night. According to the article that appeared in the *Dufferin Leader*, "The sighting was made about 11:00 p.m., with the first UFO sighted on the ground northwest of Graysville, Manitoba."[12]

Everyone was gathered two miles north of Carman when the object was first sighted. Jeff Bishop, Kerry Kaelin, and Al Harpley got into their car to chase the object, which was down the road west of them. They headed a mile north to stay out of the way of Martin Rugne, who was at the CBC tower with his camera pointed down the road at the light. The men also realized that the previous night the light had disappeared when people drove right at it. When they were a mile north, the team of men travelled west toward Stephenfield where the object appeared to be sitting.

"We went west five miles and then went south," Bishop said. "Just before we got back to the road that the UFO was on, I said, 'Stop the car before we get to the mile road because we don't want to jeopardize our position.'"

The Britains, along with reporter Dorsey Roberts and his wife, had gone south and then west to approach the object. "This thing was just down the road from us," Anthony told me. "It kept rising and falling like a blood-red moon through the trees. So we said, 'There has to be something out there.' Just before we left, the cameraman [Rugne] was running down the road with his camera. I was standing there right beside him, and I said to myself, 'Boy, is that guy wasting his film.' That's just before he got the shot of the thing lifting off and lighting up the whole horizon. Talk about a surprised fellow when I saw that [the CKY film] on television. Weren't we surprised!"

The Britains and Dorsey Roberts headed south in the opposite direction of the Bishop car in order to come out on the other side of the object. "Instead of going west," Anthony told me, "we went east, not realizing that we had to go two miles before you could get back onto the road we wanted."

"We put the binoculars on it and you could see it clearly," Dorsey said. "It seemed to be more or less sitting there."

Anthony tried to close in on the object when suddenly in his own words "It popped into the air. It jumped straight up. It hovered and then moved over a bit, hovered again, and then headed for the CBC tower."

The two couples watched the objects with binoculars. "It wasn't moving fast," said Anthony, "so we started racing back. I kept telling Dorsey, 'Those guys at the tower are going to look right in.'"

Meanwhile Jeff Bishop, Kerry Kaelin, and Al Harpley appeared to be the ones who had scared Charlie into the air. The problem was they didn't know where the object had gone. They were looking around for it when it was now high above them.

"I could see this big glow behind some trees less than half a mile away off to the right and ahead of us," Jeff told the *National Enquirer*. "It was smoky red, with a hazy glow, and to me the thing was higher than the tree, maybe 50 feet tall. It was about 20 feet thick and was sitting at an angle of about 45 degrees. The edges were fuzzy and not well defined. It was much like seeing a drive-in movie screen from the side."

At the same time Al was using the microwave tower at Haywood to get his bearings in the dark. "I swung back," he told the *Enquirer*, "and the glow was gone. It was gone before I could see it again. We drove around the section, but we never saw anything else."

Charlie in the trees: "It was much like seeing a drive-in movie screen from the side."

The car with Jeff, Kerry, and Al had come within half a mile of the object. This was confirmed when the Winnipeg Planetarium found significant radiation in the field where the object had rested. (See Chapter 6, "Landings," for a full report of this.)

Meanwhile, Martin was back at the tower, his camera pointed down the road at the glowing light that alternately increased and decreased in intensity. He was trying to determine when to shoot. It was completely dark, so he had no perspective. All he could see in the viewfinder was the light. He decided that the next time it brightened he would shoot, which turned out to be a lucky decision.

As the object brightened again, Martin started shooting his first-ever television clip. As he began to do so, the object suddenly jumped into the air and flew northeast back toward the camera. When it did, Martin panned the camera, following its flight path.

"Rugne told me that he had seen it come tracking across the sky, and that's when he followed it," Dorsey Roberts told me in an interview later. "He panned it and then stopped the camera. That was great foresight on his part — to stop the camera and let the object move through the frame so that later someone could tell how fast the object was moving."

"I shot, I would say, roughly between 30 and 50 feet of film by the amount of time," Martin said. "Let's say about 80 degrees from left to right. From 10:00 p.m. right up to midnight, the camera was moving. I was panning with it. After midnight and up to 12:10, between those three or four degrees, that was the only time the camera was stationary. Once it went through the camera, I picked it up again and followed it up through to about 2:00 a.m."

Martin and Dorsey made it back to Winnipeg at about 2:00 a.m. They drove by CKY and dropped off the film at the station for processing. Neither was prepared for the controversy that erupted, or the fact that the weirdest part of the story was yet to come.

The most bizarre aspect of the developed film was the order of sequences. "We always conjured up interesting things, that someone was playing tricks on us," Dorsey told me. "All the filming was done on the same roll of film and it was shot in this order — one, the light at the end of the road; two, the flash and the jumping into the air of the object; and three, the tracking across the sky.

"Yet when we got the film back from the lab the whole sequence was reversed for some reason. The film hadn't broken in the lab. It wasn't that they had edited it back together wrong. When it came to us, the track-ing across the sky was first and the other portion was on second. It was backward."

From any standpoint of camera logic, this was impossible, but those who saw the film claimed it happened. Unfortunately, the evidence was about to be lost.

"When I shot the original footage," Martin angrily recalled, "there was 45 to 50 feet of film or something like that. I was out till 2:00 or 3:00 in the morning. About noon all these characters [CKY film editors] had already chopped the film up, and the only thing that was left was two-eight inch pieces, and they had thrown the rest away. Now I've got the last two eight-inch pieces, the pieces that everyone sees, but they had thrown everything away before and after. I tried to find the rest of the film, but no one could tell me where they had thrown it.

"Everyone said, 'I don't know. I don't know.' Those suckers, either through gross stupidity or something else, they threw it out. I cannot to this day comprehend how anyone could be that stupid, but they apparently were that collectively stupid. The reversal of the sequences can't be proved now because they threw away the rest of the film. If they had left the film from start to finish in its entirety, a whole set of circumstances could be brought forward. There were a lot of things that were strange about this film. It just goes on and on … rather strange."

The reason that 97 percent of the footage ended up in the trash raises the next odd aspect about the film. There was nothing on it when Martin panned the camera, even though he could see it in the viewfinder while he was shooting. When the station editors saw nothing on these portions, they simply cut them out and threw them away.

Dorsey Roberts concurred. "The portion that Rugne panned for some reason never turned out."

"Why," Martin told me, "I don't know. The chemicals on the film react to light. They can't tell the difference between a UFO and something else." Yet only when the camera was stationary, the object was on the ground, and Martin had stopped at midnight to get a point of reference with a star he saw in the north did the film capture the light emitted by Charlie.

Even more spectacular were the strange things discovered when the 16 inches of film was studied frame by frame. The portion where the object jumped into the sky consisted of only three 1/24th-second frames. On the CKY film the object can be seen resting on the ground.

"It was rising up and down," Martin said. "I was using a farm light for reference, and every time it would rise I would push the camera a little to the south and shoot. This part of the film can be seen for about a dozen frames before the object jumped. It was suddenly there. It made its motion to jump."

Dorsey described to me the three frames of film that made up the jump. It was part of an 11-minute special he produced about the film later for the station. "In the first frame, the object was right in the corner and then for one frame the whole horizon lit up and you could make out the trees and the rolling land. In the third frame, it moved up into the left corner … the actual movement had taken place in 1/24th of a second."

In viewing the film, one can see that in the second flash frame the UFO has already jumped over half the frame and the object is more than five miles away. Because J. Allen Hynek and NASA never released their analysis of the footage, the exact number of feet the object actually shot upward still isn't known.

The flash is the most interesting part of the film. For one 1/24th-second frame and one frame only the whole western horizon lights up, just as the object lifts off. There are two distinct sections of light cast on the horizon — a large arc in the south and a similar smaller one in the north. Directly below the UFO on the frame there is a space where no light is cast.

Dustin Hope, the CKY spokesman for the film, described the flash and surrounding events. "How I can best explain it with the little physics that I know of is warped time. I asked the professor [J. Allen Hynek] about warped time and the flash on the horizon with a foreground and a background, and the UFO between them, so that I couldn't say that it was a car light or anything like that. It wasn't a car light because the beam was shining in two different directions, just as strong as when it so called disappeared, [the way] UFOs would have to do to get from one place to another. That's what I found interesting — that it might have defied the speed of light."

Even though there were 10 witnesses who were present when the object lifted off, the only person who claimed to have picked up the flash when it did so was Dorsey Roberts.

"At this point," Dustin Hope told me, "we don't know what warped time is — the speed of light? If they were able to break it, that's what a UFO would have to do to go from one place to another. That's what I found interesting — that it might have defied the speed of light."

"You know," Dorsey told me, "I kind of thought that I saw something at the time, but nobody else standing around me at the time saw it or said anything, so I thought that maybe my eyes were playing tricks. I said to myself that I hadn't seen the flash, then I saw it on the film. I remembered that it reinforced what I had seen. It happened so quickly. It was only one frame in the film."

The only possible natural explanation for the appearance of the flash on the horizon is what is called a flash frame. Martin Rugne brought up the idea and then immediately ruled it out as a very weak possibility because it only appeared on one frame. "It had 50 feet to do that," he said. "It seems unreasonable that one should suddenly appear at this point in the film."

The more logical explanation for the flash frame is that it was caused by the massive energy that would have been involved in lifting a 50-foot craft high into the air in 2/24th of a second.

On the second portion of the film, there is another perplexing sequence. Martin had stopped the camera to allow the UFO to fly through the frame. He remembered peering through the viewfinder. "It wasn't going too fast. It just seemed to float by."

This brief eight-inch piece of film also showed an odd wave pattern. It wasn't flying in a straight line. Instead it appeared to move up and down from crest to trough to crest.

Charlie Red Star had been observed flying this way even with the naked eye by many observers. The action is called bobbing, akin to what a bobber on a fishing line does in water. On the night of the CKY filming, the speed was fast enough that no one reported bobbing visually. The assumption was that the slower the speed the longer the frequency of the wave and the more apparent the bobbing would be.

When the CKY film is slowed correctly, the bobbing wave motion becomes apparent. The object travels from the left (west), drops into the wave, then rises once more as it passes clear out the right side of the lens's field of vision.

"The object," according to Martin, "was actually flying a second wave. When the film was slowed down frame by frame, it was found that there was a small wave motion that followed the single large wave."[13] Martin pointed out another interesting aspect that was discovered in this section. He indicated it to me as we screened the film one frame at a time.

As the object drops into the wave, it seems to rotate. The red object gets a small black line through its middle. This appears and disappears at regular intervals as the object moves to the bottom of the wave. Once the object starts to back up the other side of the wave, this phenomenon stops, but the object continues to pulsate.

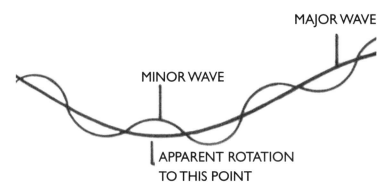

MAJOR WAVE

MINOR WAVE

APPARENT ROTATION
TO THIS POINT

Double-wave pattern of UFO on the CKY-TV movie footage.

The most unusual aspect of the second segment is the trailing objects (see echo pattern drawing on this page). Directly behind Charlie, at A, the film picks up a second object, which resembles the echo on a radar screen.[14] To make the problem more complex, detailed analysis discovered there are more echoes. At B, below Charlie, there is another one, and one more at C above him. A NASA analysis, according to Martin, even shows an echo above and ahead of Charlie at D.

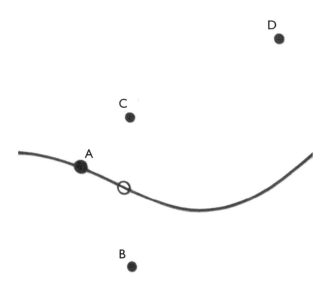

Echo pattern found on the CKY-TV movie footage.

It was, however, the main echo behind Charlie that everyone was interested in. When J. Allen Hynek first viewed the film, he stated that this effect might be linked to the inter-dimensional theory.[15]

It was plainly apparent, but nobody wanted to interpret just what the echoes were. Most people didn't even have an idea, and it might have been the appearance of the echoes that scared everyone off when it came time to hypothesize.

Those present at the filming said nothing. "I watched it all the way," Anthony Britain told me, "and there was only one object. That I'm sure of, and yet the film picked up two."

Dustin Hope at CKY told me his theory that the echo might have been a burn. "We had several photographers look at it over the years since it was shot. This could have been a burn on the film because, after all, this is a movie film. There could have been a trail left on the emulsion."

When Martin Rugne and I screened the film, we checked the burn aspect and found that it had to be wrong. After Charlie leaves the frame on the right, the echo is still there and remains so for many frames to come until it, too, flies out of the picture. The echo was something talked about by everyone but explained by no one, merely becoming another mysterious occurrence on the CKY film.

According to Dorsey, all sorts of people played back the film. Like those personally involved, they believed what they saw, but could give no explanation whatsoever for what their eyes viewed.

"We showed it to people at the planetarium," Dorsey said, "and we showed it to some air force pilots that the [Canadian] Armed Forces base sent over who were trained in night flying and night observation. They took a look at the film, and all they could say was that 'As far as we're concerned, it was definitely a UFO.' They couldn't explain what it was. We ruled out every other possibility such as swamp gas and helicopters because we checked all the places where there were helicopters and got nothing. It wasn't an airplane. That's the film we got, and there wasn't much of it, but what there was [was] very exciting."

The film made CKY famous in Carman. As Anthony Britain told me, "The CKY guys got so that they wouldn't come to our place. They wouldn't come to the airport because they wouldn't dare go through town with the CKY car. As soon as anyone saw the car, whether they wanted to watch for UFOs or not, they would follow it."

Dorsey described what happened the night after the CKY film was shot. "Martin and I were out on our own. We were receiving no pay. We just wanted to go out because we were intrigued by this. The next night we had to beat people off with sticks, the ones who wanted to come out. We had three cameramen, Martin and two others. We set ourselves up in a triangle pattern so that if we sighted this thing we'd get a fix on it with three cameras and be able to pinpoint its location. Unfortunately, we never saw it again. We stopped after that. I was getting to the point I was spending eight hours out there. Physically, we just couldn't take it anymore."

One would think that after all this interest and work on the brief three and a half seconds of film, CKY would have told the world how good the footage was, but that wasn't the case. The station's attitude was as unusual as the film itself. "As far as I'm concerned," Dustin Hope said, "it was legitimate, and everything that he [Martin Rugne] did, as well as how he presented it, was legitimate — that's over and done with now. We haven't heard of someone who's a physicist or an astronomer who's had a look at it, someone who says that this explains the unexplainable. I haven't heard of anyone."

The unexplained mysteries of the film didn't end there. When I interviewed Martin back in the 1970s, I also hoped to get my own copy of the movie. At first he was very cautious about admitting that he had the film. Finally, he admitted he had the original and that so many strange things had occurred with the movie that he wished sometimes the whole affair had never happened. In making copies of the footage, for example, some went missing. "I'm terrified of getting those things printed again," he told me, "because they almost lost them the first time I got them printed." Finally, he agreed to make a third-generation copy for me, and when I went to pick it up, screened a second-generation copy for me.

It was during this interview and screening that Martin also told me a story that had been kept secret during the controversy surrounding the film. This new fact was that he had never operated a TV camera for a story prior to capturing Charlie Red Star for all to see. On the night he took the footage, the station's acting news director said that no one could go out and shoot unless he went on his own time. But when Martin returned with the movie, it suddenly became a priceless possession.

The Second Movie

A second movie was shot in addition to the one done by CKY. It was taken by me on April 1, 1976, and has never been aired. To date, fewer than 12 people have seen the footage.

Like other photographers who got film of UFOs, I considered the shooting of my footage to be an accident. The film was taken at night with an 8 mm Bell & Howell camera using 160 ASA colour film. The location of the shoot was a bridge 10 miles south of Highway 3 on the McDonald Municipality Line.

With me at the time was my friend, Matt Cline. On that particular night we stopped at the intersection of Highways 3 and 205 East to wait for UFOs to fly by. It was just outside Sperling shortly after 7:00 p.m., with the sky beginning to darken. We had arrived at dusk, the time UFOs usually appeared.

After 10 minutes of patient waiting, we saw nothing remarkable. We did notice, however, that there were strange red/green lights starting to materialize near us. They looked like airplane navigation lights. At first there were just three — two south of us in the direction of the town of Kane, and one northeast toward Brunkild.

The lights had similarities to farm ones except they were definitely the wrong colour. We could clearly distinguish between actual farm lights and the ones we were now seeing. As it got darker, the number of red/green lights increased, so we decided to investigate, especially since there didn't seem to be any UFOs travelling about.

We drove east down Highway 205 and arrived at the first mile road where we glanced north and south but saw nothing. Continuing along the highway to the second mile road, we looked south — and there in the middle of the road was one of the red/green lights. I peered at it with 7x35 binoculars. It seemed to be about a half mile away.

Matt, who was driving, continued south to the next mile road, and strangely, the object didn't appear to get any closer. The red/green light, still sitting in the middle of the narrow gravel road, now turned into a brilliant orange ball. It was hard to tell the size, but we estimated it was much smaller than the road, which was about 12 feet across.

The sky was now quite dark, and we were completely surrounded by orange lights. The one on the road in front of us was solitary, but most of the others in the fields appeared as double oranges sitting atop one another.

After spending some time studying this peculiar situation, we discovered that all the farm fields were flooded with water. It seemed as if a huge lake covered both sides of the road right up to it. The reason, therefore, that the orange lights were doubled was that each one reflected off the water below it, giving the impression two objects were on top of each other. In other words, the bottom image was an exact replica of the top one. This might have been because there was no wind that evening and the water was quite still. The temperature was just above freezing, normal for that time of year.

The roads in this area were completely flat. In prehistoric times, the region had been at the bottom of a huge lake, and topographic maps revealed almost no changes in elevation for miles. Being a mile road, it was completely straight; being Prairie farmland, there were no trees except for the odd one in a farm field. The road we were on only had two farmyards, one at the corner as you came off Highway 205 and an abandoned one six miles away on the east side of the road.

We drove another mile south and halted again. The light still seemed to be the same distance from us and was just as bright. We continued driving both with and without our car lights until we had gone eight miles south.[16]

At that point the road changed. A wooden bridge crossed a drainage ditch, the bridge rising perhaps three feet above the road. When we approached the bridge, we noticed the orange ball was sitting on the left side of it. In comparison to the size of the bridge, the light was small. It hovered above the water just below the bridge. When we arrived on the bridge, the light suddenly disappeared. We assumed the orange ball was somewhere under the bridge, so we got out of the car with our flashlights and started hunting. It was hard to see because the level of the water was almost the same as the bridge's, and there were still piles of snow along the drainage channel, which prevented us from getting our heads low enough to actually peek under the bridge.

Finding nothing after a short search, we continued in the car south off the bridge. No light was visible on the road, but there was a small farm off to the right at the next mile road. We travelled a half mile, and seeing nothing, turned to go north again. When we looked north, we clearly saw the orange light, this time sitting on the south dike.[17] About halfway back to the bridge, I spotted the object moving toward it along the top of the dike. Its motion was erratic and bouncy, somewhat like a person with a limp trying to run.

When we were almost at the bridge, I yelled for Matt to stop the car, then jumped out and began running down the road with my 8 mm camera. At that point the orange ball dropped between the two dikes and was lost to sight again.

Once more, Matt and I got out of the car, and this time we thoroughly searched for the orange ball. After looking around and under the bridge for a few minutes without success, we headed north in the car back toward Highway 205 where our journey had started.

We had travelled north about a quarter of a mile with no further glimpse of the orange ball on the road when I glanced back and spotted it, this time sitting *on* the bridge. I told Matt to stop and suggested that rather than drive back to the bridge we should walk. Perhaps we could sneak up on it.

So we headed south on foot to the bridge, with Matt holding the binoculars and me clutching my 8 mm camera. Knowing the object could fly off at any moment, I took seven steps and shot three seconds of film. Then I took seven more steps and shot another three seconds of footage. The object had taken off twice, and I was determined to record as much as I could before it vanished again. For a third time, I stepped forward seven paces and shot three further seconds of film. We were getting closer and closer as the tension built.

When we approached the orange ball, I asked Matt what he could see in the binoculars, but not until we were 150 feet away did he say anything: "I think I see a shape."

"What does it look like?" I asked, but there was no response. In fact, to this day Matt has never told me what he glimpsed, even though we got a lot closer than 150 feet.

The next thing we knew we were at the bridge and the object was still there, maybe 50 feet away. I took another three seconds of film. It was an eerie sight. The object was round and very bright, about two feet in diameter, and as orange as the fruit. The light was so intense that it might have been another shape. There were no edges visible that I could see. I assumed the object was inside the glowing haze.

It was sitting on the right side of the bridge only inches from the structure's wooden side. My mind could only think of one thing: why was this extremely dazzling object not lighting up the side of the bridge inches away? It was so brilliant that it should have lit up everything for at least 100 yards. Yet the object merely cast a soft radiance on the side of the bridge. It was for this reason that I have always referred to such illumination as "dead light." It became a distinguishing mark of this kind of ground light.

I was now at the point of decision. We were near enough to make a run at the object, so I braced myself to do so, whispering my intentions to Matt.

He was looking around us with the binoculars. When I told him I was going to rush toward the orange ball, he said, "It looks like there's something coming down the road."

I turned and saw what at first I thought was another car coming from the north. Exchanging my camera for the binoculars, I squinted through them to see what was happening. What I saw amazed me. It seemed as if the sun was rising over *our* car. One intense blaze, a sort of semicircle, sat on top and was as wide as the car. Down the sides of the vehicle all the way to the ground was diffuse orange light that struck me as being a bit like smoke except it didn't dissipate. It looked as if a small fire had broken out inside the car, caused by the glow streaming down the sides.

"Matt," I said, "there's one sitting right on top of your car!" I began to race toward the vehicle, and Matt joined me. I was sure I hadn't taken more than a half-dozen steps when I realized what had occurred. Glancing back at the bridge, I saw that the orange ball was gone. We had been tricked! Halfway to our car, I stopped and shot some more footage.

I also took the opportunity to look through the binoculars at the car once more and now it really appeared to be on fire. The object had moved and was sitting on the hood. The interior of the car was still glowing, and the same smoky orange light flowed down its sides.

Now that the object at the bridge was gone, we resumed our scramble toward our car. By the time we got there, though, the orange ball was no longer there. We suspected it had slipped into the water.

The first thing I did when I arrived at the car was to put my hand on top of it to see if it was hot, but there was no noticeable warmth. I took out my flashlight and beamed it at the top of the car, but there was nothing out of the ordinary. My heart was pounding both from the run and from the bizarre nature of events that had taken place. Saying very little, Matt simply surveyed the interior of his car.

After a few moments, I glanced back at the bridge, and lo and behold, there was the orange ball. "It's at the bridge again," I informed Matt. "Let's go back."

Matt said he had no intention of returning. I insisted, since I was certain we could get even closer. Matt resisted, insisting he wanted to go home. Since the car was his, that was exactly what we did. The only comment he made during this frenzied period was "How did he know we'd left the car?"

I took a long pan shot of the western horizon to capture how many orange lights there were, then we headed home to tell our story. On the way back, Matt said nothing about what had transpired. Obviously, he was quite shaken. He hadn't been involved in any of the 1975 UFO sightings around Carman, so this was something new to him. He did tell me that the first thing he did when we returned to the car was to check twice for the keys, which he had left in the ignition.

During questioning by friends the next day, Matt's brother, Darryl, asked him whether he actually believed the second object at the car had been used as a decoy to pull us away from the one at the bridge. "It sure gave me that impression," Matt replied.

Ground Light Photography

During March 1976, a whole series of ground lights were encountered on the back roads of southern Manitoba. Most were within 20 miles of Sperling. A lot of photography was done on the ground lights because there were quite a few of them and they didn't really move around unless bothered by cars. We could take as many photographs as we wanted. So a great number of people got cameras, with film that varied from 200 ASA right through to infrared. Lenses ranged from 50 mm to powerful 3,000 mm (60x zoom) extender ones.

On the night Matt and I discovered the ground lights, I wasn't sure what we were seeing because we were dealing with a totally new phenomenon, one first spotted at about 10:45 p.m. on the evening of March 23, 1976. Jonathan Black, Reg Peters, and I were driving north of Elm Creek headed for the Trans-Canada Highway and Winnipeg. Down the road, we suddenly noticed a set of weird lights. The intensity of them varied from nothing to a flaring brilliant orange.

The number of lights also changed. Whenever a car came in behind it, the bottom light disappeared and the remaining orange one shifted a few feet off the west side of the road. As soon as the car passed, the objects reappeared and returned to their original positions.

After watching the lights for five minutes, we made many vain attempts to find "natural explanations" for what we were seeing. We considered parked cars, someone fixing a tractor off the road, and the possibility that the road wasn't level and we were glimpsing a series of cars approaching us from miles away.

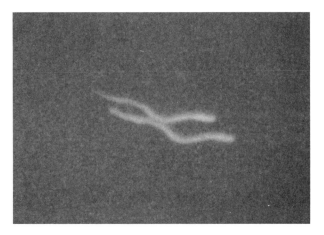

Front two lights of a triangle object creating a wave pattern in the sky.

As soon as we snapped some pictures of the peculiar lights, we moved up the road to determine if it was level and whether or not there were two cars ahead of us. All of that would give us an explanation for what we were witnessing.

We drove to where we thought the lights were and found nothing. The road was flat and straight all the way to the Trans-Canada 20 miles ahead of us. Only a single car passed us during the whole time we were there, leaving us with no explanation to explain the odd lights we had seen.

It wasn't until April 1 at the drainage ditch with Matt Cline that I was able to understand what we might be dealing with. However, I did receive a report about ground lights in the Pembina Valley from Rocky Reimer on March 31. He told me he had noticed "orange lights" while driving in the Sperling area and assumed they were the rear lights of snowmobiles but did find it curious that they were all over the place.

The night after I shot the 8 mm film of the ground light at the bridge Matt and I, with Matt's friend, Johnny Deakin, returned to see if we could duplicate our experience. I brought the movie camera and a new 50-foot roll of film. We approached the bridge from the east this time but never got to it because there were orange lights all over the countryside that distracted us. Besides us there was another car chasing the lights, so we got out of our car and tried to walk up to the objects to shoot them with the movie camera but were never able to get as close as Matt and I had the previous night.

Looking back, we probably didn't succeed because we couldn't concentrate on a single object. We would see one orange ball close to a road and give chase. Then, spotting another one on a different road, we would turn and pursue it.

The other problem we had was that we didn't keep an accurate log of what we were filming. Any orange ground light that seemed bright was shot. When screening the footage later, we realized we couldn't tell what objects we had been filming because in the darkness there were no points of reference. So we ended up scrapping the movie.

When the ground water was diverted away from the fields, the objects all moved onto the roads. The other thing they did was change colour to a brilliant arc-welding white light. When they weren't flaring, they were a triangle of small dim lights (see Chapter 7, "Ground Lights," for further details).

Once the objects moved onto the road, their numbers dropped dramatically to perhaps a dozen or so around the valley. The best and most reliable light still seemed to be on the road south of Sperling where I shot my April 1 film. That gravel road was ideal for a number of reasons:

1. Topographic maps revealed that the surrounding area was almost perfectly flat for miles, allowing for virtually unobstructed viewing.
2. There was a seven-mile stretch of road where there were no farms, so there was little worry about cars coming along or of farm lights throwing us off.
3. There was an excellent and very active light on the road dubbed Little Charlie because it produced a similar colour pattern to that seen in photos of Charlie Red Star. A photo was taken with 200 ASA colour film that was comparable to Tannis Major's third picture of Charlie (white in the middle with a yellow and then red corona around it).

There were many stories of attempts to get close to Little Charlie to obtain a good photograph, or better yet capture him altogether. Almost every imaginable plan was tried. Here I will deal with five of the ideas we acted on to get a better picture:

1. **Flashing lights at the object:** This was by far the most successful method.
2. **Chasing the object:** We tried this way the most and it was the least successful. On the night of April 4, when we got 50 feet from the object, we had two cars that chased numerous lights around for hours. These pursuits occurred at a few miles per hour, 70 miles per hour, with lights, and without lights. On one occasion, Anthony and Rachael Britain, Barry and Audrey Johnson, and I chased Little Charlie south down the McDonald Municipality Line for 15 miles and never got any closer. On the trip back toward Highway 205, Little Charlie flared brilliantly and followed the car closely.
3. **Jumping out of a car:** Because Little Charlie had followed us along

the road, we decided to try pushing him south and have some-one jump out of the car halfway. The plan was that Little Charlie would trail the car past the person hiding in the ditch with a movie camera.

We attempted this strategy when Jorg Poor from the University of Calgary and his brother asked me to drive out to the road to see Little Charlie. Along with Danny Penner, who had been there before, we visited the place where Little Charlie usually showed up. Once we got to our destination, we waited until Little Charlie flared, then headed off. After a few miles, Danny and I jumped into a ditch, while Jorg and his brother continued down the road.

Danny and I could barely see the car when it made its turn three miles south of us on its way back to us. In a state of great excitement, we checked our 35 mm camera and 8 mm movie camera as the car approached. Little Charlie, however, didn't arrive. It seemed like a long time before the car returned to pick us up. Just as the car approached, Little Charlie flamed into a full flare. After we got back into the car, the object followed us all the way to Highway 205.

4. **Approaching from a different direction:** This attempt to get nearer for a picture did meet with some success on a couple of occasions. The first time it was tried worked quite well.

I was returning to Winnipeg with Danny and Toby Penner and Rob Wheeler from a night of UFO hunting in the Pembina Hills west of Carman. The return trip led us right past the Highway 205 turnoff only a couple of miles from where Little Charlie sat.

We turned south, but instead of going two miles east before going south, we drove straight south for three miles and then east for two miles to the McDonald Municipality Line. Little Charlie frequently sat a half mile south of where the telephone wires ended. (Past this point there were no houses and therefore no need for telephone wires.) I was hoping I might trick Little Charlie and get close, so I prepared the camera as we drove south.

The trick worked. A short distance from us was an object that flared so much the light spilled right across the road. I stopped the car and pulled out the camera and tripod. Danny grabbed the binoculars and checked to make sure what lay before us was Little Charlie and not another vehicle.

Danny affirmed it was Little Charlie, and I quickly shot one photo. The object immediately ended its flare and turned into the classic two dim green lights we had seen so often.

I was about to pull out the flashlight to force a second flare when a dog from a nearby farmhouse began to bark. We moved another mile east and gazed back. Little Charlie was flaring again.

When I set up the camera and tripod once more, someone started yelling that there was another object heading down the road straight at Little Charlie, who was a mile and a half southwest of us across the field. Watching with binoculars, I saw the object glide across the mile road we were on. There were no red taillights. When everyone realized we had another ground light travelling right for Little Charlie, pandemonium broke out. I raced to set up the tripod and camera for a shot, feeling something spectacular was about to happen.

Realizing I wasn't going to get the camera set up in time, I watched to see what would unfold. My impression was that the two objects had collided. It was like witnessing an enormous explosion in absolute silence. The lights blazed with incredible intensity and then dimmed rapidly, as Danny Penner said later.

I continued to set up the tripod, hoping the objects would separate again. After about 20 seconds, they did, so I used a cable release and was able to catch the event with a time exposure.

It was 2:30 a.m. now. Despite this, Danny and I decided to walk across the field toward Little Charlie. It had already been a good night of filming and we hoped we could sneak up on the light. We strode through the field, which turned out to be very wet and muddy. Shooting some 8 mm film, we got closer. Little Charlie must have seen us coming, because when we finally arrived at the road, we noticed he appeared to be sitting.

All of the still shots we took that night turned out and were some of the best we ever got. We shot all 50 feet of the 8 mm film, but it didn't turn out, which was strange because Danny had said he could clearly see Little Charlie in the lens.

5. **Using a powerful 60x telephoto lens:** The lens was provided to us by Carl Bachmanek and Paul Dawkins. They had a good look at Charlie Red Star just north of Carman at the CBC tower. When they came to see Little Charlie, they brought along a 60x telephoto lens to get a good photo. They had been warned that it was very hard to get close to the object.

The date was May 13, 1976, exactly a year to the day after the CKY film was shot. There were scattered clouds, with a three-quarter moon. The temperature was chilly. Also present from Carman were Anthony and Rachael Britain and Jack McKinnon, who was employed as an analyst of aerial crop photographs.

Through the telephoto lens we saw a single orange light with a reddish border. The picture was quite fuzzy and wavy because the lens not only amplified the object but also the dust and heat coming off the road.

Anthony and I had seen ground lights dozens of times and had come to the conclusion that the reason this object was so far down the road was partly because of the lens being used. We got no decent photographs and learned nothing from this attempt to shoot ground lights with a powerful telephoto lens.

LANDINGS

They're out there — no doubt about it.

— Edwin Fuhr, Manitoba Farmer

During the two-year flap of UFO sightings, there were to my knowledge probably 20 landings in Manitoba. Some were witnessed and others were discovered later as swirl patterns or burnt circles in farm fields. The different landings were part of a worldwide phenomenon that came to be known as UFO landing trace evidence.

Late in September 1974 the landings in Manitoba might have been predated by a similar occurrence a few miles west in Langenburg, Saskatchewan, when five swirled patterns were noticed in the canola field of farmer Edwin Fuhr, along with a silver disk that was still spinning in one of the circles when Fuhr found them. The "saucer nests" and Fuhr's sighting made headlines across Canada and the world. They were investigated by the FBI along with the RCMP, whose tracking dogs refused to enter the circles.

The number of Manitoba landings wasn't high considering how many sightings there were. The landings do, however, represent a phenomenon that has come and gone in ufology. At the time of the Manitoba UFO flap, UFO landings were common around the world. The same could be said for sightings of aliens in and around landing sites. Now, more than 40 years later, landings and sightings of aliens around landing sites are no longer recorded — a well-documented fact that generates little discussion in UFO literature.

In order to obtain "trace samples" from a landing sight, the ufologist must be on the scene as soon as possible. In most cases, due to witnesses suppressing the event, this wasn't possible for the majority of Manitoba cases. Members of the Winnipeg Planetarium, though, did some analysis.

The Little Man

One of the most bizarre landings in Manitoba occurred near Bagot, about 20 miles northwest of Carman. Rather than writing up a summary, I include the full notes I made after interviewing the witness:

> This is the account of a UFO sighting made by Terry Orlando who lives in Bagot, Manitoba. The story of the event was given to me on March 15, 1978. The incident took place in 1972 or 1973.
>
> It was 1:00 a.m., and Terry was travelling east toward Bagot in a truck with his girlfriend when he spotted a light in a field north of the road he was on. Out of curiosity, he stopped his truck on a crossover road (a small crossing road over a ditch where tractors and combines drive onto a field from a road). He then walked into the field to see what was going on.
>
> As he approached the object, he noticed it was a saucer-shaped craft sitting in the field. Terry got to within 100 yards of the object and halted, fearing to go any closer. He saw heat waves coming off the object and heard a low hum.
>
> The craft was about 12 feet across and about eight feet high. Atop the saucer section of the object Terry saw a dome with something resembling three antennae sticking out. On the top of each antenna was a red light. The object glowed yellow and a

brilliant white light emanated from its edges. Terry couldn't see any doors or windows.

Fearing to get any nearer to the craft, he circled it, looking for something to give him a hint about what the thing was. When he got halfway around the UFO, he suddenly became aware that the craft was now between him and his girlfriend in the truck. So he decided to turn back, taking the same path back around the saucer.

Terry arrived back at the truck, which was parked 100 feet down a mile road off the main highway. To get back on the highway, he had to back up. As he turned, his lights naturally swung across the field. In the gleam, someone became visible striding through the ditch. The "Little Man," as Terry described him, was completely dressed in silver.

The Little Man didn't seem to notice that Terry had spotted him, or at least he didn't seem bothered. He simply ambled along the ditch and back up the other side, heading toward the saucer.

Terry figured the Little Man had made a large circle walking in behind the truck. Terry's girlfriend came to the same conclusion, because she suddenly became very frightened. Terry decided to take her home as quickly as possible. When they got to her place, he dropped her off and raced back to where the saucer had been sitting. The trip took him 10 minutes.

When he arrived back at the scene, the saucer had lifted off the ground and was hovering and shimmering in the air. After a few minutes, it flew northwest at an incredible speed, which Terry described as like a bolt of lightning going into the sky.

Such a story would have been questionable had it not been for the events that followed the initial sighting. Terry's neighbours went into the field two days later where Terry had seen the craft. The field had recently been cleared of trees and brush, and the men found an area where the stumps and grass were burnt. They also noticed footprints where Terry and the mysterious visitor had walked.

A couple of days after the sighting RCMP officers showed up at Terry's place, even though he hadn't reported the sighting.

They asked him a whole bunch of questions about what had occurred and what Terry had seen. They were, according to Terry, a bit shocked by what he told them.

Later, Terry received a call from a man in Ottawa. He identified himself, but Terry couldn't remember his name. When I questioned Terry about what the man had asked him, he replied, "The same things you're asking." Sometime after, the Ottawa man called back and asked the same questions.

Years later I saw the declassified RCMP files on UFOs. I looked in 1972 and 1973 and found no evidence of Terry Orlando's story or the Ottawa investigation. These types of UFO cases disappearing from official government files never surprise me.

More Little Men

The Roland farm of Bill Wheatley was six miles south of Carman. The Wheatley family was famous in the area for growing giant pumpkins. In fact, Bill's father, Roger, once held the *Guinness Book of World Records* for a 423-pound pumpkin.

In October 1976 (the same year as the world-record pumpkin), Bill and a group of other combiners were combining cattle corn. Bill stated that one of the combines (operated by Devlin Faester, a neighbour) came across a 25-foot swirled area of corn. Figuring that the combine had broken down, Bill went over and saw the combiner staring at the four- to five-foot-high corn now swirled down to 12 to 18 inches. (Anyone who has ever tried to pull corn and break it up to dispose of it at the end of the season knows the pressure required to do this.)

Bill related what he had found to the *National Enquirer*.[1]

> We got off and looked closer. You could see burnt marks up, say, six to eight inches from the ground. The stalks go up six inches and then they are burnt for a little bit, three or four inches. [The burn marks were only on the stalks at the edge of the circle. They were on both sides of the stalks and looked as

if the scorching had been done with a blowtorch.] It was easy to see.

Then I guess we noticed the tracks, really odd tracks. I've never seen anything like them in my life. They were round — I guess maybe five inches in diameter, almost perfect circle as I remember it. You see, it had rained a few days before, so these showed up quite well. They were sunk in the ground about an inch.

They were approximately five to six inches in diameter but there were little marks to each one of these. It was just a round pad mark and there were little claw marks about this size [very thin] … and they sunk into the ground about an inch. It was something very heavy, but it didn't look like they were machines.

They looked like some kind of animal because these claw marks would go away from the spot, but they didn't follow a pattern like an animal would [to the way it walks], but this didn't have a pattern. It was just helter-skelter and yon.

It didn't have a pattern, and wherever these claw marks seemed to be there were cobs picked off the corn. The ears were picked right out of the husks. You wouldn't have noticed unless you went and grabbed the husks and there was nothing in it. You

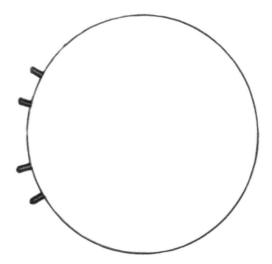

Footprints found in a corn circle.

know how the husks are dry in the fall? The husks were hanging there and there was no ear inside of it. It was gone! This is what was really weird, as far as we were concerned.[2]

All of the prints were outside the circle and extended 20 to 25 feet away from it. All of the claw prints were pointed in the same direction, as opposed to tracks of a normal animal in which the claw marks would have pointed in different directions.

There were 12 to 18 husks checked where the prints were, and they were all missing the ear of corn. When I interviewed Bill in probably 1977, I asked if the farmers had kept one of the stocks missing the ear or one of the burnt stocks. Bill said they hadn't. It was the busy harvest time and they just drove over the circle after looking around.

Neither Bill, his father, Roger, nor Devlin Faester had seen any of the UFOs. They did admit they had heard many stories about people in Roland (three miles away) having seen "the lights."

Roland

In the midst of the 1975 flap, there was a landing right in Roland. The landing happened on the night of a very violent thunderstorm in the area. The brilliant red light hovered low in the town, and some witnesses actually thought a fire had been caused by the thunderstorm. The emergency fire volunteers were called to put out a fire they couldn't find.

The next day in the corner of one front yard a burn mark was discovered that looked somewhat like an X. When I went out to see it months later, the X was still visible. It indicated an object that wasn't very big, more the size of a car than a house.

Portage la Prairie

Betsy Clinton found two horseshoe burns in a pasture near her home. They were 13 to 14 feet in size and were clearly defined. The grass on either side was tall and unscathed by whatever had burned the horseshoe print. They simply appeared one day.

Morden

This landing is discussed in detail in the "And Now Others See" section of Chapter 2. This landing location was very close to the northern edge of the Grand Forks missile silos in North Dakota.

Halbstadt

This landing occurred on July 2, 1975, in Halbstadt at the peak of the flap in southern Manitoba. The incident happened in the early growth of a sugar beet field. The site was discovered when a farmer, Elmer Friesen, found a 30-plus-foot-wide area where the beets were either dead or withering moving out from the centre of the circle.

On closer inspection, Friesen discovered three peculiar markings in the shape of a triangle in one part of the circle. The pod marks were 17 inches across and three inches deep.

Three staff members from the Winnipeg Planetarium — Dennis Targ, Elliot Slater, and Tibor Bodi — investigated the site. They eliminated

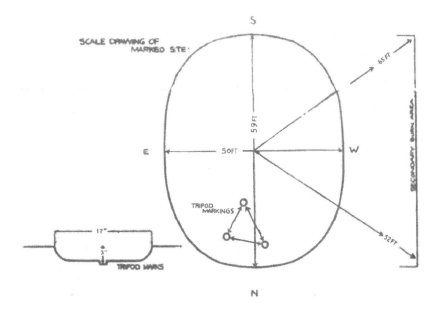

The Halbstadt landing site.

fertilizer burns, lightning, and a host of other possible causes for the strange dead section in the middle of the field.[3] The team found no radiation at the site in contrast to the Carman location (see the next section).

The CKY Movie Landing Site

The complete story of the CKY film is told in Chapter 5, "Cameras, Photographers, and Charlie Red Star." Eight days after that event the Winnipeg Planetarium's Elliot Slater and Dennis Targ (an electronics technician) went out to the spot north of Carman to check for signs that an object had been there, as the 10 people involved in the TV film claimed.

Dufferin Leader publisher Jeff Bishop led them to the site where he had seen the object. He had previously described it as "smoky red, a hazy glow, and not higher than the trees, maybe 50 feet tall. It was about 20 feet thick and sitting on an angle of about 45 degrees. The edges were fuzzy and not sharply defined. It was much like seeing a drive-in movie screen from the side."

After getting his bearings, Jeff pointed to the area he believed the saucer had been in. The farm was owned by Kenneth Roth. Dennis Targ took background radiation counts and found that they were 10 milliroentgens. As he examined the rest of the field, he came up with four hot spots. "In the centre of these four particular spots, he said, "I had readings of 38 to 40 milliroentgens, dropping off to 25 in the outer edges of the circles. These patches were about 50 feet in diameter and were 75 to 100 feet apart. They weren't in an absolutely straight line but were in a little swoop, as if they were part of a very large circle. That was the first time I found readings that high."[4]

All possible alternate explanations for the high readings were considered and rejected.

On June 8, two weeks later, Roger Haskins, a geologist with the Mineral Resources Department of the provincial government, his wife, Susan (also a geologist with the same department), and Dennis Targ from the Winnipeg Planetarium, made a second trip to the spot Jeff Bishop had identified as the place where the saucer had sat at a 45-degree angle on the night of May 13, 1975.

The farmer had since planted and there had been a couple of major rainstorms. Readings taken in the circles were only slightly higher than background radiation. It was likely that the radiation from the saucer had been washed away.

GROUND LIGHTS

In 1976, as mentioned earlier in this book, we started to discover what we referred to as "ground lights" on many of the mile roads in the UFO flap area. We gave them that name. Years later the same sort of objects were described by other researchers in other parts of the world as orbs, spook lights, and monitors.

A lot of work went into researching these ground lights to see if they were connected to the large UFO, and if so, what their role was. As the research progressed, many theories were raised to explain these objects.

Possibilities

Distant cars as a possible rationalization for ground lights were given a lot of study. Of the 100-plus people who had seen Little Charlie, the only ones who continued to insist, after seeing the phenomenon, that it was caused by car lights were the photographers Carl Bachmanek and Paul Dawkins. These two men had seen Charlie Red Star, and one night they brought a 60x telephoto lens to the road Little Charlie frequented, hoping to film him.

This was the only evening someone would insist Little Charlie was a natural phenomenon. When Carl, Paul, Anthony and Rachael Britain, and I arrived, Little Charlie seemed to know what was about to happen. He had moved far down the road and could barely be seen with the naked eye. Even with the powerful telephoto lens, he appeared no closer than usual.

Carl and Paul, however, had never seen Little Charlie before. They were convinced that what everyone was looking for was nothing more than approaching car lights 20 miles down the road.

An argument ensued between Anthony and the two photographers about how far one could see down the road before the horizon became a factor. When the two photographers insisted that a car could be seen on a flat road 20 miles away, Anthony got so upset that he and Rachael left. I stayed with the two photographers for another 45 minutes, but Little Charlie didn't flare a single time. It was pitch-black at the end of the road for the most part.

I was greatly disturbed by the fact that Paul and Carl assumed the object to be car lights, so I spent some time checking into how far the actual horizon was. A human's line of sight regarding the horizon would have a height of about five feet, but for the skeptic's sake, let's make it six feet. A car's lights would be about two feet off the ground, but again for the skeptic's sake, let's also make it six feet. The point at which the lights

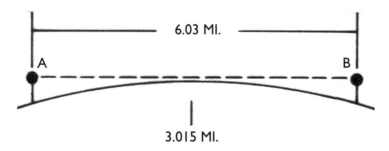

LINE OF SIGHT (AB) AT A DISTANCE OF
6 MILES FROM A HEIGHT OF 6 FEET

Calculation of the distance to the horizon.

would disappear over the horizon would be three miles, or a little more than 10 percent of the 20-mile claim made by Paul and Carl.

The two photographers weren't the first people to claim we were watching cars coming at us. Usually, I asked such skeptics how far down the road they thought the object was. When they guessed, I asked how fast they thought the car might be moving. The usual estimate was 40 to 50 miles per hour. A quick calculation would give a time when the car would then pass us. After the object didn't come 15 minutes after the person's prediction, almost everyone quickly admitted the car theory was wrong.

The other reason we ruled out cars as a possible explanation was because we had already determined from past experience and observation that the ground lights were dead lights. It was very easy to tell there was no car coming when looking through a high-powered telephoto lens like the one Paul and Carl had brought with them.

As mentioned in "The Second Movie" section of Chapter 5, the first night I was able to get close to Little Charlie I noticed that though the object was very bright it didn't cast light outward the way a normal incandescent bulb does. It was more like a light that had been placed inside a bag.

Later, when viewing both Little Charlie and approaching cars through binoculars, I perceived a distinct difference. Car headlights are built to cast light down the road to illuminate it. With binoculars the actual beams can be seen.

When observing Little Charlie, these beams weren't visible. The light might be very bright, but it was more like a self-contained glow. In later observations with ground lights that sat on other roads, it was possible to tell exactly when a car would approach from behind the object. The beams of light suddenly appeared, and we would know there was a car behind the object. Then the object would move off the road, and within a couple of minutes a car would pass us. After that the ground light would return to the road and flare.

Thanks to a number of years taking tours of people to Little Charlie's road, I had exhausted my ideas and patience. Once they heard the stories of the lights, many people would propose an idea to get closer. Usually, it

A ground light on a dirt road at night.

was something we had already tried. In the end, I would draw a map for the tourists of where the road was and when to go.

Ground Light Collision

One of the more spectacular sightings during the two years I was in an around the area where the UFOs were being seen occurred in the summer of 1976. I was with the regular trio of students who often came with me: Rob Wheeler and Danny and Toby Penner. We were up in the Pembina Hills, looking for a vantage point to gaze over the valley to see if anything appeared. After a couple of hours seeing nothing, we headed back east toward Winnipeg. The time was very late — well past midnight.

As we passed Sperling, we turned south to see what Little Charlie was up to. This time, rather than going two miles east and then three miles south to where he usually sat, I went three miles south and then two miles across, hoping that by coming from the side we could catch him off guard. The plan worked. As we crossed the second mile road, there he was — brilliant and appearing to be only a quarter mile from us. I quickly set up the tripod and took a picture. By then Little Charlie had moved back but was still pretty close.

We thought we were onto something, which prompted us to continue driving a mile east so that the object was southwest of our position. It was still bright and appeared to be no more than a half mile from where we had taken the picture.

Stopping to watch, we hoped we might be able to walk the mile across the field and sneak up on the object for a second time. It was at that point I noticed another object travelling from the north on Little Charlie's road, heading right for him.

We couldn't tell if the object was a car or another ground light. I scrambled to put the camera on the now-folded tripod that we had just taken down moments before. (For those who haven't shot a camera in pitch-black, think of it as like trying to assemble the whole thing by feel.) As the object passed the east-west mile road, I urged everyone to look for red, since a car driving across the field of vision would have red taillights.

As the light passed, everyone called out at once that it wasn't a car but another ground light racing straight for Little Charlie. I fumbled to get the camera ready, but there was no time. As the two objects came together, I stopped my struggle with the camera and watched.

It was an incredible sight — and a vision — that is still as clear to me today as if it had occurred yesterday. As the two lights merged, there was a huge explosion and the intensity of the light increased at least 10 times. However, there was absolutely no noise; it was like watching a film of an atomic bomb going off without the sound. Then the intensity immediately dropped but stayed much higher than normal. By then I was able to get the camera ready and took a picture.

Bright aftermath of two ground lights colliding on a road.

We had now experienced two unique sightings one after another, so everyone was excited about walking right up to Little Charlie while he wasn't looking. The trip across the field, however, wasn't easy. It was wet and we picked up lots of mud on our shoes. Our progress was very slow, but everyone was determined to finish.

Just as in the case of driving up to Little Charlie with a car, we didn't seem to get any closer as we fought our way across the field. When we finally got across, Little Charlie still seemed to be in the next field. We concluded that we might have been looking at a farm light. Disappointment set in, since no one was prepared to hike through yet another muddy field. So we prepared to head back to the car and end our night of searching.

However, something wasn't right. We could hear a loud buzzing. Such a sound under a hydro line, where we stood, wasn't uncommon, but this was particularly piercing. It was like being inside a beehive. Jennette Frost, who lived only a mile east of where we were, had mentioned the intense buzz in connection with the appearance of UFOs. She had had many sightings and had recorded them in a journal.

The hydro line ended only a few feet south of us. I looked north and south down the road and saw nothing, yet there was a strong feeling experienced by all of us that something strange was present.

Stepping out from under the hydro line toward the road, I spotted something — a small brilliant white ball of light sitting seven poles (a couple of hundred feet) south of my position. It was only visible for a couple of seconds and then was gone, along with the almost deafening buzz.

The light exhibited a strange characteristic that I was already aware of: it could only be seen from certain angles. From where we were under the hydro line, nothing blocked the view of the object, yet it wasn't visible. Moving three feet in another direction made it evident.

We had seen this characteristic while watching Little Charlie. From the middle of the road, the object was apparent, but when we moved to the shoulder it sometimes disappeared — one more mystery we were never able to explain.

Charlie Fights Back

Without a doubt the scariest moment of the entire flap for me happened one night in April 1976 while chasing a ground light south of Brunkild, a town on Highway 3 between Carman and Winnipeg.

On the evening in question, we were tracking triangles that had been flying around for a couple of weeks. One of my friends was in the front seat busily writing down descriptions of object after object, while Danny and Toby Penner and Rich Willow were in the back seat.

One of the objects hovering near the Brunkild microwave tower was a triangle with two red lights in front and a green one in back. It veered off southwest, and we were headed that way, too, when I noticed a pair of ground lights right in front of the car. (Ground lights usually came in pairs — one bright and one dim.)

I drove down with lights on and lights off until I came to a point eight miles south of the highway where the gravel road ended and dirt started. There were deep ruts in the road, and I assumed it was safer to stop here than risk getting stuck in mud far from any town.

Leaving the car with Toby Penner, I walked toward the object, flashlight at the ready. I told the others to remain in the car and that we would be right back. As we approached the object, I discovered strange white impact marks in the mud (four inches long, almost one and a half inches wide, and one and a half inches deep). White outlined the holes and there were white spots in the bottom of it, providing another mystery we never solved. Turning back to the lights at the end of the road, we experienced an incredible encounter, one I will let my notes from that night describe:

> I saw that they [the lights] were still there but that the less intense one was on the left. I gave three bursts from my flashlight toward the one that appeared to be on the ground. After about three seconds, to my great surprise, the object pulsed back three times. What is meant by this is that during a period of about 1.5 seconds the object would rise and fall in the intensity of its light. This the object did three times without moving.
>
> Next I took the flashlight and made a long vertical line up and down in the air. In response, after a few seconds, the object rose to double its height and then dropped back down.
>
> I took the flashlight and made a long vertical line back and forth along the horizon. In response, the object moved back and forth across the road in a motion resembling a falling leaf.
>
> I repeated all the motions, three flashes, this time two up and two across. The object repeated all the motions.
>
> Suddenly, the thing started to make noise. Although there was a small breeze, the sound was very clear. It sounded at first like Morse code. The start was a short-short-pause-long. At this point Toby said, "Look, he's doing everything you're doing."
>
> I told him to listen to the noise.
>
> The noise was still there. It was short beeps like a type of code, but now I realized that instead of using beeps it was using a whistle noise. Later, Toby and I discussed the sound and concluded that it was a beep and a whistle at the same time.
>
> Toby started back to the car, and I asked him to send one of the other people to watch the objects. The noise had now continued

for about 20 seconds, but I wasn't paying much attention. This is because I had begun to think that I was losing control of the situation. The object had been responding to the light, but now with the noise it was doing things I hadn't ordered.

It appeared that this was some kind of small observation craft or a monitor and that I had annoyed it. The noise stopped, and I heard Toby yelling at the car. I quickly turned and ran back to find Toby telling everyone about the amazing stuff that was going on down the road.

I took Danny, Toby's older brother, to see the object. I was hesitant to get as close as the first time and stopped at the white holes in the road. I repeated all the flashlight motions — up/ down and sideways. The main bright light repeated all the actions.

Suddenly, I got the distinct impression that we should return to the car, and we did. When I got back, I related to the others what had occurred. As I talked, I suddenly noticed a familiar object visible in the back window — a bright arc welding light hovering low on the horizon. It was flying east along the southern horizon very close to us and appeared headed right toward the two objects on the road.

From the time I first saw that object until it arrived at the other two objects, I didn't watch. I was too busy panicking. All I could recall, as I stared out the front window, was Danny, Toby, and Rich fighting for one of the two sets of binoculars in the back seat. It sounded as if they were having a great time. Later the kids who were watching said that the object began to pulse red as it came toward the two ground lights.

Just after the object crossed south of us, I saw it seemingly pause for a moment and then continue east. "Are you ready?" I asked my companions.

Someone asked, "Ready for what?"

The object began to brighten. "Here he comes," I warned.

The battle for the binoculars continued; one set was now missing. It turned out that someone was partially sitting on it.

I did up my seat belt — why I still don't know. The whole affair had frightened me terribly because it seemed like a nightmare that had come true. I could do nothing, and this object was now calling the shots.

Rich and I were in the front seat and seemed to be the only ones disturbed by what was happening. Even when Toby and I had walked down the road in pursuit of the two objects, Rich had been very unhappy. At the time he had said, "I wish we'd leave it and go the other way."

The object, as feared, stopped travelling east. It made a turn north, then west, and was now hurtling toward us. Someone in the back seat said, "This is neat, eh?"

Asking for my binoculars, I held them against the windshield of the car. This was necessary because my hands were shaking so badly that I couldn't keep them still.

The triangle object was quite familiar to me. There were two red lights in front and a green one in back. I had seen the object twice before: earlier that evening moving over the Brunkild microwave tower headed southwest, and a few weeks earlier when Reg Peters and I had spotted it east of Carman. The lights appeared in formation, but I was sure they were attached to the same craft.

The object appeared to be tilted, with the far side down and the front tilted up. I didn't know how; it just seemed that way. It was coming at us and wasn't very high — maybe 500 feet.[1] The kids in the back seat were having a wild party.

The lights kept coming toward us until I was staring almost straight up at them. I was never so scared in my life. The object paused for a second, shifted a bit to my left, then started moving north. As it made the slight shift, like a small jerk in a film, my fear instantly vanished. I went from being more afraid than I ever recalled being to having no fear at all.

When I put down the binoculars and stopped watching, Danny said, "That's the same one we saw earlier. Do you think it's the same one? Or another one with the same lighting?"

"Same one," I replied.

"It came from the same direction we saw it go," Danny added.

"Probably the same one."

"That's the same one I saw," Danny insisted. "It's the one I saw before you."

"Yeah," I agreed.

"Let's stay all night," someone in the back suggested.

The object easily took up the majority of the field of vision in the binoculars, and as with the two prior sightings of it, there were gaps between its three huge lights.

The whole event seemed to take about 20 minutes from the time the object left the two small ground lights until it went north away from our car, but it was probably only a couple of minutes.

Suddenly, there was a bright white light behind us, and the interior of our car was lit up. I got out and saw that an RCMP vehicle had pulled up behind us.

An officer stepped out of the police car and walked over to my window. "Trouble?" he asked.

"No," I replied.

He beamed his flashlight through the window. "Okay, what's going on here?"

"We're just watching those lights at the end of the road," I said.

"What lights?"

"Turn off your car lights and I'll show you. You can't see anything with them on."

The officer strode back to his car and turned off the lights. The four kids in my car got out. It had only been a minute or so since the triangle of lights had flown over, so I pointed to the object as it travelled toward Brunkild along with another light that had just materialized.

"Do you see those two objects there?" I asked the officer.

"Yeah ..."

"Okay," I said, "take a look at this."

The kids were very excited; they knew what was about to happen.

We moved down the road to where only one of the objects was visible, and then only barely. I made a long vertical line in the air with my flashlight. The object moved up into view, then dropped to the left side of the road.

"Are you sure it isn't a farm light?" the officer asked.

"We've been chasing it for six miles," I said, though it turned out to be eight miles when measured later.

"Oh, well," the officer said, "it's probably just a couple of guys down the road having a couple of beers."

"It's not a couple of guys down the road having a couple of beers," I insisted. "We've been following it for miles."

The officer started moving back to his car. "Oh, well, I'll see you guys around." He hopped in his car and pulled away.

"Don't let him get away!" I cried. "Get his licence plate number."

A couple of the kids ran after the RCMP officer's car, pointing their flashlights at it.

"Got it!" Rich shouted in triumph. "BLT-147."

I made plans to interview the RCMP officer after finding out what detachment he was stationed at but changed my mind, thinking it would be hard on the man to explain the lights in the sky and on the road.

The Monitor Connection

While researching the UFO flap, I was also working on the story of Wilbert Smith, who had headed up the official Canadian government flying saucer investigation from 1950 to 1954. I had received Smith's story and his activities from a radar technician named Ernie Epp, who was working at the Department of Transport in Winnipeg. Ernie had been a technician for Smith in a flying saucer detection building that the latter had constructed on Department of National Defence property outside Ottawa. Smith had experienced a UFO sighting after travelling to Carman during the flap.

The Smith story encouraged me to travel in 1977 to Ottawa to meet with the man's widow, Murl. She in turn put me on to a defence research scientist who had worked privately with her husband from 1956 until Smith's death in December 1962. The man, Art Bridge, was now living in Morden, only 20 miles south of Carman.

I had a number of secret meetings with Art. He was still interested in the subject of UFOs but had no intention to go public with what he had done for Smith or the Canadian military. In the 1970s, when I talked to him, he wasn't doing anything related to science.

During one visit with the former scientist, I brought up the ground lights we were seeing and told Art about our attempts to capture, film, and explain them.

"You mean monitors?" he asked after hearing my tale.

I had absolutely no idea whatsoever what he was talking about but pretended I did. "Yes, monitors."

"We had those things all over in the time I was in Ottawa. They were tracking what Wilbert and the rest of us were doing." He then told me about the time they spotted a monitor hiding in the ditch in front of the house. Later, I realized it was the same story Wilbert Smith had told on an audiotape years earlier:

> We saw one of the monitors do exactly that trick. We did believe that a certain conversation we were having was being monitored by one of the little fellows. So when we came out of the house we made a definite effort to locate it. We did. It was lying down in the ditch right in front of the house, and as soon as we spotted it, apparently the people who were controlling it became aware of the fact. As soon as we spotted it, we saw what appeared to be a heat wave about a foot in diameter and what popped right out of it was a little disk and it just took off and disappeared into the great blue yonder. I think the whole operation took place in less than about two seconds. We were looking right at it. There were three of us, and we all saw the same thing.

It suddenly occurred to me that Murl Smith had talked about these monitors, as well, but I didn't recall her using the same name. She had basically told me that the objects made a nuisance of themselves around her yard. One of the things she said was that they burned out a whole row of beans in the garden. She also mentioned they had done damage to a neighbour's tree, which led the neighbour to say to Smith, "Wilbert, I don't know where your little friends are from but could you please tell them to stay out of my yard?"

Murl had told me the objects were around all the time. It was probably these monitors that had led to the stories inside the Department of Transport that Wilbert was losing touch with reality.

Ernie Epp, the radio technician who had put me on to Smith, stated he had asked Smith about the aliens, and Wilbert had told him they were landing in his yard all the time. The fact was monitors *were* in the yard, and Epp, unfamiliar with them, assumed big flying saucers were landing and visiting Smith.

James Smith, Wilbert's eldest son, also spoke of the monitors. He was 17 when his father died in 1962, so he remembered many of the strange events that occurred in and around the house as he was growing up. In an interview with Errol Bruce-Knapp, host of the radio show *Strange Days ... Indeed*, James recalled the monitors:

> At our home when this flying saucer club met in the basement there were windows, and on many occasion there would be small monitor saucers looking in the windows listening to what was going on. In terms of size, they would have been about 30 to 36 inches across and a foot thick, looking, very much like a jelly doughnut.
>
> I came out of the porch steps one evening just after dark. There was one sitting about three feet out on the front lawn where it could look in the front window and monitor what was going on. We just stood there and looked at each other for about 20 or 30 seconds and then it just took off straight up. The grass underneath it was virtually sterile for the next 10 years. Nothing would grow. There was this great patch of nothing. Similarly, the trees at the side of the house with access to a window — our neighbours used to complain, "Smith, keep your saucers in your own trees." These things would sit up there and virtually burn all the leaves and branches around them. There would be this dead clump, this dead hole in two or three trees that had access to the windows.

Whether or not the objects on the ground in southern Manitoba were the same as the ones Smith had seen in Ottawa in the late 1950s was hard to determine. The same could be said for the small balls of light reported in British crop circles throughout the 1980s and 1990s.

The British crop circle lights looked very much like our Manitoba balls of light. The British researchers, too, weren't able to determine much beyond the fact that the lights were a real phenomenon associated with crop circles. Further investigation into these lights will hopefully produce an answer someday.

The other key place the ground lights/monitors were reported was in Wilton, North Dakota, near the Minot Missile Base. The local newspapers had done articles on these strange balls of lights but couldn't come to any conclusion about what they were.

I travelled to Wilton in 1977 to present my slides of the balls of lights we had chased around the roads of southern Manitoba, and it appeared from the reaction of the full room of townspeople who showed up for the lecture that we had all seen the same thing.

THE NUCLEAR CONNECTION

Since 28 Oct 1975, numerous reports of suspicious objects have been received at the NORAD CU; reliable military personnel at Loring AFB, Maine, Wurtsmith AFB, Michigan, Malmstrom AFB, Mt, Minot AFB, ND, and Canadian Forces Station, Falconbridge, Ontario, Canada, have visually sighted suspicious objects.

— Commander-in-Chief, North American Air Defense Command, November 11, 1975

Most ufology researchers know and accept the close connection of UFOs to nuclear missiles. Researcher Robert Hastings, in fact, wrote a book on the connection called *UFOs and Nukes*. In 1975, however, the connection wasn't as well known.

While the sightings were occurring in Manitoba, I knew we weren't the only place experiencing such incidents. People in four states bordering Canada — North Dakota, Minnesota, Montana, and Wisconsin — also witnessed numerous UFOs in 1975, as did Ontario residents, who spotted more than a normal share of them.

I knew these were all connected because I was the background researcher for the *National Enquirer*'s Daniel Coleman, who was working on UFO stories in each area.

When I returned to Carman in 2004 almost 30 years after the UFO events of the 1970s, I expected everyone would be ready and willing to give me insights into what the UFO flap had meant and how it had changed their lives but that didn't happen.

Only Anthony Britain seemed eager to reflect on what had occurred. When I asked him why the UFOs had been in Carman, he said, "You know why they were here."

"No, I don't," I replied.

"I told you all about it."

"Anthony, in 30 years I've never known why they were here."

"The missiles ... I told you we'd sit in the hills and watch the objects coming in from the United States."

As soon as I heard the word *missiles*, I knew he was right. By 2004, researchers had become aware of the nuclear connection. It all made sense.

Growing up in Winnipeg, we all knew about the Grand Forks and Minot U.S. Air Force bases in North Dakota and their Minuteman III intercontinental ballistic missiles (ICBM) silos. We knew that if there was ever a nuclear exchange between the Soviet Union and the United States we would be the first to go. Every 10th Soviet missile would fall short right on top of us. We also knew there were 300 ICBMs, each with three warheads, in North Dakota. That meant that if North Dakota had been a country in 1975 it would have been considered a nuclear superpower.

Anthony reminded me of the conversation he had with a U.S. Air Force pilot at Jack's Place Bar in Windygates, Manitoba, on the border with North Dakota. The pilot was from Minot Air Force Base. He told Anthony that he had been on a mission with an order to ram. This was all confidential. He said four pilots ran into something sitting over a silo. It came right up through the formation, and he said it had no intention to veer off. The object came right through, and the pilot was in the way, so he avoided it and let it come through. The pilot said he wasn't going to die for that.

I knew about the highly publicized Sandy Larson abduction case in August 1975. It had happened very close to two Grand Forks Air Force Base missile silos outside Buffalo, North Dakota.

Then there was the story of UFO abductee Katarina Sharma, who told me of an encounter with a UFO at the A-10 Blitzkrieg missile silo three-quarters of a mile north of Karlsruhe, North Dakota. Katarina was about nine at the time. She and two friends were outside the gate of the silo when a UFO rose through the metal lid that covered the missile. The perfect spherical ball the size of a garbage can lid ascended 25 feet and spun. Its colour was a shiny metallic bronze with burn marks. The ball's glow could have been a reflection from the sun. Hesitating for a moment, it then quickly flew away.

Finally, there were the same ground-light-type objects we spotted in Manitoba that appeared just southwest of Karlsruhe around Wilton. As I mentioned earlier, I travelled to there in 1977 after the local newspaper did a story on the small balls of light that were seen on the nearby roads following cars around. When I did my lecture in Wilton, the room was full. Many who had seen the Wilton ground objects agreed that what they had witnessed appeared similar to what I was showing on slides of the objects observed in Canada.

UFOs have always seemed interested in nuclear weapons and power plants, a connection that dates back to 1945 when the modern UFO era began. What follows is a chronology of such events:

1945: A couple of weeks after the atomic bomb was dropped on Nagasaki in August 1945 a young U.S. Marine named Ed Rogers arrived by ship in the devastated city. While there he took a series of photographs. In the 1990s, it was discovered there were UFOs in many of the pictures. The Marine made arrangements for the photographs not to be released until after his death, which occurred in 2014.

1947: A UFO crashed outside Roswell, New Mexico. At the time the Roswell U.S. Army air base was the only operational atomic

Disk-shaped object over the harbour in Nagasaki, Japan, in August 1945 only days after the atomic bomb was dropped on the city. Credit: Marie Udea.

bomb unit in the world. The pilots from Roswell made up the crews that dropped the two atomic bombs on Japan. In addition, the first atomic bomb test took place only 120 miles to the west in July 1945.

1947–1952: In the years after the Second World War, UFOs continued to show a great interest in nuclear weapons and nuclear power plants. The correlation was first made public by Captain Edward Ruppelt, who directed the U.S. Air Force investigation into UFOs back then. He reported to *Life* magazine that when viewing a folder of 63 unexplained UFO reports that had been plotted on a map of the United States he discovered that it showed an ominous correspondence with the location of various atomic energy installations. "These sightings," he told *Life*, "were pinpointed on a map. Soon afterward, it was seen by a Pentagon representative who noted that a number of concentrations duplicated exactly the area of atomic energy installations. The Pentagon man excitedly reported back to his headquarters. A conference was called immediately in Washington. Intelligence had to tell the Pentagon that they had no evidence that the flying saucers are spying on or threatening our atomic program. But this fear still lies deeply in some responsible minds."[1]

1952: On November 20, 1952, George Adamski appeared, only three days after the *New York Times* announced to the American people that the first hydrogen bomb had been tested. He went down in history as the first contactee (a person claiming to have talked to occupants of UFOs). Adamski said Orthon, the alien he communicated with, was worried that the atmospheric nuclear bomb tests would kill all life on Earth, spread into space, and contaminate other planets.[2] Other contactees in the 1950s and 1960s came forward with similar nuclear messages.

1979–1980: Paul Bennewitz, a physicist who operated a small electronics company called Thunder Scientific Corporation outside Kirtland Air Force Base in New Mexico, reported UFOs over the Manzano Nuclear Weapons Storage Facility. His reports circulated widely inside the UFO research community. The U.S. Air Force intelligence people at Kirtland met with him about his sightings and then set up a program to discredit Bennewitz and what he claimed he had witnessed.

1980: On three nights, December 26, 27, and 28, the twin air force bases of Woodbridge and Bentwaters, England, were visited by a series of UFOs that shot beams of light into the nuclear weapons storage area and reportedly affected the tactical nuclear weapons stored there. A connecting aspect seemed to be the fact that the American military was on high alert, since at that time the Soviets had moved troops to the

Polish border in a possible move to invade Poland for a second time. The nuclear weapons stored at Bentwaters were the type of tactical nuclear weapons that might have been used if there was a new war over Poland.

1986: During the Chernobyl nuclear power plant meltdown on April 26, 1986, there were reports that a bronze-coloured fiery sphere came to within 1,000 feet of the damaged Number 4 reactor at the height of the fire. It reportedly shot out two bright red rays at the reactor. The radiation levels reported fell from 3,000 to 800 milliroentgens per hour. After three minutes, the UFO flew northeast.

Final Thoughts

For the purposes of this book, the most important nuclear connection came in 1975 following the U.S. military loss to the Communists in Vietnam, Laos, and Cambodia. It was a very unstable moment in American foreign policy. The "domino theory" was the predominant political and military strategy. It embodied the fear that one country after another would fall to the Communists until they controlled the world if the United States didn't prevent that from happening.

After the Vietnam defeat, U.S. military planners were likely trying to figure out which country would topple to the Communists next. Would they move to seize South Korea, the Philippines, or Indonesia? Because there were insufficient American troops on the ground in these nations would nuclear weapons have to be deployed to draw a line in the sand and stop the spread of communism? It is very possible that when the Vietnam War ended in disaster in April 1975 the status of the ICBMs was secretly raised.

Whatever the U.S. strategy was the records reveal a great interest by UFOs in nuclear weapons in 1975. NORAD Command Director's Logs show numerous encounters with UFOs in or around the nuclear weapons storage areas at various Strategic Air Command (SAC) bases along the Canadian border. These bases had stockpiles of nuclear weapons and also headquartered the huge B-52 bombers loaded with nuclear weapons for their daily Cold War–era deterrence missions.

Consider, for example, the written record of UFO encounters at Loring Air Force Base in Maine in October 1975. SAC documents refer to the objects as helicopters, as if someone were able to get a helicopter inside the weapons storage area and escape unscathed.

The initial incidents at Loring created concern at the highest levels of the American government: "The incidents drew the attention of the CIA, the Joint Chiefs of Staff, and the Secretary of Defense. Though the Air Force informed the public and the press that individual sightings were isolated incidents, an Air Force document stated that Security Option III was implemented and that security measures were coordinated with fifteen (15) Air Force bases from Guam to Newfoundland."[3]

The UFOs spotted at Loring penetrated the nuclear weapons storage area at an estimated 300-foot altitude. The event went on for two nights and one incident lasted at least 40 minutes. On both nights the events ended with the object flying toward the Canadian border, 12 miles to the east.

Another case highlighted by the NORAD documents was an encounter at Wurtsmith Air Force Base on the Michigan-Ontario border. The base wing commander, Colonel Boardman, ordered a KC-135 in the area to intercept the object, but the mission failed.

Then there was Great Falls, Montana, where Sabotage Alert Teams guarding the nuclear weapons at Malmstrom Air Force Base dealt with UFOs a few weeks later. As with the incident at Loring, the UFOs did what they pleased. F-106 interceptors were scrambled in response to multiple reports of UFO visits to nearby missile sites at Moore, Harlowton, Lewistown, and several sites around Malmstrom. Most strikingly, it was also reported that computer codes in the missile warheads were altered.

Then, on November 10, 1975, there was a UFO encounter at Minot Air Force Base directly south of Carman. The base's experience was with a mysterious automobile-sized object.

At the same time there was also activity on the Canadian side of the border. Police and military officers and NORAD radar saw and tracked UFOs that alternately hovered and darted at high speed at the NORAD Falconbridge radar station near Sudbury, Ontario. As in the SAC occurrences, NORAD scrambled two F-106 jets but to no avail. The Department of National Defence headquarters in Ottawa also became involved.

In the midst of all the UFO visits to nuclear bases, logger Travis Walton claimed he was abducted in Snowflake, Arizona. The case became one of the most famous abduction stories ever, made headlines around the world, and is still the subject of numerous documentaries because it lasted five days instead of the normal one or two hours. The abduction almost seemed, as with the hovering of UFOs over nuclear missiles, to be a sort of dramatic alien warning to governments about the dangers of such weapons.

So how do all the SAC base nuclear incursions along the border tie into the long series of sightings in the Carman area? As mentioned earlier, Anthony Britain had maintained that the Carman sightings were tied to the Minuteman III missiles at the Grand Forks and Minot installations and that he had talked to a U.S. Air Force pilot who had been involved in a jet scramble involving a UFO over a missile silo.

On July 3, 1974, the Soviets and the Americans signed an additional protocol to the SALT I Treaty that stated each country could build an anti-ballistic missile (ABM) site to shoot down each other's ICBMs. This was the ground-based version of what would later become the Star Wars anti-ballistic missile shield. Each country would be allowed 100 new nuclear missiles.

The United States selected its ABM site near Nekoma, North Dakota, about 80 miles as the crow flies south of Carman. Soon there would be 400 nuclear missiles within a couple of hundred miles of Carman. In the centre of the missile complex was a huge pyramid with the top cut off. The structure was built to house the most advanced radar unit in the world and was constructed to withstand the direct effects of nuclear weapons. The enormous complex contained the Missile Site Phased Array Radar and computers necessary to track and destroy incoming Soviet ICBMs. Locals referred to the building as Nixon's Pyramid.

"Nixon's Pyramid" at the Stanley R. Mickelsen Safeguard Complex in Nekoma, North Dakota — a huge radar installation set up to detect Soviet ICBMs. It was capable of triggering 100 nuclear missiles to destroy incoming missiles from the enemy.

Separate long-range detection radar was located almost on the Canadian border near the town of Cavalier, North Dakota. This radar facility was only a few miles from the Halbstadt, Manitoba, UFO landing site.

The $6 billion ABM base was called the Stanley R. Mickelsen Safeguard Complex and became the only ABM unit ever to go into official operation in the United States. The installation of the missiles began in early 1975 at the same time as the UFO sightings started in Manitoba. The plan was that Spartan five-megaton missiles would try to intercept Soviet ICBMs while they were still outside the atmosphere. If that failed, the much faster one-megaton Sprint missiles would be launched to intercept the Soviet ICBMs as they approached the North Dakota missile fields.

By April 1975, eight Spartan and 28 Sprint missiles were operational. Then, as the UFO intrusions at the SAC bases began late in 1975, "the full complement of 30 Spartans and 70 Sprints became operational."[4] On November 18, 1975, the U.S. House of Representatives and Senate voted to take the Mickelsen site off alert. It was determined that with high costs and the Soviet use of multiple warheads the plan was doomed to fail. The idea of mutual assured destruction (MAD) seemed to be a better plan to deter a Soviet first strike.

The decommissioning of the site commenced on February 10, 1976, and as the 100 nuclear missiles were removed, the UFOs stopped being reported in the Carman area. The records show that they left and never returned. It was as if some intelligence agency had placed UFO drugs in the Carman water in March 1975 and took them out in early 1976.

Aerial photograph of the Stanley R. Mickelsen Safeguard Complex in Nekoma, North Dakota. It went into operation in 1975 when the Charlie Red Star flap occurred. When the installation was decommissioned and the missiles were removed the following year, the UFOs departed, too. Credit: Library of Congress, Prints and Photographs Division, HABS ILL, 16-CHIG, 33-2.

I asked Anthony Britain in 2010 how many UFOs he had seen in 1975–76, since he was out every night with visitors, researchers, newspaper reporters, and movie crews. He estimated he had experienced about 150 sightings. Asked how many UFOs he had witnessed in Carman in the 35 years after the flap he replied, "None."

The UFO flap in Carman was over. Charlie Red Star appeared to have left for good, and the citizens of Carman returned to their normal lives. I, on the other hand, fell down the UFO rabbit hole and have been chasing the mystery ever since.

Carman Poll Evaluation, November 30, 1976

This poll was taken at Carman High School.

Poll Questions

1. How many of you believe (without having to decide what the origin might be) that there is such a thing as a flying UFO?

   No: 9.6%   **Yes:** 72.1%   **Undecided:** 17.3%

2. How many of you believe that you have seen something in your life-time that could be classed as a UFO?

   No: 36.5%   **Yes:** 62.5%

3. How many of you believe that you have in the past two years seen something that could be classed as a UFO?

   No: 46.2%   **Yes:** 52.9%

4. Of those of you who answered Yes to Questions 2 or 3 or both, were you close enough to actually see an object as opposed to a light in the sky?

    No: 76%   **Yes:** 23%

5. Of those of you who answered Yes to Questions 2 or 3, were you within 100 yards of the object?

    No: 90.4%   **Yes:** 9.6%

6. Of those of you who answered Yes to Questions 2 or 3, did you see any people in or around the craft?

    No: 98%   **Yes:** 0.96%

7. Of those of you who answered Yes to Questions 2 or 3, after seeing the UFO, did you experience a time lapse, a period of time where you couldn't account for what happened?

    No: 91.3%   **Yes:** 7.7%

8. Do you know of anyone else (other than the people in this school) who have seen a UFO?

    No: 63.5%   **Yes:** 35.6%

9. How many of you have, without the aid of mass media, TV, or news-papers, ever seen a Boeing 747 jumbo jet? That is, how many of you have actually seen one in person or on the ground?

    No: 44.2%   **Yes:** 54.8%

10. Have you ever read a book on UFOs — this includes Erich von Däniken?

    No: 42.3%   **Yes:** 47.1%

The results of the Carman poll were very much what I expected. The sightings were more numerous than in Sanford (a town 20 miles east that experienced many sightings, as well) and were of a much higher quality.

This is shown in the large number of responses to Questions 4 and 5. In fact, almost 50 percent of the respondents reported being close enough to actually see an object rather than just a light in the sky, which is usually the case for most UFO sightings.

The most stunning result, however, was in the comparison of the responses to Questions 3 and 9. According to those polled, more students claimed to have seen UFOs than saw Boeing 747 jumbo jets.

Of those polled, it was found that 85 percent of the students had either seen a UFO themselves or personally knew someone who had.

The results were so strong in Carman that they dwarf those in other Manitoba areas. A comparison to the national poll shows that personal experiences of UFOs in Carman are six times the country's average. Nationally, only 11 percent claim to have seen a UFO, and only 54 percent believe in the possible existence of them.

The numbers seem to back up the statement that in 1975 and 1976, at least, Carman was the UFO capital of the world.

Charlie Red Star Poetry

"Charlie Red Star" by Roger Currie and Kent Anderson

Twinkle, twinkle, UFO
How we wonder where you go.
Up above the world so high
Like a bright light in the sky.
As you shine your big red light,
Carman's people stay up at night.

"Chief Charlie Red Star" by Frances Stagg

Who rides the night on his fiery steed,
Crossing all barriers at unfathomed speed?
Riding the wings of the clouds tossed on high,
Drifting by moonlight o'er soft silent sky.

'Tis Chief Charlie Red Star
The great warrior bold
From a Cree Indian legend by the campfire I'm told.

His headdress aflame with bright feathers of red
As in days long ago on his pony he sped.
He rides through the buffalo past the stars
Hunting the Great Plains from Pluto to Mars.

With soft silent footsteps that no man can hear.
For he brings only joy and never a fear.
As embers die out on our campfire bright
And the daybreak arrives to give light to the night.

The Indians know he is happy at last
Reliving old memories and dreams of the past.
When he hunts through the night, we won't question why.
Good night, Charlie Red Star — Old Chief of the Sky.

Notes

INTRODUCTION
1. A flap is a prolonged series of UFO sightings.

CHAPTER 1: THE ARRIVAL OF CHARLIE RED STAR
1. Chris Rutkowski, *Aliens & Abductions: What's Really Going On?* (Toronto: Dundurn, 1999), 27.
2. Ibid.
3. Ibid.
4. Ibid., 28.
5. Jess Stearn, *Edgar Cayce: The Sleeping Prophet* (New York: Doubleday, 1967), 257.
6. Daniel Coleman investigated the series of sightings in all three places. The actual reporter's stories sent back for all three areas can be found at the end of this book. The Wisconsin sightings led to another major event in UFO history. In March 1976, Jimmy Carter was campaigning for president in Wisconsin at the time of the flap. During a question-and-answer session, he was asked what he would do about the UFO situation. Carter replied that if elected he would release all government information on UFOs. The comment became famous, and Carter is still asked about the matter from time to time.
7. On January 7, 1948, Air National Guard Captain Thomas Mantell, a very experienced pilot and a Second World War veteran, was ordered to check out reports of an unidentified flying object in Kentucky airspace. Mantell and his three fellow P-51D Mustang pilots, all of whom were already in the air, proceeded to do so. After pursuing something unknown for a while, three

of the pilots returned to base, but Mantell continued on, eventually crashing near Franklin, Kentucky, on the border with Tennessee. What he was chasing remains a mystery, but there are plenty of theories — see www.ufocasebook. com/Mantell.html. As for the Arizona logger Travis Walton, he claimed he was abducted by a UFO on November 5, 1975, and held for five days. See the logger's own book *The Walton Experience* (New York: Berkley, 1979); also entitled in a later edition as *Fire in the Sky: The Walton Experience* (Boston, MA: Da Capo Press, 1997), which includes material about the movie *Fire in the Sky*, based on Walton's ordeal.

8. Debbie Lyon, "Have You Seen Any UFOs Lately? The Manitoba Center Wants to Know," *Winnipeg Free Press*, June 4, 1977.

CHAPTER 2: WITNESSES AND TESTIMONIES TO CHARLIE RED STAR

1. "*UFO Report* Interview with Jim and Coral Lorenzen," *UFO Report*, August 1977.
2. Josiah Thompson, *Six Seconds in Dallas: A Micros-Study of the Kennedy Assassination* (New York: Bernard Geis/Random House, 1967), 25–29.
3. For a full description, see "The CKY-TV Movie" section of see Chapter 5, "Cameras, Photographers, and Charlie Red Star."
4. Joseph McCann also claimed that the UFO activity had affected the 115 horses in the north pasture. He told the *National Enquirer*: "You know my 115 horses up in the north pasture, they're going crazy up there. They're getting wild up there. Last year they were tame but now they are getting wild. Whatever they're [UFOs] doing to them, they're getting crazy up there."
5. These photographs by Tannis Major were the best ones ever taken of Charlie. A full account of the events involved in taking the pictures is given in the section called "The Tannis Major Photographs" in Chapter 5, "Cameras, Photographers, and Charlie Red Star."
6. This is exactly the same type of description given to me by Jennette Frost at Sperling, who described the two lights she had seen on one object as similar to the type of lights used on old Model T cars.
7. This exact reported effect of close encounters with UFOs appeared as part of the plot in Steven Spielberg's movie *Close Encounters of the Third Kind*. As the Manitoba cases were never made public, Spielberg must have obtained his example from some other UFO sighting in which the same event occurred.
8. See the "More Little Men" section in Chapter 6, "Landings."
9. The lack of objectivity from Constable Wotherspoon might have come from the fact that the first two officers who had talked to the media were transferred out to less friendly environments. In Canada the RCMP has many outposts in the North or in the bush, which isn't exactly where many officers are dying to go.
10. The Staggs had witnessed the same thing on May 6, 1976. This incident was different in that the Staggs described a fourth object that flew by the car very low to the ground.

11. This is particularly true in light of the fact there were three other cases in which animals disappeared in heavy UFO sighting areas.

CHAPTER 3: CLASSICS

1. The jerking motion was identical to the one described by the McCann children in 1975. I also saw it on the second night I spotted a UFO in Carman in June 1975. It was called the bouncing Ping-Pong ball by the McCann children, and that was exactly the way it looked — a white ball bouncing randomly in the sky.

CHAPTER 4: IT'S FUNNY THEY SHOULD BE THE SAME

1. Years after the Manitoba UFO flap there were many reports of triangles. The 1990s brought the famous cases of triangles that were seen and tracked by the military in Belgium, and by a dramatic series of triangle sightings witnessed by most of Phoenix, Arizona, in 1997. This led to many new reports of triangles around the world. It should be remembered that triangles were a collective reality many years before.

2. In the 1990s and 2000s, reports of objects being dropped off by a larger entity in the sky became commonplace in sightings around the world. In these reports, the number of objects ranged from a couple to hundreds. Many of them, especially in Mexico, were videotaped and can be found on YouTube.

3. This identical docking manoeuvre was sighted just north of Elm Creek by Frances Stagg and her husband, Art, on November 17, 1975, and May 6, 1976.

4. Wendelle Stevens, "UFO Tracks in the Sky," *UFO Report* 2, no. 5 (Fall 1975).

5. Daniel Coleman's report to the *National Enquirer* concerning a sighting in Two Harbors, Minnesota.

6. The Brunkild microwave tower sighting is described in more detail in the "Charlie Fights Back" section of Chapter 7, "Ground Lights." A second identical event occurred at Homewood, Manitoba, on March 19, 1976.

7. Exactly the same three-light triangle description was given to me by a family of six living north of Carman. Just as the Manitoba UFO flap was ending, triangle articles started to appear in UFO magazines around the world. Examples are Richard Hall, "The Weirdest UFOs I Have Known," *Official UFO* (May 1977): 20. Also see James A. Hudson, "Trail of the Triangle UFO," *True Flying Saucer UFO Quarterly* 7.

8. This sighting by Anthony Britain compares to those of Charlie, who usually flew 1,000 feet or lower.

9. John Womack, *I Was Picked Up by a U.F.O.* (Cullman, AL: Helms Publications, 1975). This "flow" property of light was similar to light coming off an object sitting on a car in April 1976. It looked much like smoke that floated around and moved more like a fluid than a beam.

10. J. Allen Hynek and Jacques Vallée, *The Edge of Reality: A Progress Report on Unidentified Flying Objects* (Chicago: Henry Regnery, 1975), 273.

11. Probably the most famous case of UFOs, hydroelectricity, and blackouts concerns the many reports during the 1965 Northeast Blackout. Numerous UFOs were observed just before the blackout, and many people think they might have played a role in what happened. Even the U.S. Office of Emergency Planning named "unknown phenomena" as one of the things being looked into in its investigation of what caused the blackout. It never did reach a conclusion.

12. In a North Dakota tape supplied to me by Richard Faflak of a woman who recorded from one device to another when a UFO flew close to her house, the same double-sine wave appears when put on an oscilloscope.

13. See the "The Second Movie" section of Chapter 5 and the "Possibilities" section in Chapter 7 for more discussion of the dead light phenomenon.

14. Similarly, experiences with ground lights showed that the small ones were very sensitive to light. The correlation here was much more repeatable.

CHAPTER 5: CAMERAS, PHOTOGRAPHERS, AND CHARLIE RED STAR

1. See the section called "The Second Night — Charlie Takes Off" in Chapter 2.

2. Not getting it on the spool might happen in the field because loading a camera was often done just by touch because of the pitch-black conditions and the fear of losing night vision by turning on a light to change film while something flew around.

3. Daniel Coleman, *National Enquirer*, June 17, 1975.

4. Ralph Mayher took the picture on July 29, 1957, in Miami Beach. See Todd Zechel, "The CIA and UFOs," *Official UFO*, September 1977.

5. The local RCMP officers had sightings of Charlie Red Star and talked to reporters. However, both officers involved in the incident were transferred shortly after and never claimed they saw UFOs again.

6. A.G. McNamara, "UFOs: What Are They?" *Journal of the Canadian Air Traffic Control Association* 8, no. 1 (1977): 9–12.

7. Interview with Bob Pratt, *National Enquirer*, August 3, 1976.

8. When I received the developed film back, I looked for the frame where the object had crossed behind the telephone pole. The object was clearly visible: a long red line across the horizon with a break in the line. Few photos taken of UFOs have all the items seen by the photographer. This picture of mine was one of the few where the shot corresponded to what had actually been seen.

9. In many important UFO sightings, mysterious "men in black" or MIBs sometimes haunt the case. They harass witnesses and seem more interested in destroying important evidence. Wendelle wrote to me about all this in a letter dated February 23, 1977.

10. Personal interview with Dustin Hope, March 16, 1976.

11. See Chapter 4. Various other people, including Jennette Frost, saw Charlie on May 12, 1975, too.

12. *Dufferin Leader*, January 7, 1976.

13. See Chapter 4 for more discussion about this wave theory.

14. The image is faint and cloudy in comparison to the actual object.

15. As described more fully at the beginning of Chapter 4, the inter-dimensional theory toys with the idea that UFOs might be linked to parallel dimensions.

16. Because these Manitoba roads were perfectly straight with few if any turns, we often travelled them at high speed without lights. If the moon was out, there was usually enough illumination to see the road faintly. Another reason for driving without lights was that we had discovered that ground lights were very sensitive to anything else that glowed.

17. There were dikes on either side of the drainage ditch to prevent water from flowing back onto the fields. The land here was so flat that the water had to be channelled away.

CHAPTER 6: LANDINGS

1. Interview with *National Enquirer* reporter Bob Pratt, August 28, 1976.

2. I first read the *National Enquirer* interview with Bill Wheatley in 2004. I interviewed Bill probably the year after Coleman from the *National Enquirer*. Although I have misplaced my notes, what Bill Wheatley states in this interview is identical to the story I recall him telling me.

3. F. David Penner, "Strange Markings Studied," *Red River Valley Echo*, July 16, 1975.

4. Bob Pratt, *National Enquirer*, June 17, 1975.

CHAPTER 7: GROUND LIGHTS

1. At night it is hard to determine size and distance because there are no reference points. This object was either very low or very big based on the field of vision in the binoculars.

CHAPTER 8: THE NUCLEAR CONNECTION

1. Robert Moskin, "Hunt for the Flying Saucer," *Life*, July 1, 1952.

2. It wasn't until the hydrogen bomb was developed that it was possible to destroy the world. Physicist Herbert York summed up the implications of the first test of a hydrogen bomb: "[T]he world suddenly shifted, from the path it had been on to a more dangerous one. Fission bombs, destructive as they might be, were thought of as limited in power. Now, it seemed, we had learned how to brush even these limits aside and to build bombs whose power was boundless." See Herbert F. York, *Arms and the Physicist: An Eye-Witness Report on a Half Century of Nuclear-Age Drama* (Woodbury, NY: American Institute of Physics, 1995), 11.

3. Air Force Security Police message to 15 U.S. Air Force bases, November 10, 1975.

4. Robert Johnston, "Multimegaton Weapons: The Largest Nuclear Weapons," April 6, 2009. Accessed at www.johnstonsarchive.net/nuclear/multimeg.html.

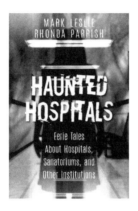

**Haunted Hospitals: Eerie Tales About Hospitals, Sanatoriums, and
Other Institutions**
By Mark Leslie and Rhonda Parrish

**A look inside the hospitals, asylums, and sanatoriums in which formal
spectral residents refuse to move on.**

Hospitals are supposed to be places of healing, places of birth, and places
of hope. But with all of the varying highs and lows that are experienced
in these buildings, is it any wonder when echoes linger indefinitely?
How about asylums, which house some of society's worst offenders
and troubled inmates, or sanatoriums, places where the mentally and
physically ill find themselves trapped, even after death?

Journey inside the history of these macabre settings and learn about
the horrors from the past that live on in these frighteningly eerie tales
from Canada, the United States, and around the world.

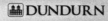